A Nation Forged by Crisis

ALSO BY JAY SEXTON

Debtor Diplomacy: Finance and American Foreign Relations in the Civil War Era, 1837–1873

The Monroe Doctrine: Empire and Nation in Nineteenth-Century America

A Nation Forged by Crisis

A New American History

JAY SEXTON

BASIC BOOKS
New York

Basic Books
Hachette Book Group
1290 Avenue of the Americas
New York, NY 10104
www.basicbooks.com

Printed in the United States of America

First Edition: October 2018

Published by Basic Books, an imprint of Perseus Books, LLC, a subsidiary of Hachette Book Group, Inc. The Basic Books name and logo is a trademark of the Hachette Book Group.

The Hachette Speakers Bureau provides a wide range of authors for speaking events. To find out more, go to www.hachettespeakersbureau.com or call (866) 376-6591.

The publisher is not responsible for websites (or their content) that are not owned by the publisher.

Print book interior design by Six Red Marbles Inc.

Library of Congress Cataloging-in-Publication Data has been applied for.

ISBNs: 978-1-5416-1723-0 (hardcover); 978-1-5416-1722-3 (e-book)

Library of Congress Control Number: 2018015890

LSC-C

10 9 8 7 6 5 4 3 2 1

This book is dedicated to a group of Americans who made sacrifices on behalf of the nation in one of its greatest moments of need:
Melvina Sexton and Army Staff Sergeant J. D. Sexton
and
Betty Collier and Marine Sergeant Creighton "Dude" Collier

Contents

Introduction

No words in American history are better known today than those of the second paragraph of the Declaration of Independence, which assert "all Men are created equal, that they are endowed by their Creator with certain unalienable Rights, that among these are Life, Liberty and the Pursuit of Happiness." Americans have struggled to fulfill those ideals ever since. The bar could not have been set higher. "The United States was the only country in the world that began with perfection and aspired to progress," as mid-twentieth century historian Richard Hofstadter memorably put it.[1]

But for all the implications of the Declaration's second paragraph, few at the time of its drafting considered it the most significant section of the document. It was the first and final paragraphs that were then understood to contain the most critical lines. Their objective was constitutional and diplomatic, not ideological. These passages were an attempt to demonstrate to audiences at home and abroad that the diverse inhabitants of the thirteen colonies were "one people" ready "to assume among the Powers of the Earth, the separate and equal Station to which the Laws of Nature and of Nature's God entitle them." The Declaration concluded not with ideologically charged rhetoric but with a description of the political authority, power, and unity of what was now given, for the first time, a name: "the UNITED STATES OF AMERICA…and that as Free and Independent States, they have full Power to levy War, conclude Peace, contract Alliances, establish Commerce and to do all other Acts and Things which Independent States may of right do. And for the support of this Declaration, with a firm Reliance on the Protections of divine Providence, we mutually pledge to each other our Lives, our Fortunes, and our sacred Honor."[2]

Thomas Jefferson drafted the Declaration at a moment of international instability and opportunity. The political crisis in Britain's North American colonies threatened to trigger a second world war in as many decades. France awaited the opportunity to strike back at its British nemesis, whose 1763 victory in the Seven Years' War had left it as the dominant European power in North America—and with the burdens that led it to levy new taxes and assert its authority over its colonies. The rapidly growing population and economy of North America further destabilized the international order of the mid-eighteenth century. As North America boomed, thanks in part to an unprecedented increase in immigration and Atlantic trade, the political institutions of the British Empire struggled to adapt. Patriots declared themselves independent at a moment in which the aggregate power of the thirteen colonies was rapidly growing. Linkages between the Old World and the New were stronger than they had ever been. In fact, much of the patriots' strength came from relatively recent British connections. The blockbuster pamphlet that had given the cause of independence such momentum, Thomas Paine's *Common Sense*, published in January 1776, was authored by one of the era's many British emigrants—in Paine's case, one who had arrived in North America less than two years earlier. The printing press of John Dunlap, an Irish-born Philadelphian who printed the initial run of the Declaration of Independence, was one of the many British imports of this period that empowered the patriot cause. The roads and communication systems that the British built in North America during the recent Seven Years' War became the circuits of patriot resistance.[3]

The Declaration of Independence was a bold gambit aimed at convincing wavering observers at home and abroad—particularly France, the Americans' longtime enemy but now potential ally—that the patriots had established a new country worthy of recognition and support. "It is not choice then but necessity that calls for Independence," Virginian Richard Henry Lee pointed out in June 1776, "as the only means by which foreign Alliances can be obtained; and a proper Confederation by which internal peace and union can be secured." Establishing political legitimacy was the critical next step for the rebellion, for it would pave the way to diplomatic alliances as well as further material support and foreign loans. This diplomatic goal was inseparable from—indeed, dependent upon—the union of the thirteen states. "Foreign Powers could not be expected to acknowledge Us," John Adams argued in 1776, "till We had acknowledged ourselves, and taken our Station among them as a sovereign Power, and Independent Nation." The position in which the American rebels found themselves offered them that rarest of political opportunities, a chance to create the world anew. "The present time," Paine argued in 1776, "is that peculiar time, which never happens to a nation but once, viz. the time of forming itself into a government. Most nations have let slip the opportunity, and by that means have been compelled to receive laws from their conquerors, instead of making laws for themselves."[4]

The nation's founding document, in short, was not only a statement of timeless principles but also an outward looking and innovative act of statecraft during a moment of crisis. This is not to demote the historical significance of those admirable ideals of the Declaration's second paragraph, which have inspired so many over the course of American history. "We hold these truths to be self-evident," stated the 1848 Declaration of Sentiments of the women's rights convention in Seneca Falls, New York, "that all men and women are created equal." "Very seldom, if ever, in the history of the world," Martin Luther King Jr. declared a century later, "has a sociopolitical document expressed in such profound, eloquent and unequivocal language the dignity and the worth of human personality." Rather, it is to suggest that the animating ideals of the Declaration's second paragraph have been entwined, from the very beginning, with its opening and closing paragraphs, which navigated a course for a hastily constructed ship of state through stormy international waters.[5]

THIS BOOK TELLS the history of the United States through the greatest periods of crisis in each century of its existence. It opens with the eighteenth-century Revolution and founding, when the thirteen colonies broke from the British Empire and created a new political union. Next comes the Civil War—America's "second revolution"—which witnessed the abolition of slavery and accelerated the nation's international rise. Then we reach the protracted and interrelated crises of the mid-twentieth century: the Great Depression, the Second World War, and—finally—the onset of the Cold War. These periods of crisis were like violent earthquakes that forever altered the nation's political landscape.

Traditionally, historians of the United States have given primacy to internal factors when explaining the nation's development: long simmering social and political struggles that periodically have come to a boil, such as the campaign against slavery in the nineteenth century and the civil rights movement of the 1950s and

1960s; the emergence of new political practices, alignments, and institutions—for example, the collapse of the Whigs and the rise of the Republican Party in the 1850s; and specific leaders, as in "the age of Jefferson." Some historians have suggested that there are peculiar rhythms or cycles within American history involving flurries of reform and innovation. Wars undeniably have been powerful drivers of transformative change at home in that the demands of mobilizing resources and political will have necessitated changes to America's domestic institutions. It is no coincidence that all the periods examined here occurred in the midst of intense conflicts.[6]

There is merit to these explanations, many of which inform the pages that follow. My argument is not that they are wrong, but rather that they are incomplete. The history of the United States—particularly its moments of crisis—cannot be understood in a vacuum. Nations are more than repositories of individual rights and political traditions; they are configurations of power forged by geopolitical pressures. The United States that we know today bears the imprint of the international forces that have been placed upon it in the past: the booms and busts of the global economy, the ebbs and flows of human migration, and the violent fluctuations in the international order. The old shibboleth of American "exceptionalism"—that most persistent of nationalist myths, which posits that the course of US history has been the unique product of its internal formations, institutions, and ideology—has obscured the ways in which the volatile forces of global integration have conditioned its development. Far from being an exceptional nation walled off from the world, the United States has always been entangled within it—even in those times in which Americans have attempted to limit their connections to the international system.[7]

What follows is less a description of the domestic fault lines that opened up during periods of crisis than it is an assessment of the distant, yet powerful, forces that shifted the underlying tectonic plates of historical change. When we broaden our perspective beyond the nation in this way, things look different: a new set of determinants of historical change become visible; familiar stories unfold in unexpected ways; contingent moments in which the course of American history—and world history—might have played out differently come into focus.

Three aspects of America's foreign relations, in particular, emerge as drivers of its history. The first is what we today call national security. The development of the United States, particularly in moments of crisis, has been shaped by international pressures, foreign threats, and imperial rivalry. For most of its existence, the United States has been a vulnerable nation, one weaker than the traditional European powers as well as one whose innovative but untested system of constitutional democracy was in danger of imploding. Native peoples, revolutionary ideologies, and foreign cultures have struck fear into the hearts of the citizens as well as the leaders of the United States. Anxiety and insecurity have been as important to US history as have confidence and national triumphalism. Even archnationalists, operating at moments of relative stability, have feared the worst. "Within five years from this time," Henry Clay predicted in the midst of the high tide of early nationalism in the aftermath of the War of 1812, "the Union would be divided into three distinct confederacies." Yet for all these anxieties, what is most striking when one takes the long view of American history is the extent to which the United States has been the beneficiary of geopolitical reconfigurations. The age of revolutions, the era of mid-nineteenth-century nation making, and the global crisis of the 1930s and 1940s all ended with the United States occupying a more secure and profitable position within the international system.[8]

National security has been more than merely a matter of diplomacy and foreign relations; it also has molded domestic politics, fueled the growth of the federal government, and fostered America's ardently nationalist culture. International crises have been the catalysts of political innovation. The 1787 Constitution—the world's oldest written national constitution—aimed not only to balance liberty with order but also to enhance the security of the imperiled former British colonies. The specter of foreign threats similarly prompted the creation of the modern national security state in the mid-twentieth century. And it was sometimes the absence of external threat that made all the difference. It was no coincidence that the Civil War unfolded at a moment of newfound security for the Union, nor that the destructive partisanship and culture wars of our own era have occurred against the backdrop of America's Cold War triumph.

Second, the development of global capitalism has played a key role in the making of the United States. Here, too, America has benefited from broader developments. Over the course of the last two and a half centuries, the United States has been one of the greatest beneficiaries of the economic processes that we now call globalization. It has attracted foreign capital at relatively low rates of interest, it has been a magnet for laborers seeking work, and it has accessed lucrative foreign markets and resources as well as attracted competitively priced imports. The development of the American economy, including the establishment of the immense internal market that has been the material foundation of US power, has been inseparable from the broader formation of global capitalism. The pursuit of wealth and economic power has been as central to the course of American history as has the pursuit of equality. "Our plan is commerce," Paine averred in his 1776 pamphlet, "and that, well attended to, will secure us the peace and friendship of all Europe; because, it is the interest of all Europe to have America a free port."[9]

But for as much as the international economy helped give rise to the US economic juggernaut, it also has been the source of internal discord and political conflict. The United States has never been a single economic unit; rather, like most nations, it is a conglomeration of different economic interests, many of which pursue their own objectives in the wider international order. Competition between different economic, sectional, and social groups has generated political tensions, which in turn have been intensified by the financial panics and economic downturns that have been an inescapable feature of global capitalism. The result has been divisive debates over economic questions, including tariffs, trade policy, foreign investment, and imperial connections. The international economic order, in short, has deepened internal divisions and contributed to crisis even as it has made the United States the wealthiest nation in world history.

Last, but certainly not least, is immigration. The inflow of people is a defining feature of the history of the United States, a "nation of nations." The largest numbers of immigrants arrived in the half century between 1870 and 1920 as well as in our own era since 1980. In both of these periods, the percentage of the population that was foreign-born climbed into the teens, triggering heated debate over immigration policy (the historic high is 14.8 percent in 1890; in 2016, the figure stood at 13.4 percent). But these were not the only times in which immigration created political controversy. Two of the periods that witnessed the largest proportionate increase in the population that was foreign-born often come as a surprise. The decade after 1845 saw some three million newcomers arrive on America's shores at a time when the 1850 census counted twenty-three million people in the United States. This wave of immigration, which was driven by the Irish potato famine and dislocation in Europe, particularly in Germany, accounted for a remarkable 13 percent of America's population. The span between the end of the Seven Years' War and the outbreak of the American War of Independence saw a similar surge of new arrivals, who came both voluntarily (from the British Isles and Germany) and against their will (enslaved Africans). The new arrivals of the 1760–1775 period amounted to an estimated 10 percent of the overall population of the colonies. The sudden bursts of immigration in these periods destabilized existing political institutions, contributing in both cases to the breakdowns that were to follow.[10]

Immigration has been of greater importance than merely functioning as a wedge issue debated by "native" Americans. Those who landed upon America's shores brought with them new ideas and political agendas. Immigrants arrived not to a monolithic society but rather to one with its own social fault lines, above all, those related to African American enslavement and its legacies. Immigrants and their children—even in eras such as the mid-twentieth century, when the percentage of the US population that was foreign-born plummeted to its all-time low of less than 5 percent as a result of federal immigration restrictions—have shaped the culture and politics of their new home just as much as the United States has changed them.

THE QUEST FOR national security and global power, America's shifting position in the international economy, and fluctuations in immigration have made the United States the nation that it is today. America's foreign relations have conditioned its history not only in their cumulative effects over the long haul but also as a result of their volatility. In periods of crisis, America's position in the world has lurched in unexpected directions. For as inexorable as the rise of the United States appears in retrospect, there have been contingent moments in which the very existence of the nation was up for grabs.

This is the essence of crisis: the world turned upside down; the known replaced by the unknown; panic reigning as people struggle to maintain their balance amid shifts in the very ground beneath their feet. "It came with a speed and ferocity that left men dazed," *New York Times* correspondent Elliot Bell wrote of Wall Street's catastrophic collapse in October 1929. "The market seemed like an insensate thing that was wreaking a wild and pitiless revenge upon those who thought to master it." Crises are contagious, spreading like viruses from one realm to another. It is not without reason that the word *crisis* was associated with medical conditions and health scares in the nineteenth century. Each of the periods under consideration in this book were less a singular crisis than a set of interlinked crises—a political crisis could trigger an economic panic, which in turn could intensify social conflict, and so on. As these pandemics spread throughout the body politic, crisis itself was normalized, becoming an almost accepted characteristic of an age.[11]

Just as foreign crises have spread to the United States, domestic ones have spilled outside its borders, unsettling foreign countries and peoples as well as reconfiguring America's connections to the world. Consider the fateful winter of secession that followed the 1860 election of Abraham Lincoln. The crisis over slavery that divided the Union into warring sections also led to a series of sharp reversals in America's position in the global system. The immigration surge of the 1840s and 1850s was followed by a span that saw the lowest number of foreign arrivals in a century. The foreign capital that had rushed into the roaring American economy in the preceding decades suddenly began to flee; indeed, more capital left the United States in 1860–1862 than came into it, also a once-in-a-century occurrence. One of the world's most valuable commodities and America's largest export—Southern cotton—was confined to the ports of the Confederacy as a result of Richmond's ill-fated diplomatic strategy, leading to unemployment and social unrest in the British textile towns of Lancashire. The most unexpected reversal was how the national security that the United States had attained after the war against Mexico in the 1840s was suddenly imperiled, with European powers encroaching once again upon the Western Hemisphere. Meanwhile, Confederate emissaries crossed the Atlantic in search of an alliance with Britain.

"Our country, after having expelled all European powers from the continent," Secretary of State William H. Seward lamented in early 1861, now threatened to "relapse into an aggravated form of its colonial experience, and, like Italy, Turkey, India, and China, become the theatre of transatlantic intervention and rapacity."[12]

A wider view of American history that looks beyond the nation's borders brings into focus not only the migration patterns, economic flows, and international rivalries that have connected the United States to the world but also those rare moments in which the very existence of the nation was in question. Perhaps none was more pregnant with implications than the autumn of 1777, when the fate of the patriots' bid for independence hung in the balance. Having proclaimed their independence to the world the previous fourth of July, their cause had stalled, on the battlefield and in the diplomatic courts of the Old World. "I think the game is pretty near up," Washington privately confessed at year's end. "To accomplish their independence is not quite so easy as to declare it," the English philosopher Jeremy Bentham haughtily remarked. But then a series of events forever changed the course of modern history: the stunning patriot victory at the Battle of Saratoga in October; the drafting of the Articles of Confederation in November that, for all its limitations, further demonstrated the political resolve of the Americans; and, most of all, the alliance signed with France in February 1778, which provided the patriots with the resources, military assistance, and naval power that ultimately tipped the scales in their favor.[13]

There are comparable "Saratoga moments" in other crises of US history, as we shall see. These contingent moments played out in their own distinctive ways but are joined by a common denominator that has been curiously forgotten in our age of US global power: foreign states and peoples have played decisive roles in the critical moments of American history. As we make our way through

our own era of global instability in an unprecedentedly interconnected world, there is perhaps no more important lesson from the
past to keep in mind.

"CRISIS MAY BEGET crisis," Franklin D. Roosevelt said as his administration transitioned from battling the Great Depression to enter-
ing the Second World War, "but the progress underneath does not
wholly halt—it does go forward." Like so many of Roosevelt's public statements, this one reveals a truth even as it conceals others.
The United States came out on the other side of its greatest crises
as a stronger and more efficiently organized nation, as Roosevelt
suggested. The process of mobilizing resources to counter threats
catalyzed innovations in political economy, such as the creation of
a national financial system during the Civil War and the economic
reforms of the New Deal. Previously marginalized social groups,
particularly women, African Americans, and immigrants, secured
new political rights, not least because of the sacrifices they made
on behalf of the nation in its moments of need. In the bigger picture, the United States came to be the most powerful nation the
world has ever known because of the stress tests it endured, the
rivals it overcame, and the power it accrued during its moments of
trial.[14]

But as true as all of that is, such Whiggish notions of the forward progress of the United States are misleading. The crises that
forged the nation saw rights taken away from social groups, as well
as granted to them. The new nation of the 1780s was founded upon
slavery as well as freedom. The political rights earned by African
Americans during the Civil War were rolled back in the era of Jim
Crow; loyal Japanese Americans were rounded up into internment
camps in the 1940s; and "Rosie the Riveter" was welcomed into the
workforce during the Second World War, only to then be told to
return home after 1945. Crisis moments might have catalyzed the

rationalization of the political system, but they also perpetuated inequalities and sowed the seeds of future troubles.[15]

When we view American history from a global perspective, we see a nation that has been prone to abrupt reversals in its relations with the wider world. The United States has gyrated between free trade and economic nationalism, between encouraging immigration and restricting it, and from expansionist foreign policies to those aimed at limiting its commitments abroad. Old enemies have been embraced as new allies, only then to revert to rivals. Amid all these twists and turns, there is a discernable—and curiously underappreciated—pattern: geopolitical shifts that enhanced American security and power have devolved into periods of instability at home. Moments of international triumph have quickly transitioned to political crisis. A mere dozen years lay between the 1763 victory in the Seven Years' War and the 1775 "shot heard round the world" at Lexington and Concord; the conquest of Mexico in 1848 and the collapse of the Union in 1860; the decisive US intervention in the First World War in 1917 and the Wall Street crash of 1929; and the fall of the Berlin Wall in 1989 and the terrorist attacks of 9/11. America's global ascent has not unfolded in a linear manner, even if the historical trendline—at least until recently—has been the growth of US national power.

As we navigate through our own iteration of what Lincoln called "the stormy present," it behooves us to take a new look at our history to see how past moments of crisis have made America the nation that it is today. Furthermore, in an age in which our political crises are entangled with the volatile processes of modern globalization, we would be well served to revisit the nation's history from a global vantage. When we do this, the familiar story of America's history looks different. To return to the metaphor of the ship of state, far from being one that has inexorably sailed forward in pursuit of its founding ideals, the United States is one that has been blown in unexpected directions and whose rudders have sharply turned when tossed about in tempestuous waters. This book aims to show that American history does not move consistently in any direction, that US citizens alone have not determined their nation's destiny, and that the interconnected nature of the modern world ensured that the crises that forged the United States were not confined to its borders. These realities were evident in the very beginning, at the unexpected founding of a new nation, a crisis to which we will now turn.[16]

CHAPTER 1

An Unexpected Result

"THERE IS SOMETHING ABSURD," Thomas Paine wrote in *Common Sense*, "in supposing a continent to be perpetually governed by an island." It is testament to the subsequent success of the American experiment that Paine's words ring far truer today than they did when written in 1776. To the majority of those living in British North America in the mid-eighteenth century, there had been nothing absurd about remaining connected to the empire that they celebrated as a guardian of their British liberties. "I never had heard in any conversation from any person drunk or sober," reported Benjamin Franklin in 1775, "the least expression of a wish for a separation." It was with the regret of a spurned lover, not the anti-imperial zeal of a separate people, with which patriots moved toward political independence. "We must endeavor to forget our former love for them," Jefferson wrote in the original rough draft of the 1776 Declaration of Independence. "We might have been a free & great people together."[1]

That thirteen of Britain's North American colonies came to seek their independence was the unexpected result of a volatile international environment. The United States was the by-product of an age of European expansion and world war. The struggle for mastery over North America—the site of Europe's largest overseas settlements and most lucrative markets—helped to trigger a series of broader conflicts between Britain and France, which intensified in the mid-eighteenth century and didn't come to an end until the defeat of Napoleon at Waterloo in 1815. But it wasn't just the world wars of this period that led to the unanticipated result of American independence. The mid-eighteenth century witnessed a sudden developmental burst in North America. The growing American colonies did not drift apart from the mother country in the mid-eighteenth century, but just the opposite: immigration boomed, transatlantic trade dramatically increased, and the aggregate power of British North America multiplied. This breakneck pace of growth placed new strains on the underdeveloped political institutions of the Britain's North American empire.

At the very moment that the Atlantic shrunk like a contracting accordion, the defeat of France in the Seven Years' War reconfigured the geopolitical landscape, giving Britain and its colonists the upper hand in North America, including nominal control of the lands west of the Appalachians. Here were the roots of the looming crisis. The old political institutions of the British Empire were unsuited to this new context of high war debts, rapid growth and expansion of the North American colonies, and persistent conflict with Native peoples. New circumstances demanded political change. The peoples of the British Empire on both sides of the Atlantic debated how to adapt to this new context, unleashing a polarizing process of political sorting that ultimately erupted into war with the 1775 "shot heard round the world" at the battles of Lexington and Concord.

The ensuing American Revolution was less an anticolonial rebellion or social revolution than it was a crisis of integration, a civil
war waged over political control of a booming North America. For
as much as we today remember this as a struggle for freedom and
liberty, it was also a conflict about power and authority. This civil
war, however, did not play out in isolation from the broader international order. The 1778 internationalization of the American
conflict, in which France entered the war as allies of the patriots,
did as much as any other factor to determine its result. But, as was
so often the case in this age of world war, the conclusion of the
conflict in 1783 did not settle matters. The American republic remained vulnerable, threatening to collapse in the face of persistent
foreign pressures and internal discord in the ensuing years. The
two founding documents of 1787, the Constitution of the United
States and the Northwest Ordinance, stabilized the former colonies, providing them with a political framework engineered for the
international habitat to which the new nation had been born. But
for all the genius of the US founding, lurking within the nation's
new political system was a fatal flaw that in time would erode it
from within.

I

Of all the characteristics of British North America in the mid-
eighteenth century, none did more to shape the volatile politics of
the period than did its remarkable growth. In the early eighteenth
century, Britain's American colonies were sparsely populated outposts of the Old World. In 1730 its European settler population was
only 629,000, most of whom were huddled close to the Atlantic seaboard. By 1770, the colonial population had surpassed two million,
thanks in large part to the high birth rates of colonial America—
what Benjamin Franklin called "the American multiplication table"

in which the population nearly doubled every twenty years. "If they should continue to double and double," Samuel Johnson wrote of the colonies in 1775, "their own hemisphere would not contain them."[2]

A dramatic upswing in immigration also fueled the growth of the American colonies. After stagnating in the early eighteenth century, emigration from the British Isles to North America started to accelerate; emigrants in the period 1700–1740 totaled only 39,400—a figure nearly matched in the following decade alone. This increase in migration of the 1740s and 1750s portended a much larger wave in the 1760–1775 period, which witnessed an estimated 125,000 arriving from across the British Isles. The largest number of arrivals now came not from England, but from Ulster and Scotland, thus diversifying the British population of the colonies. Other arrivals came from further afield. Of particular note were Germans, large concentrations of whom settled in Pennsylvania, as well as an estimated 84,500 enslaved Africans who were brought against their will to the colonies, which would soon become a proslavery republic. The total arrivals in the decade and a half after 1760, including those brought to the New World against their will, comprised roughly 10 percent of the population of the thirteen colonies in 1775. In terms of the proportionate increase in the percent of the population that was born overseas, this was one of the most significant immigration surges in American history.[3]

The increase in immigration was part of a broader integration of Britain's Atlantic economic system. The movement of people generated a corresponding increase in the exchange of mail and news across the Atlantic. Trade and investment also ballooned; exports from Britain to North America increased an astounding 360 percent between 1740 and 1770. The growing population of British North America only partially accounts for this increase. Per capita consumption of British goods in colonial America grew by 50 percent. Living standards rose across North America.

A threefold increase of shipping capacity made this commercial boom possible. So, too, did innovations in transatlantic systems of credit and insurance, which developed to meet the rising demand of an economic system that was fast becoming a single unit. Although the population of the colonies was becoming more diverse, its economic connections to the Old World were becoming more British.[4]

The goods that crossed the Atlantic introduced British material culture into the daily lives of the inhabitants of the North American colonies. The products that colonists imported in this period extended far beyond the items needed for survival, a characteristic of early colonial trade. The mid-eighteenth century witnessed the birth of a consumer society fueled by the symbiotic forces of British manufacturing and increased colonial demand. Colonists mothballed their homespuns in favor of imported textiles; they indulged in imported tea and sugar; they purchased the mid-eighteenth century's must-have furniture item—the glass-paneled corner cupboard—to display their growing collection of Staffordshire ceramics. "The quick importation of fashions from the mother country is really astonishing," remarked one Englishman in Maryland in 1771. "In short, very little difference is, in reality, observable in the manners of the wealthy colonist and the wealthy Briton." What was most significant about the spread of British consumer goods in this period was that it happened in multiple places at the same time—in the tidewater of Virginia as well as the towns of New England, and in the diverse cities of the middle colonies, not to mention in old England itself. Social customs such as tea time helped colonists to imagine themselves as part of a transatlantic British community, one that consumed similar goods, expressed allegiance to the same king, and—most of all—were united in opposition to the shared enemies of French Catholicism and France's Native American allies. "Every drop of blood in my heart is *British*," wrote future founding father from Pennsylvania

John Dickinson in 1766. But not all in North America narrowly defined Britishness in ethnic terms. In its most capacious sense, to be British meant to be an equal member of a diverse transatlantic cultural and political community.[5]

The dramatic growth of Britain's Atlantic empire in the mid-eighteenth century did not invariably foster imperial unity. Indeed, the scale and pace of change unsettled old colonial institutions and networks, which struggled to keep up. On both sides of the Atlantic, observers began to express new anxieties about how North America's sudden growth spurt might disrupt the status quo in commerce, culture, and politics. Elites in the home isles became gripped by fears that emigration to North America deprived Britain of skilled labor and threatened to undermine its dominance in manufacturing. In this zero-sum calculation, the strengthening of the colonies constituted a threat to Britain. "Every sensible person must foresee that our fellow subjects in America, will, in less than half a century," one London paper opined, "form a state much more numerous and powerful than their mother-country. At this time, were they inclined to throw off their dependency, it would be difficult for this kingdom to keep them in subjection."

British observers took note of the character of those who chose to cross the Atlantic, seeing omens of future trouble. "Men who emigrate are, from the nature of the circumstances," remarked the English agriculture writer Arthur Young, "the most active, hardy, daring, bold and resolute spirits, and probably the most mischievous also." As officials in London sought to restrict further emigration by prohibiting the American colonies from offering enticements to prospective settlers, some in North America became concerned that their societies would come to be dominated by other immigrant groups. "Why should Pennsylvania, founded by the English," Benjamin Franklin wrote, "become a colony of *Aliens*, who will shortly be so numerous as to Germanize us instead our Anglifying them, and will never adopt our Language or Customs any more than they can acquire our Complexion?" Franklin was not alone in opposing attempts to restrict British immigration to the colonies. Indeed, one of the grievances leveled against King George III in the Declaration of Independence was that "he has endeavoured to prevent the population of these States."[6]

The booming economy of the colonies also placed new pressures on British mercantile regulations, which dated back to the mid-seventeenth century. American colonists and merchants became experts at finding loopholes and weak spots in Britain's hoary Navigation Acts, whose purpose was to increase customs revenue for the Crown by regulating colonial trade. British commercial and political leaders understood that the growth of the North American market carried with it the risk that foreign competitors would profit from illicit trade that the colonists themselves facilitated. The case of one of the era's most sought-after commodities—tea— is revealing: an estimated 75 percent of the tea consumed in North America was thought to be smuggled in from Dutch sources in the West Indies in violation of Britain's protectionist Navigation Acts. Lord Townshend worried that the "great commercial system, on which the strength and prosperity of Great Britain and the mutual interest of both countries, vitally depended" would be undermined by "the foolishly ambitious temper of a turbulently ungrateful people" in North America. Such thinking lay behind the future Tea Act (1773), which though it actually reduced duties, nonetheless infuriated colonial merchants in that it undercut their business by propping up the exports of the monopoly British East India Company. In short, the rapid growth of the population and economy of North American presented new challenges to a British mercantile order that had taken root in an earlier age characterized by colonial dependence and relatively slow economic development.[7]

At the very moment that the British Empire wrestled with how to adapt to the growth of North America and the Atlantic economy, conflict with the old foe of France intensified. There was nothing new about war between Britain and France, who clashed from 1743 to 1748. War beget war. Even when Britain and France were at peace in this period, they were paying for the most recent conflict and preparing for the next one. And it wasn't just the formal wars that were of significance to mid-eighteenth century North America. The Anglo-French rivalry drew in the Native peoples of North America, who shrewdly played the European powers against one another in pursuit of their own objectives. "The importance of the Indians is now generally known and understood," remarked an English trader in 1755. "A Doubt remains not, that the prosperity of our Colonies on the Continent will stand or fall with our Interest and favour among them." The escalating rivalry with France and her Native allies required constant political attention at the very moment an Atlantic boom was transforming the colonies' social and economic foundations. Managing these entwined, structural shifts placed acute strains upon the political institutions of the British Empire.[8]

In 1754 the Anglo-French rivalry again flared up, ultimately erupting into the Seven Years' War, known in America as the French and Indian War. This global conflict deserves the label of a "world war" given its reach from North America to eastern Europe, West Africa to the Caribbean, and Bengal to Manila. It all began in the contested interior of North America, where a young Virginian named George Washington led an ill-fated British military expedition to push the French and their Native allies out of a contested area in the Ohio Valley, near present-day Pittsburgh. Washington's defeat set in motion a chain reaction, first in North America, where Britain (and her colonies) escalated the campaign against France. Within a few years, the war had spread around the globe. "The turmoil in which Europe finds itself," Frederick the Great wrote, "began in America.... But, thanks to our century's statecraft, there is now no conflict in the world, however small it may be, which...does not threaten to engulf the whole of Christendom."

coastal hinterlands, such as Florida (acquired from Spain in the 1763 treaty), thus advancing Britain's strategic interests. The Royal Proclamation Line, as it was called, shocked and enraged colonists, who had long railed against the attempt of Catholic France to use her Native allies to contain British expansion in the very regions that they had fought to control in the recent war. In their eyes, the imperial state in London had betrayed them, denying them the fruits of their victory. A distant government was micromanaging their affairs, signaling disrespect and superiority in the process. The suspicion of central power that would become such a feature of American history was powerfully on display in the aftermath of the Seven Years' War.

At the very moment that the furor over the Royal Proclamation played out, British officials also sought to address their crisis of public finance. Britain's ability to mobilize capital was a decisive factor in the outcome of the Seven Years' War. But when the war ended, debt became a question of mathematics. There simply were not enough inlays to cover the outlays. The national debt ballooned from £72 million in 1755 to £146 million at the war's conclusion. Furthermore, the new strategic liabilities in North America came with an estimated £225,000 yearly bill. Once again, there were no good options—only a series of bad ones. Once again, British officials made a bad situation worse. They turned to the colonists to shoulder their share of the burden after a costly war that had resulted in new military commitments in North America. It was widely recognized that the colonists paid only a fraction of the taxes demanded of Englishmen—by one estimate, the per capita imperial tax burden in North America was one shilling, whereas it was twenty-six shillings per head in England. "The great object," declared Prime Minister George Grenville in 1764, "is to reconcile the regulation of commerce with an increase of revenue." Viewed from London, the colonists were beneficiaries of British military spending. North America's growing economy and population now enabled the colonies to shoulder their fair share of the costs of the empire that had so demonstrably advanced their interests.[11]

II

What unfolded next was a radicalizing process of political sorting. In a series of controversies over the next dozen years, imperial reformers in London attempted to assert political power over the colonists to get them to contribute more to the costs of the British Empire. Parliament passed a cascade of acts aimed at increasing revenues and establishing its authority in North America: the Sugar Act, the Stamp Act, the Declaratory Act, the Tea Act, the Boston Port Act. Each time Parliament made its move, resisting colonists—who came to call themselves patriots—countered with one of their own, and did so with surprising vehemence, sophistication, and, as time progressed, unity. Their responses included founding the Sons of Liberty, orchestrating consumer boycotts, publishing the Massachusetts Circular Letter, dumping tea into Boston Harbor, and convening the Continental Congress in 1774 to establish a more unified front in the face of Britain's policies. The harder each side tugged, the more intractable the crisis became and the more difficult it was for Britons on either side of the Atlantic to maintain a middle-of-the-road position somewhere between the widening poles. Eventually, American patriots severed their political links to the British Empire in the 1776 Declaration of Independence.

The tug of war started soon after the conclusion of the Seven Years' War. In the eyes of an emerging group of British political elites, the empire's old administrative and political institutions were not up to the new task that confronted them. Although the British were victorious against their French rival, the war had revealed the deficiencies of the administration and financing of their empire. During the conflict, Whig statesman William Pitt in London had incentivized the cooperation of the North American colonies by committing the British treasury to reimburse some 40 percent of the war expenditures made by colonial assemblies, thus creating the financial hole that required new revenue streams to fill. But the legacies of the war were not all perilous. By necessitating the growth and integration of Britain's imperial apparatus, the long struggle against France had cracked open the door to the centralization of political power within the empire. Measures like the 1765 Stamp Act of the Grenville ministry not only sought new sources of revenue but also aimed to impose order upon an undisciplined fiscal and imperial system, particularly where its power was weakest—in the colonies themselves. The desired result was a more centralized and efficient empire, one with the political institutions to match its newly expanded territorial and commercial reach. The Stamp Act had its share of critics in Britain as well as the colonies. But even some of the most vociferous opponents of the measure saw the need to defend the powers of Parliament. "When two countries are connected together, like England and her colonies, without being incorporated together," William Pitt asserted in a speech otherwise known for its conciliatory tone toward the American colonists, "the one must necessarily govern; the greater must rule the less."[12]

These imperial reforms were highly unpopular in the colonies, which had grown accustomed to home rule—"salutary neglect," as Edmund Burke labeled Britain's North American policy of the early eighteenth century. Those loyal to the British Empire in North America had their work cut out for themselves. Defenders of British rule dug in upon unfavorable terrain in the 1760s and 1770s, grouped as they were with the unpopular policies that emanated from London: restrictions on attractive western lands; the enforcement of mercantile regulations; and, most of all, the levying of taxes by Parliament.

The problems facing the estimated 20 percent of the colonies' population that would remain loyal to the British Empire in the ensuing civil war went deeper than the unpopular policies with which they became associated. Those who came to be called *Loyalists* or, less affectionately, *tories* were often outsiders from numerically small or even marginalized social groups. At the top stood those elites who enjoyed the spoils of royal patronage. These were the colonial governors, imperial officials, Anglican clergy, and wealthy merchants whose social status and positions of authority relied upon British rule. These elites lacked the common touch and popular appeal required in an era marked by increased public participation in politics. But Loyalists were not simply elites; they hailed from diverse social backgrounds, including many from regions of ethnic and religious diversity in the mid-Atlantic colonies and the backcountry of the South. These common Loyalists feared the public committees and dictates of their fellow colonists—with reason, it should be added—more than that of the distant Parliament in London. In the eyes of these Loyalists, British rule was desirable because it could counteract the power of a coalescing patriot majority that threatened the property and even security of those who opposed them. When the fighting had begun in the 1770s, one Marylander believed that "it was better for the poor people to lay down their arms and pay the duties and taxes laid upon them by King and Parliament than to be brought into slavery and to be commanded and ordered about as they were" by patriot leaders.[13]

Loyalists' reasons for defending British rule did not have wide appeal, at least in the comparatively populous and prosperous North American colonies. The story was different elsewhere in Britain's American empire, where fourteen colonies remained loyal. The common denominators among those that did not join the rebellion of the thirteen mainland colonies are revealing. Those in the West Indies, such as Jamaica and Barbados, remained more dependent upon British power for security against imperial rivals—and internal dangers of slave rebellion—than did the thirteen colonies. Many of the owners of the plantations in the British Caribbean continued to live in England. These absentee slave masters sought to buy their way into the British aristocracy, not challenge its legitimacy. In Nova Scotia, which also remained loyal, crown-appointed officials held more power than they did in the colonies to the south. Economically, those colonies that remained loyal also tended to be more reliant upon British markets, imports, and credit.[14]

These conditions of dependence did not exist in the dynamic and more economically diverse thirteen colonies of the mainland, where a group of self-labeled patriots led the resistance to Britain's attempts to impose its authority. The patriots operated from a position of political advantage—they dug in on higher ground. The colonies that became the United States were not only less dependent upon British power than were those of the West Indies but also possessed a relatively liberal social and economic order that primed them for political innovation. For all of the elaborately formulated fears about the creep of Old World hierarchies, Americans remained comparatively free from the ecclesiastical establishments, fixed social hierarchy, and central political power that they were so quick to denounce. Some British imperial officials recognized the near impossibility of imposing Old World forms of authority upon the peoples of the New World. "The British form of government, transplanted into this continent," wrote British imperial governor Sir Guy Carleton in 1768, "never will produce the same Fruits as at Home, because it is impossible for the Dignity of the Throne, or Peerage to be represented in the American Forests." It was in this fertile soil that the seeds of patriot resistance—and future American democracy—took root.[15]

If the social foundations of the rebelling colonies set them apart, the secret to the patriots' success was how they appropriated

British ideas, institutions, and infrastructures of power. Although remembered today as revolutionaries, those colonists opposed to British imperial centralization were a rather conservative group when it came to defending existing political institutions, at least in the early phases of the imperial crisis. These self-proclaimed patriots celebrated their English rights, the powers of their colonial assemblies against intrusive royal governors and acts of Parliament, and the status quo of a decentralized British Empire. "It was precisely because they saw themselves as British," Sir John Elliott has written, "that the Americans would stand up for their rights."[16] That peculiar American tradition of "moving forward while facing backward" can be seen in the patriots' political thought. The political crisis prompted a rediscovery of the old British "country Whig" ideas from earlier in the eighteenth century that had identified corruption and centralized power as existential threats to the collective political community. The early phases of the imperial crisis also saw colonists embrace royalism as a means of opposing the centralizing ambitions of Parliament. A group of Massachusetts opponents of the Stamp Act opened their petition by proclaiming that they were "True and Loyal Subjects to our King." In this formulation, it was the imperial reformers of London who were threatening to undermine the integrity of the British Empire—the true Britons were those in North America.[17]

Patriots commandeered more than just old British political languages. They also harnessed the power of the empire's political and economic structures on behalf of their cause. The colonial assemblies evolved into being almost miniature parliaments in each colony, the printing presses churned out the era's rich pamphlet literature and newspapers, and the roads and communication systems that had been central to Britain's victory over the French in the Seven Years' War became the circuits through which colonists coordinated information about resistance to British policies after

1763. Even docks and wharfs were commandeered by the colonists in sensational acts of resistance, such as the Boston Tea Party. As is so often the case in civil wars, the side that took control of existing institutions of political power and networks of exchange gained a decisive advantage.[18]

Patriots ingeniously built new political networks on top of these colonial foundations. Nowhere can their political creativity be seen more clearly than in their exploitation of the era's booming consumer marketplace. When Parliament raised duties and taxes, colonists responded by orchestrating surprisingly effective consumer boycotts. These nonimportation and nonconsumption protests achieved two objectives. First, they struck back at Britain by restricting the American markets to which British manufacturers were coming to rely upon. Second, and just as important, the boycotts became an effective method of fostering political unity within the colonies. The public committees and petitions of the colonial boycotts staked out the rationale and form of colonial resistance while also broadening political participation. Those unable to vote in elections for colonial assemblies made their voices heard by participating in boycotts. "The people, even to the lowest Ranks," John Adams observed as early as 1765, "have become more attentive to their Liberties, more inquisitive about them, and more determined to defend them, than they were ever before known or had occasion to be." Women took part in boycott associations and other political arms of patriot agitation, strengthening the patriot cause and sowing the seeds of female empowerment and political participation that would become a defining feature of nineteenth-century America. "Tho a female," the New Jersey poet Annis Boudinot Stockton wrote, "I was born a patriot and cant help it If I would."[19]

There was, however, a darker, suppressive side to this activity. Patriot organizations and public committees deployed shaming, intimidation, and violence to achieve their political objectives. Those colonists who disregarded nonimportation and boycott campaigns, for example, were named and shamed in local newspapers, losing their reputations and credibility in the process. Extralegal public committees of patriots sprang up to enforce boycotts by brute force and intimidation. A key feature of the imperial crisis of the 1760s and 1770s was its escalation. The tarring and feathering of British tax collectors provoked heavy-handed British reprisals, which in turn further inflamed patriot resistance. Nowhere was this more so than in Boston, a hotbed of resistance to British authority. This intensifying cycle of political conflict was evident across British North America. In Virginia, the patriot cause was fueled not only by the call of "no taxation without representation" but also by the move of Lord Dunmore, the royal governor, who responded to the escalation of patriot resistance in 1775 by attempting to enlist the enslaved on behalf of defending British rule. The scheme ultimately backfired. Yet again British policies made an unfavorable situation even worse. The effect of Dunmore's proclamation was to bolster the ranks of the patriots and push them toward the radical political position of embracing independence. In the British Caribbean, concerns about the stability of slavery fostered imperial loyalty; in Virginia, in contrast, anxieties about slave rebellion fueled patriot resistance.[20]

In disrupting the relationship with the imperial center in London, as well as introducing intimidation and suppression into the equation, the patriot cause destabilized a range of social institutions and relations. New possibilities emerged as the imperial crisis progressed. This was when the unexpected began to unfold. The most significant departure was how patriots transitioned from attempting to beat back the centralizing tendencies of the post-1763 British imperial state to the more radical moves of declaring independence and joining together in a new political union. Even after the opening battles of the civil war at Lexington and Concord in April 1775, the majority of the patriots stopped short of calling for full independence, hoping instead for some advantageous negotiated settlement. This soon would change.

It was in this period of flux that an English immigrant named Thomas Paine arrived in Philadelphia in 1774. More than any other individual, it was this newcomer who lit the fuse that would detonate the original political fireworks of the Fourth of July. The genius of *Common Sense*, Paine's pamphlet published in January 1776, was how it presented the radical step of breaking from Britain in terms understandable to an increasingly politicized and excitable public. Paine avoided the impenetrable, high-brow prose of the era's political pamphlets, a point signaled in his title: common people could understand the arguments of *Common Sense*. Paine rhetorically smashed the foundations of British politics—above all, the monarchy and mercantilism—in order to clear space for his vision of an independent, republican union of the former American colonies. Rather than emphasize the British precedents for colonial demands, Paine declared that "the cause of America is in a great measure the cause of all mankind." *Common Sense* did not seek merely to reclaim English rights; rather, it sought to promote "natural rights of all mankind." Paine's common-sense argument extended to the foreign relations of an independent America. "It is the true interest of America to steer clear of European contentions," Paine wrote, "which she can never do, while by her dependence on Britain, she is made the make-weight in the scale of British politics." The economic interests of America, Paine likewise contended, pointed toward independent internationalism, in which America could "shake hands with the world—live at peace with the world—and trade to any market." Once freed from the shackles of British trade regulations, America could expand and diversify its export markets. Open markets would serve American interests for as long as "eating is the custom of Europe." Paine's liberal economic vision was one that shared traits with another landmark publication of 1776, Adam Smith's *The Wealth of Nations.*

Common Sense popularized the arguments that would soon find expression in the Declaration of Independence and the liberal economic internationalism of the Jeffersonians. Paine was a brilliant political thinker and pamphleteer. But *Common Sense* was the product of not merely individual genius but also the integration of the British Empire: the burst of migration to British North America that brought Paine to Pennsylvania; the exchange of ideas— liberal and radical, in Paine's case—across the Atlantic; and the new possibilities opened up by a political crisis that destabilized political institutions, commercial regulations, and social hierarchies. The most influential case for the independence of the colonies was less the culmination of some distinctly American political tradition than it was the unanticipated product of the growth and integration of the British Atlantic system. It was thus fitting that the byline of the first edition of *Common Sense* informed readers that it was "written by an Englishman."[21]

III

What is now called the American Revolution did not totally upend a social order in the way the French Revolution would. Nor was it an anticolonial rebellion, at least not in the modern terms of a unified people rising against foreign colonialism in all its forms— racial ideology, labor exploitation, resource appropriation, political domination. Rather, the Revolution is best understood as a civil war waged over control of the political institutions of the British Empire that required adaptation to the new contexts of the post-1763 era. This was a civil war in a double sense: the struggle pitted American colonists against their brethren across the Atlantic as well as against one another. To call the conflict a civil war is not to impose some newfangled meaning upon it but rather to recover how many observers at the time made sense of what was unfolding. Shortly after the opening shots were fired in the battles of Lexington and Concord in April 1775, a Rhode Island newspaper announced the commencement of "the *American Civil War*, which will hereafter fill an important page in history." The conflict was called a civil war, particularly in its early years, by those across the political spectrum in Britain and in the colonies.[22]

The outcome of this civil war would be determined not only by the relative strength of each party but also by the actions of foreign powers. The winds of international rivalry filled the sails of the Patriot cause. The greatest geopolitical advantage of the American rebels, somewhat paradoxically, was the unrivaled power of their opponent. Britain's position of international strength after 1763 stoked resentment and anxiety across Europe. The relative dominance of a single power deranged international relations to the fortuitous benefit of what came to call itself the United States.

Still reeling from its defeat in the Seven Years' War, France waited for an opportunity to strike back against its old rival. Foreign Minister Comte de Vergennes devised a new strategy. France would negate Britain's greatest strength—its maritime dominance—by embarking upon an ambitious program of naval buildup. French diplomacy would stay out of costly European disputes so as to concentrate its power on countering the British. The nation known for meddling in Europe uncharacteristically steered clear of a diplomatic crisis in Bavaria in 1778. But the French did not just stand back. They also constructed a coalition of those aggrieved by Britain's rapid expansion. They negotiated their most important alliance in 1779 with Spain, who wanted to reclaim Florida, Minorca, and—above all—Gibraltar, which Britain had captured in the War of Spanish Succession in 1704. Other powers seized the opportunity to chip away at British dominance. Even Britain's traditional ally Holland morphed into an enemy in the Fourth Anglo-Dutch

War (1780–1784). "We have no friend or ally to assist us," Lord Sandwich, First Lord of the Admiralty, explained in 1779, "on the contrary all those who ought to be our allies except Portugal act against us in supplying our enemies with the means of equipping their fleets."[23]

The outbreak of civil war in the American colonies played into France's hands. But Vergennes was a patient diplomat, one who was well aware of the Americans' traditional anti-Catholicism and hostility to France's long-standing Native American allies. Furthermore, with its program of naval buildup still ongoing, France chose to wait for the right moment to strike, rather than rush headlong into another conflict. Such considerations did not preclude early covert support for the Americans, which came in the form of war materials smuggled into the rebelling colonies. The patriots needed all the help that they could get. They required imported gunpowder in the war's early years, and their lack of a national financial system and historic reliance upon British credit presented obvious challenges to funding the war effort. "The world wondered that we so seldom fired a cannon," Benjamin Franklin explained. "We could not afford it." The American patriots quickly grasped the geopolitical calculus of their rebellion: to attain independence, they needed foreign support; but to secure foreign support, they needed first to declare their independence and unify into a single political entity. "It is not choice then but necessity that calls for Independence, as the only means by which foreign Alliances can be obtained; and a proper Confederation by which internal peace and union can be secured," Richard Henry Lee of Virginia wrote in June 1776.[24]

The 1776 Declaration of Independence was more than an articulation of timeless political principles. It was the cornerstone of American wartime statecraft, the nautical chart that determined the course taken by the world's newest ship of state. The Declaration sought to create momentum and confidence in the cause of independence, both at home and abroad. It proclaimed to the world that the thirteen rebellious colonies were united and independent, ready "to assume among the powers of the earth, the separate and equal station to which the Laws of nature and of Nature's God entitle them." Most significant of all, the Declaration committed the patriots not only to independence but also to union among the colonies. The statecraft of the new republic was in equal parts outward facing and inward looking; independence and union had been fused in a symbiotic relationship whose interlocked fortunes would wax and wane until a second civil war settled matters nearly a century later.[25]

There was no going back from the words Jefferson wrote in 1776. "A more impudent, false and atrocious Proclamation was never fabricated by the Hands of Man," grumbled British admiral Lord Howe. The Declaration boldly raised the stakes of the conflict. The target European audiences, however, did not immediately rush to the newly declared nation's aid. France and Spain remained to be convinced that the rebellious Americans could withstand conflict against Britain. With George Washington's ragtag and outnumbered army on the run after evacuating New York City in the autumn of 1776, the patriot cause looked bleak. It wasn't just the military situation that made the French think twice about formally jumping into the fray. Although the rebelling colonies had announced their unity and ambition, the Declaration was prospective, rather than descriptive, racing ahead of the institutional development and political integration of the thirteen states. The question remained: Were the rebelling Americans really "one people" that had formed a political regime strong enough to stick around?[26]

Two developments in 1777 provided the answer. The first occurred on the battlefield. The American victory at Saratoga in October derailed a British offensive under General John Burgoyne that aimed at separating the northeastern colonies from those to their south. It was a stunning victory. One Yankee observer spoke for many around the world in declaring the battle "perhaps an unprecedented Instance that near 6,000 British & foreign Troops, under the command of an accomplish'd General, should surrender themselves Prisoners of War *in the field* to an Army of raw Continental Troops & Militia!" Saratoga did not guarantee victory in the war for the Americans, but the triumph of the force of General Horatio Gates demonstrated that the American rebels were capable of holding their own against the mighty British. News of the American victory sent shock waves across the Atlantic. One French advocate of the American cause was in such a rush to propagate news of the battle when it reached Paris that he jackknifed his carriage. "We have the honor to acquaint your Excellency," the now Paris-based US diplomat Benjamin Franklin informed Vergennes, "with advice of the total reduction of the force under General Burgoyne." It appears that when word of Saratoga arrived in Versailles, the French were already of the view that war with Britain was inevitable. The extent of the American victory even raised concerns that Britain might make enough concessions to lead to a peaceful compromise with her rebelling colonies, placing the two Protestant, English-speaking entities back on a collision course with their traditional rival, Catholic France. "The question we have to solve," Vergennes wrote shortly after hearing rumors that Britain was preparing to make peace with its colonies, "is to know whether it is more expedient to have war against England and America united, or with America for us against England."[27]

The news of Saratoga was soon followed by another breakthrough for the Americans that increased their prospects of becoming a permanent player on the international scene. This one was of a political nature. In November 1777, the Continental Congress, a governing body of delegates representing the thirteen colonies, announced the completion of a new political framework for their association, the Articles of Confederation. The Articles envisioned a union that was little more than an alliance among independent but like-minded states—"a firm league of friendship," as it was called in Article III. The thirteen states, which drafted their own constitutions during the war, retained the real power under the Articles. It would not take long for the unwieldiness of the Articles to become clear; disputes over ownership of western lands delayed its ratification until 1781. But despite its ill-fated future, the Articles were heralded as a step in the right direction at a critical juncture in the war for independence. This new constitutional framework centralized US foreign policy and extended to Congress power to borrow money—something which in time led the states to "consider themselves as one body, animated by one soul," as John Adams later remembered. "More than any other consideration," Congress declared in the covering letter that it circulated with the new Articles, "it will confound our foreign enemies, defeat the flagitious practices of the disaffected, strengthen and confirm our friends, support our public credit, restore the value of our money, enable us to maintain our fleets and armies, and add weight and respect to our councils at home, and to our treaties abroad." However tentatively, the rebelling Americans were beginning to construct a political apparatus that Europeans could recognize as a central state worthy of doing business with. The initial announcement of the Articles—coming on the heels of the victory at Saratoga—further demonstrated to the world that far from being just a group of rebels, the thirteen British colonies were coalescing into a single country. The drafting of the Articles of Confederation served a vital constitutional and diplomatic purpose at a critical moment in the war.[28]

The climax of this Saratoga moment was the Franco-American treaty of February 1778, which transformed the course of the war. The civil war had been internationalized. The most immediate implication of the alliance was that it thwarted an attempt by Lord North's British government in 1778 to negotiate a peace with the

Americans in which they were to be offered effective home rule within the British Empire. Emboldened by the support of the powerful French, the American rebels rebuffed an offer that they might well have accepted just a few years earlier. The collapse of this attempt at a negotiated peace intensified the conflict. In the coming years, the United States needed every bit of the foreign assistance it received from France (and, to a lesser degree, from Spain after its alliance with France in 1779). Loans from France, Spain, and Holland helped to fill the gaping hole in the budget of the Continental Congress; French military support and war materials greatly enhanced the capabilities of the Continental Army; and French naval power set the stage for the decisive 1781 Battle of Yorktown—it was the French naval force commanded by Comte de Grasse that bottled up Cornwallis's army in Virginia, making it vulnerable to a siege by a joint Franco-American army under Washington's command. American independence from Britain was ultimately achieved by interdependence with its old French enemy.

The United States also benefited from the geographic expansion of the conflict that resulted from its 1778 internationalization. France sought to strengthen its position in the Caribbean, India, and on the high seas; Spain was intent upon taking back Gibraltar; Holland sought to advance its commercial and shipping interests. For a time in 1779, there was even the prospect of a Franco-Spanish invasion of Britain itself, an invasion fear not unlike that of 1940. The expansion of the war diverted British resources from North America, including in the west, where the United States accelerated operations against the Iroquois, Shawnee, and Cherokee. At the same time, the expansion of the conflict revealed an irony: American interests were served by British success outside of North America. The British would be more willing to entertain American independence if they were offset by imperial gains elsewhere. That is more or less how the civil war came to an end. Cornwallis's surrender at Yorktown was followed by significant British victories

in the Caribbean and India. Britain accepted the loss of her thirteen colonies and turned her back on old Native American allies
who were not represented at the negotiations that led to the 1783
Treaty of Paris. In exchange, the British strengthened their positions in Canada, the Caribbean, and—most of all—India, which
was now on its way to becoming the "jewel in the crown" of the
British Empire. France and Spain, in contrast, came away with little
to show for their costly intervention. Indeed, by greatly increasing
the French debt, the war helped to set in motion a chain of events
that would lead to the French Revolution in 1789.[29]

Foreign intervention in the civil war brought into the world a
new nation that might well not have established its independence
on its own. The United States was born premature, successfully delivered by its French midwife. Military and political leaders recognized that the end of the war in 1783 did not guarantee the survival
of the new nation. "Without an entire conformity to the Spirit of
the Union," Washington asserted at the war's end, "we cannot exist
as an Independent Power." There were, however, grounds for optimism. The experience of shared sacrifice and victory against the
mighty British Empire was a powerful incubator of patriotism in a
new republic that purged from its borders sixty thousand Loyalists
at war's end, many of whom ended up relocating within the British Empire, particularly Canada. New "continental" (as opposed to
"colonial") institutions created during the war, such as the Articles
of Confederation and the national debt, lived on after 1783, per-
petuating and institutionalizing connections across state lines. "A
national debt, if it is not excessive," Alexander Hamilton wrote,
"will be to us a national blessing." The war, in sum, tied the steel
rebar and poured the first layer of concrete in the national foundation of the United States.[30]

But the foundation of this new nation remained shallow and
unstable. The peace of 1783 saw the centripetal forces of union
gave way to the centrifugal forces of fragmentation. The loose

constitutional framework of the Articles of Confederation, in which individual states retained sovereignty and ultimate power, quickly proved unworkable. Operating under the new state constitutions drafted during the Revolution, newly elected state legislators— many of whom came from modest, backcountry backgrounds and embodied the era's emerging populist spirit—wielded more power than the national government created by the Articles. They focused on fiscal policy, the most pressing issue at hand. In the mid-1780s, states confronted the worst of all possible scenarios: high debts combined with deflation at a time of conflict between coastal elites and backcountry farmers. There was no easy answer—nor uniform response. Rhode Island prioritized the interests of small debtors through inflationary policies of printing more paper money. At the other end of the spectrum, Massachusetts doubled down on austerity and high taxes—taxes that were several times higher than those that had precipitated the patriot agitation back in the 1760s. Despite the different policies pursued in Rhode Island and Massachusetts, both witnessed social conflict and political instability.

As the individual states plotted their own ways forward, the infant union remained vulnerable. In North America, the independence of the United States triggered countermoves from the established imperial powers of the Old World. Britain had recognized US independence, but it maintained regional footholds in the West Indies and in Canada, whose population was bolstered by the arrival of Loyalists who understandably wanted to settle scores with the republic that had expelled them and expropriated their property. Even within the heart of North America, Britain provocatively maintained relations with its old Native American allies, continuing to occupy its forts in the Great Lakes region that lay within the borders of the United States. Meanwhile, London banks turned the screw on American debtors during a credit crunch in the mid-1780s. The new nation's problems did not end with the persistent power of the former colonial master. Spain sought to reinforce its position in the New World by strengthening its footholds in Florida and Louisiana that would protect its imperial core further south. The old Iberian empire demonstrated its power in 1784 when it cut off American access to the Mississippi River in New Orleans. The response of the United States in the unratified Jay-Gardoqui Treaty of 1786, in which Secretary of State John Jay of New York negotiated commercial benefits for the Northeast while forgoing American navigation rights on the Mississippi, inflamed sectional tensions at home. As Americans debated how to respond to the closing of the Mississippi, Spanish agents in the continental interior attempted to lure settlers and Native peoples into their orbit by offering generous land grants and trade opportunities. The signs pointed to a protracted imperial struggle to determine North American mastery—a competition for which the decentralized United States was ill prepared. "England is at heart inimical to us; Spain is jealous," wrote Henry Knox. "It would be no strange thing if within ten years the injustice of England or Spain should force us into a war; it would be strange if it should not within fifteen or twenty years."[31]

As external pressures mounted, cracks emerged in the new republic's shallow and unstable foundations. Alternative political possibilities appeared. Angry debtors and backcountry farmers rose against the Massachusetts establishment in Shay's Rebellion. Leaders of independent Vermont toyed with the possibility of re-entry into the British Empire. Western settlers considered allying with Old World imperial powers, particularly Spain. Some settlers sought to secede from established states; indeed, a new state of Franklin within the western territory of North Carolina was temporarily created. John Jay, a proponent of federal power, feared that unless meaningful political reform along national lines was adopted "every [American] state would be a little nation, jealous of its neighbors, and anxious to strengthen itself by foreign alliances, against its former friends." North America threatened to descend into a third major war since 1754.[32]

IV

The founding fathers who convened at the Philadelphia Constitutional Convention in 1787 did not have to compromise with one
another. They did not see eye to eye on the fundamental issues
of political representation, the institutional composition of government, regional interests, the powers of the state, or the future
of slavery. The list could go on. But for all their differences, the
statesmen assembled in Philadelphia were brought together by a
heightened perception of threat. They understood that they and
their nation faced a series of unacceptable risks. They shared the
belief that reforming, innovating, and empowering their constitutional system—however difficult that task might be—was more
desirable than risking the fate of political fragmentation and Old
World recolonization. "We have seen the necessity of the Union,"
James Madison wrote, "as our bulwark against foreign danger, as
the conservator of peace among ourselves, as the guardian of our
commerce and other common interests."[33]

It was one thing to recognize that strengthening the union between the states was the best hope for their political stabilization.
Finding a way to achieve that objective was an altogether different matter. At its most fundamental level, the greatest challenge
confronting the statesmen at the Philadelphia convention in 1787
concerned how to construct a central state capable of survival in
a volatile international order within the limits of a political environment in which most Americans remained suspicious of central
power. Americans wanted stability, order, and prosperity, but they
associated a strong central state with the actions of the British Parliament in the 1760s and 1770s. Madison summed up the dilemma
by acknowledging both the precarious international position of the
new republic and the legitimacy of the concern that "the means
of defense against foreign danger have been always the instruments of tyranny at home." The Constitution delicately walked this

tightrope: it created a new government powerful enough to maintain its independence in a world in which it faced foreign rivals and threats but not one so powerful that it would collapse under its own central weight by reawakening the very impulses that had triggered the break with Britain. The Constitutional Convention's many compromises sought the middle ground, none more so than the "great compromise" concerning the contentious issues of political representation and the geographic distribution of political power. The pragmatism of the eventual "great compromise"— which created a bicameral legislature with a lower house based on population and an upper house in which each state had two representatives—typified the US founding in that none of the delegates demanded total victory or the unconditional surrender of their opponents.[34]

The founding fathers did not seek to spread their revolution in foreign lands as did the French after 1789 and the Soviets after the Bolshevik take-over in 1917. Rather, the international objective of the postrevolutionary America was hard-headed realpolitik: to consolidate the gains of the Revolution by constructing a political system capable of securing the territories of the trans-Appalachian west as well as advancing the new republic's interests in the international arena. The Constitution empowered the new government to make treaties, lodge diplomatic protests, and more broadly, pursue its national interests. Furthermore, it gave authority to the central state to raise the taxes required to fund future wars. On this score, as in others, the Congress and the executive would need to collaborate. There were limits to the powers of the executive when it came to foreign policy, not least the two-thirds Senate majority required to ratify a treaty. It should come as little surprise that this precarious new republic riven by internal tensions would seek to implement constitutional safeguards against tyranny. The genius of the founding fathers of 1787 can be found in how they achieved two very different objectives at once: the Constitution was a bulwark against central tyranny—bolstered by the ratification of the Bill of Rights in 1791—even as it vested the new federal government with sufficient powers to compete with the monarchical, fiscal-military states of the Old World. "If we are to be one nation in any respect," Madison wrote in *Federalist 42*, "it clearly ought to be in respect to other nations."[35]

Of all the achievements of the Constitution, perhaps the least appreciated today is how the political stability it established fostered economic growth. The former colonies now united into a single, open economic market, one whose material integration would in time deepen its political unity. "A unity of commercial, as well as political, interests can only result from a unity of government," Alexander Hamilton argued in *Federalist 11*. The Constitution went further, endowing the new central state with the powers it needed to pursue the nation's international economic interests. The US objective of breaking down the restrictive mercantilist systems of the Old World had been impossible to achieve under the decentralized Articles of Confederation. By empowering the federal government to regulate overseas commerce as well as foreign relations, the Constitution enabled the new government to make a more vigorous attempt to "open all the foreign markets possible to our produce," as Jefferson put it in 1789. Just as important as breaking down foreign barriers to commerce was the ability of the new government to impose customs duties, or tariffs on imported goods. Import duties were by far the most important source of revenue for the US government in its early years, comprising more than 90 percent of federal revenue during Hamilton's time as secretary of Treasury. The new state thus had a vested interest in promoting international trade, as its revenue depended on it. But this dependence upon customs duties was not without its problems. It tethered the government's finances to international trade, which was volatile in an era of European war and rivalry. Furthermore, the power to tax imports opened the door to contentious political debate over the regional distribution of taxation and the prospect of using tariffs not only to fund the government but also to advance political and economic interests, such as protecting American manufacturers from foreign competition.[36]

The Constitution further enhanced the international position of the United States by demonstrating to financial markets that the new republic had the wherewithal and durability to stick around long enough to do business with. The central government now possessed explicit powers to regulate commerce, to raise capital, and to tax to pay for its operations and services. Just as important as the Constitution itself were the early actions of the new government that inspired confidence in financial markets on both sides of the Atlantic. The federal assumption of state debts from the Revolution as part of the "compromise of 1790" opened European capital markets to the United States. In the Funding Act of 1790, the new US government adopted British principles of debt management, including the principle of nondiscrimination among creditors, which enhanced the new republic's credit rating abroad. "Every farthing of foreign capital," Alexander Hamilton wrote in 1791, "is a precious acquisition." By 1803, half of the US national debt was held abroad. Indeed, it was the London bank of Baring Brothers that extended credit to the United States so that it could pay France for the Louisiana Purchase in 1803.[37]

Foreign capital was not the only import that the new republic attracted from abroad. Most of the founders embraced immigration as a means of promoting economic development and national power. Madison argued shortly after the new government was created that it was "no doubt very desirable that we should hold out as many inducements as possible for the worthy part of mankind to come and settle amongst us" on the grounds that it would "increase the wealth and strength of the community." But such sentiments were accompanied by fears that foreign arrivals might retain sympathies to their homelands and old monarchs, thus undermining America's independence and republican form of government. It was for this reason that the Constitution included citizenship requirements for federal officeholders and a clause that prohibited the federal government from extending titles of nobility to citizens. The Constitution also prevented government officials from receiving emoluments, or payments, from foreign states. The objective was to limit foreign interference in the fragile republic's politics.[38]

There was reason to be concerned about such foreign meddling in the ideologically charged and internationally unstable context of the early republic. In the presidential election of 1796, French minister to the United States Pierre-Auguste Adet openly worked to defeat John Adams. "Foreign influence," Washington warned in his 1796 farewell address, "is one of the most baneful foes of Republican Government." Similar attempted interventions would occur throughout the nineteenth century, as enterprising revolutionaries from Ireland, Europe, Latin America, and the Caribbean traveled to the Yankee republic with the intent of influencing US policy and elections. But just as dangerous as foreign meddling was the prospect of US overreaction to the threat, made clear by the Federalists' draconian Alien and Sedition Acts of 1798, which infringed upon the freedom of speech and led to the politicized deportation of foreign nationals within America.[39]

The naturalization acts of the 1790s established early regulations concerning the extension of citizenship to new arrivals. The US naturalization system was liberal; in contrast to the Old World conception of "perpetual allegiance" in which citizenship was immutable, the United States created a system of volitional citizenship in which newcomers could choose to become members of the new US political community. Nonetheless, these early acts placed limits upon the right of naturalization. They restricted citizenship along racial lines to "free white persons" as well as along political lines by requiring that those naturalizing "absolutely and entirely renounce and abjure all allegiance and fidelity to any foreign prince, potentate, state, or sovereignty whatever." Naturalization became a divisive issue, with Federalists in favor of stricter limits as means of countering their Jeffersonian Republican opponents, who drew power from the resurgence of immigration in the 1790s, a decade in which an estimated 97,900 people arrived in the United States, many from Ireland. As in the case of customs duties, the new constitutional order portended future conflict over immigration and naturalization.[40]

The movement of people—from both within and outside of the United States—was at the heart of the "forgotten" founding document of 1787, the Northwest Ordinance. The Confederation Congress, still operating under the Articles of Confederation, passed the Ordinance at the very moment the Philadelphia convention was taking place. Just like the Constitution, this founding document arose from internal divisions and geopolitical rivalry—put another way, from anxiety. The fear in this case was that the white settlers and land speculators west of the Appalachians would have little reason to remain loyal to the Eastern Seaboard. They might even respond to overtures from foreign powers. The settlers in the Northwest Territory did not want to be ruled over by a distant metropolitan government that was unresponsive to their needs. They did not want a repeat of something like the old Proclamation Line of 1763. But this did not mean that they simply wanted to be left alone. Settlers wanted stability, protection from Native Americans, and integration into the markets of the Eastern Seaboard and beyond. One thing was certain: the weak US government under the Articles could not compel loyalty, even though it possessed titular authority over the region of the Ohio Valley and the Great Lakes. "If they declare themselves a separate people," Jefferson informed Madison in 1787 regarding white settlers in the West, "we are incapable of a single effort to retain them. Our citizens can never be induced, either as militia or as soldiers, to go there to cut the throats of their own brothers and sons, or, rather, to be themselves the subjects instead of the perpetrators of the parricide."[41]

The Northwest Ordinance addressed this challenge by mixing central power and home rule, thereby echoing the compromises of the Constitutional Convention. The Northwest Ordinance—first drafted by Jefferson in 1784 and then passed by Congress in a revised form three years later—bucked the eighteenth-century trend of imperial centralization by establishing the conditions in which new states could be carved out of western territories and enter into the union on equal terms, rather than as dependent colonies of the states in the East. When Jefferson spoke of an "empire of liberty," he referred to this decentralized union of equal states.[42]

The Ordinance was in effect a deal struck between, on the one hand, white settlers and land speculators and, on the other, the US government. The inhabitants of the West pledged their loyalty to the new nation and agreed to congressional oversight and control during an initial phase overseen by a federally appointed territorial governor. In exchange, the US government offered settlers a long-term deal that no other imperial power could match: eventual self-government and political equality within the union once the population threshold of sixty thousand inhabitants had been reached; the promotion of public higher education (which led to the founding of Ohio University in 1804); federal support for the development of infrastructure; and, perhaps most important, the deployment of military power when needed in relations with Native Americans. If anything, inhabitants of the West inverted the traditional colonial model by taking more from the metropole than they gave. Each newly admitted and still sparsely populated western state, for example, would elect two senators, giving the settlers' disproportionate political power. This was imperialism practiced as much from the outside-in as from the inside-out.

The success of the Ordinance was not purely due to how it secured the support of white settlers by offering them political equality once the criteria for statehood had been met. Just as important was how, in conjunction with the Constitution, it empowered the federal government to manage western territories and to assert control over the Native Americans who lived in them. The federal government did not offer Native Americans the same terms available to white settlers. Rather, by promoting white colonization into the continent's interior, the Northwest Ordinance would lead to countless violent encounters between settlers and Natives. The Northwest Ordinance was in this regard a more traditional instrument of colonial rule and expansion, a founding document of American empire. The costs of the Northwest Ordinance for the Native peoples of the West was made clear in the Ohio Valley in the 1790s. When Native Americans refused to cede their lands to white settlers, the Washington administration dispatched a force under the command General Anthony Wayne, who defeated a Native coalition at the Battle of Fallen Timbers in 1794. The following year's Treaty of Greenville opened the Ohio Valley to a rush of white settlement. The power of the United States in the continental interior had been demonstrated. The stage was set for the forced removal of Native Americans in the coming decades.[43]

V

"Tis done!" exclaimed Benjamin Rush upon the ratification of the Constitution, "America has ceased to be the only power in the world that has derived no benefit from her declaration of independence." The political genius of the Constitution and the Northwest Ordinance was that they turned liabilities into strengths. Rather than seek to thwart or micromanage settler expansion to the west, the Northwest Ordinance harnessed the power of westward migration on behalf of national interests. Instead of ham-fistedly imposing rule upon the states, the Constitution delicately stitched together a political system with built-in safeguards of checks and balances that alleviated persistent fears of central rule while still creating a government capable of survival in a world marked by international rivalry.[44]

This distinctive American ship of state proved seaworthy in the turbulent "age of revolutions" and great power rivalry that lasted into the 1820s. The French Revolution of 1789 not only upended the social system of France but also destabilized the international order, triggering in 1793 a further period of European war that would last until 1815. Its effects could be seen across the Atlantic as well, in France's colony of Haiti, where slaves led by Toussaint L'Overture achieved freedom and independence from their white enslavers, and in Spanish America, where Creole elites such as Simón Bolívar led struggles for independence that would meet with success in most of Spain's colonies by the 1820s. Here was another fortunate break that went the way of the new United States. The fact that its revolution came first gave the new republic a head start in developing a nation strong enough to withstand and profit from this age of revolutions.[45]

The French Revolution was initially applauded by most Americans as confirmation of the universality of their own revolution, but its violent turn in 1792–1793 divided the United States along ideological lines. Indeed, this foreign revolution was one of the primary drivers behind the formation of the new national political coalitions of the Republicans and Federalists. Led by Thomas Jefferson, Republicans remained suspicious of British power and saw their recent ally France as a sister republic. Federalists, conversely, feared that the social disorder in France, which was so vividly symbolized by the guillotine of the Reign of Terror in 1792–1793, would undermine social order and political stability in the United States. The Federalist Washington administration went further, effectively scrapping the 1778 alliance with France when it aligned with Britain in the 1795 Jay Treaty, whose principal achievement was to postpone hostilities between the two English-speaking countries. The prospect emerged that the contagion of ideological conflict and great power rivalry might cross the Atlantic to the new republic. The new party politics of the 1790s were bare-knuckled and divisive. But for as much as they fractured the new republic along ideological lines, the new parties also paradoxically strengthened the union by establishing political coalitions that crossed state lines. Indeed, it was the very depth of the ideological divisions of this era's politics that legitimized new national institutions and political practices. The peaceful handover of power from the Federalists to Jefferson in the "revolution of 1800" set the precedent of the losers accepting the results in exchange for the right to live to fight another day, a noble pattern that would be followed until 1860–1861. There might have been duels in the politics of this period, but in the 1790s there was no guillotine in the United States.

For all their rancor, the partisan politics of the 1790s did not preclude the new government from getting down to work. The decade saw the new union stabilize national finances, construct a navy, and implement neutrality legislation aimed at avoiding entanglement in the European war that erupted in 1793. The United States remained a minor power in this era, but it did hold its own against France during the naval "quasi-war" of 1798–1800 and Britain in the looming "second war of independence" in 1812. Important traditions of statecraft and diplomacy were born, none more enduring than the nationalist foreign policy articulated by George Washington in his 1796 farewell address. Washington's "great rule" of having "as little political connection as possible" with foreign nations was not an end in itself but rather a means of mitigating the partisan conflict and sectional tensions that threatened the union from within. Washington wanted to insulate the United States from these pressures while at the same time maintaining ties to foreign markets. Washington trumpeted the extension of "our commercial relations" with foreign markets and anticipated a time "when we may defy material injury from external annoyance;...when we may choose peace or war, as our interest, guided by justice, shall counsel." Rather than a dogma of isolationism, as it is often described today, Washington's farewell address was a call for internal unity and nation building so that the United States could acquire the power necessary to hold its own in a volatile international system.[46]

The trend line of this age of revolutions was one in which the United States consolidated its international position while European empires unraveled in the New World. The Haitian slave rebellion terrified Southern slaveholders in America. But after a brief period of policy experimentation in the late 1790s Federalist administration of John Adams, the United States settled upon a policy of nonengagement with the hemisphere's only black republic, a policy that would last until the Lincoln administration during the Civil War. The Haitian rebellion brought the United States a territorial windfall in that it led Napoleon to unload the vast Louisiana territory in 1803. The hemisphere's greatest slave rebellion had the paradoxical effect of expanding the territory of President Jefferson's slaveholding "empire of liberty." The Spanish American revolutions, which unfolded over the course of the first decades of the nineteenth century, also strengthened the hand of the United States and opened new markets to Yankee traders. The Monroe Doctrine of 1823 declared that "the American continents, by the free and independent condition which they have assumed and maintain, are henceforth not to be considered as subjects for colonization by any European powers." This high tide of early US nationalism portended the more assertive and expansionist foreign policies of the coming decades, even as it presented the United States as an anti-imperial power. Monroe's 1823 message found support across the political spectrum. International affairs will "create no divisions of opinion among us," declared archnationalist Henry Clay in 1823. "We shall, in regard to it, be 'all federalists—all republicans.' "[47]

By the time of the Monroe Doctrine, peaceful relations with Britain had returned after the War of 1812. Indeed, the Monroe administration announced its doctrine only after learning that Britain also opposed attempts of European powers to restore Spain's American empire. This emerging convergence of interest with Britain was premised upon a renewed surge of activity in the Atlantic economy. In the decades that followed 1815, the British Isles became America's most significant source of investment, finished goods, and immigrants. The United States was the largest foreign market for British capitalists, manufacturers, and emigrants. Indeed, the independent former colonies were of more economic importance to the British in this period than was the rest of the British Empire combined. The stewards of this mutually profitable relationship, a group of sophisticated Anglo-American banking houses led by the London-based firm Baring Brothers, reaped windfall profits. To be sure, the close economic relationship brought with it risks as well as rewards. The great financial panics of the nineteenth century—above all, those in 1819, 1837, 1857, and 1873—were transnational phenomena that rippled back and forth across the Atlantic. But with these risks came the benefits of cheap capital and profitable trading relations with the world's greatest economic power. The accordion of the Atlantic economy contracted once again.[48]

In the big picture, the outcome of the Anglo-American civil war meant that the costly, bloody, and divisive project of the conquest and settlement of the continent was transferred from Britain to her former colonies. The silver lining for the British of the loss of the thirteen colonies was that it spared them the overhead costs involved in this enormous job by effectively outsourcing it to the United States. At the same time, because the United States was its prime trading partner, the old colonial master would profit from the process, like the seed capitalist who reaps a windfall from a spin-off of a long-ago speculative investment. The independence of the United States established a more efficient political framework to guide the processes of the settlement of North America and the integration of the booming Atlantic economy. The unexpected turn of 1776 did not stop those processes—indeed, by rationalizing the political institutions that oversaw them, it accelerated them.[49]

BUT FOR ALL the success of early US statecraft—for all the creativity the founders demonstrated in establishing a new state custom designed for the international context in which it operated—there was a critical defect within the political system of the new nation: slavery. The union created by Americans in the age of the founding was geared toward certain political ends. Managing a protracted and ideologically charged internal conflict between sections was not one of them. In fact, the way in which the founders dealt with slavery revealed that the union was designed to do the opposite: to side-step the issue and, when that was not possible, to follow the path of least resistance in the hope that the matter would somehow magically disappear.

In the long term, there was no going back from having declared "all men are created equal" in 1776. The genie was out of the bottle. But the implications of those words were not immediately apparent to most of the framers huddled in Philadelphia in 1787, not least among the half of the delegates who owned slaves. Most of the founders, including many of those who were themselves slaveholders, envisioned a future in which slavery would diminish in political and economic importance, perhaps even be phased out completely, as would happen in the northern states in the coming decades. That wishful thinking served as a convenient rationalization for those who prioritized the security and stability offered by the Constitution over its protections of slavery. Meanwhile, the Southerners who pressed for advantage in Philadelphia were of the view that the greatest threat to slavery was not a more powerful federal government but rather threats along the south-western flank of the union, where Native peoples and European powers remained active along the Gulf Coast. Indeed, many Southerners already understood what would become a pillar of their statecraft in the nineteenth century: central power was essential for the preservation of slavery. "Without Union with the other states," Charles Pinckney of South Carolina said in support of the Constitution during his state's ratification process, "South Carolina must soon fall."[50]

In a convention marked by compromise, it should not be surprising that the framers sought to find a middle ground on the slavery issue when it could not be avoided. The problem was that the compromises relating to slavery functioned as endorsements of it. Slavery would not magically disappear if the Constitution propped it up. The compromise provisions did exactly that. The three-fifths compromise, which counted slaves as three-fifths of a person for the purposes of the apportionment of political representation, inflated the political power of states with large slave populations. The fugitive slave clause that required the return of escaped slaves who had crossed state lines extended a powerful precedent of the federal promotion of slaveholder interests to future generations. To be sure, the Constitution was not uniformly proslavery. Although the clause on international slave trade prohibited the federal government from interfering in that noxious trade until 1808, it empowered the central government to act against it thereafter. "If there was no other lovely feature in the Constitution but this one, it would diffuse a beauty over its whole countenance," declared Pennsylvania's James Wilson. "Yet the lapse of a few years, and Congress will have power to exterminate slavery from within our borders." Nonetheless, on balance the Constitution upheld the interests of slaveholders by creating a new political order that recognized the right to hold slaves and, indeed, set precedents for how central power could support the institution.[51]

The territorial ordinances of the founding period also set the stage for the future political crisis over slavery. These ordinances were every bit as important to the future politics of slavery as was the Constitution, perhaps even more so. The Northwest Ordinance prohibited slavery, whereas the 1790 Southwest Ordinance condoned it. This contrast is explained by the fact that the western territories were not virgin lands but rather former European colonies or possessions. When it came to slavery in the territories, the federal government led from behind. The almost complete absence of slavery in the Northwest Territory explains the famous prohibition of Article VI of the Ordinance. Likewise, every federal endorsement of slavery in western territories—the Southwest Territory (1790), Kentucky (1792), the Mississippi Territory (1798), Louisiana (1804), and Missouri (1805)—confirmed the existing labor system in those places. To have imposed an antislavery agenda on these territories would have triggered constitutional crisis, perhaps even geopolitical crisis, for the savvy inhabitants of the southwest had other suiters, particularly the Spanish Empire.[52]

Far from resolving the slavery question, the Constitution and territorial ordinances of the founding period sowed the seeds of future competition between advocates of free and slave labor in the western territories. This confrontation was more than just a political conflict between the emerging groups for and against slavery. It was a clash of rival labor systems, a protracted cold war waged between two different, but related, social orders that raced to accumulate the most economic might, popular support, political power, and international legitimacy. The greatest crisis of US history—the second civil war in less than a century—loomed on the horizon. But, just as was the case with the first, the origins of this one extended beyond North America and unfolded in unexpected ways.

CHAPTER 2
The Wrecking Ball

SLAVERY LAY BEHIND the greatest crisis in American history. Of that there is no serious debate. It was clear to Americans at the time that the future of slavery in the federal territories of the West—and by extension the future of slavery itself—was "somehow the cause of the war," as Lincoln put it. It was also clear that the slavery question was more than a conventional political controversy or wedge issue. It was a wrecking ball that demolished the social, economic, and political institutions that held the Union together.[1]

What made the slavery question so destructive was the remarkable growth of the South's peculiar institution. In the late eighteenth century, many Americans had predicted that slavery was on the road to extinction. By the mid-nineteenth century, however, the astonishing expansion of slavery, along with the political power amassed by the Southern master class, led many to conclude that, in the future, forced labor might well extend beyond the South. "We shall *lie down* pleasantly dreaming that the people of *Missouri* are on the verge of making their State *free*," Lincoln warned in his 1858 "House Divided" speech, "and we shall *awake* to the *reality*, instead, that the *Supreme* Court has made *Illinois* a *slave* State." The ambitions of some Southern slaveholders extended beyond the horizons of the United States. "I want Cuba," thundered Mississippi senator Albert Gallatin Brown, "I want Tamaulipas, Potosi, and one or two other Mexican States; and I want them all for the same reason—for the planting or spreading of slavery."[2]

The political crisis that culminated in civil war in 1861 is most commonly understood as a domestic one. But its roots extended beyond America's borders. The crisis of the Union played out within a moment of world history characterized by the development of global capitalism, ideologically charged political conflict, and revolutionary advances in communications and transportation. "In place of the old local and national seclusion and self-sufficiency," wrote Karl Marx and Friedrich Engels in 1848, "we have intercourse in every direction, universal interdependence of nations." The growth of American slavery in the first half of the nineteenth century that caused the sectional crisis was fueled by a British-led international economic order that developed an almost insatiable appetite for cotton, "white gold," as it was called at the time. As slavery became ever more entrenched into Southern life and ever more central to the international economic order, it disrupted the fragile political balance within the Union. A growing number of people within and beyond the United States passionately devoted themselves to either advancing or destroying slavery as the institution grew in size. Policies and ideas that once had unified Americans on either side of the Mason-Dixon line, ranging from the tariff to evangelical Christianity, now tore them apart along sectional lines. Slaves became increasingly shrewd political actors whose daily struggles to improve the terms of their bondage, if not free themselves from it altogether, ensured that the slavery question could never be swept under the rug of national politics.[3]

As the slavery debate intensified, shifts in the international position of the United States increased its vulnerability to the deepening sectional divide. Most important was the increased power of the United States, which was made clear by its conquest of northern Mexico in 1848. With the European powers acquiescing to US continental dominion, the old security rational for national union faded away. The greatest threat to the Union now derived from the management of its new continental empire. This danger assumed the form of a simple question. Would America's vast western territories be open to slavery? As the political system struggled to contain the morally charged debate unleashed by this question, it was simultaneously shaken to its core by a sudden surge of immigration, whose principal driver was a devastating potato blight on the other side of the Atlantic. International forces powered, rather than contained, that wrecking ball as it battered the structures of the Union during the political crisis of the 1850s.

I

Until relatively recently, the Old South was viewed as a social and economic anachronism, a curious throwback destined to be overwhelmed by Yankee capitalism. According to this view, slavery was a quasi-feudalistic institution that stunted the region's economic development. In the nineteenth century's race of material development, the backward-looking, slaveholding South ran the wrong direction around the track. Few interpretations of the American past have been as thoroughly revised as this one. Far from a feudalistic holdout, the slaveholding South is now seen as a driver of capitalist development. The growth of American slavery was central to the emergence of new global systems of political power, financial services, transportation, and commodity markets. At each plantation and farm, the master class wielded power over its bonded laborers. But sustaining that power required more than just maintaining discipline on the plantation. It required an imperial power structure, a hospitable international economic order, and a powerful proslavery culture and ideology.[4]

By nearly every measure, the slaveholding South grew at a frenetic pace in the first half of the nineteenth century. The slave population dramatically increased, almost entirely through natural reproduction after the closing of the international slave trade in 1808. This set the South apart from the slave systems of the Caribbean that required continuous importations of new slaves from Africa. The first US census of 1790 found there to be roughly seven hundred thousand slaves in the nation. Twenty years later there were nearly 1.2 million. By the eve of the Civil War, there were some four million enslaved people in the United States. Agricultural production based on slave labor, particularly that of cotton, which flourished in the black belt region of the states of the Deep South, grew at a similar pace. Before Eli Whitney's 1793 cotton gin expedited the labor-intensive process of separating cotton seeds from fiber, the United States produced three thousand bales of cotton per year. Seventy years later, the slaves in the South produced four million bales of cotton. The cotton boom altered the demography of slavery, shifting its geographic concentration from the old tobacco complex of the Virginia tidewater to the new cotton kingdom in the states of the Deep South and the Mississippi River valley. An estimated one million slaves endured a forced migration in the South at some point in their life. American slavery, in sum, was not a static institution stuck in the past; it was a dynamic social and labor system that rapidly expanded, overcoming seemingly all obstacles in its way. "The slaveholding South is now the controlling power of the world," South Carolinian James Henry Hammond triumphantly declared in the 1850s. "No power on earth dares to make war upon it. Cotton is King."[5]

American slavery rested upon racist assumptions of the inferiority of people of African descent. But another of its foundations was an emerging global economic system that had an insatiable appetite for its staple crops of tobacco, sugar, and—above all—cotton. At its mid-nineteenth-century height, the slaveholding South produced the lion's share of the cotton consumed by the textile mills of Britain (77 percent), the United States (nearly all), and Europe (90 percent in France, 60 percent in Germany, and 92 percent in Russia). The most important market for Southern cotton was Britain. The textile mills of Lancashire transformed the raw material into finished textile goods, which were then transported to markets around the world, particularly within the British Empire. As the nineteenth century progressed, the cotton South became a key component to Britain's economy and imperial system. Some in Britain raised concerns about the "alarming fact that Britain is almost entirely dependent on foreign supply for this article," which *The Economist* estimated sustained in one way or another nearly one fifth of the British population.[6]

Southern slavers shrewdly leveraged their white gold to attract foreign investment. Without credit, there would have been no slave empire. American slaveholders were blessed with ample land—once the Native peoples of the Deep South had been dispossessed of their territories in the era of the War of 1812—and, owing to high birthrates among the slave population, labor. But, like the new American republic as a whole, the South needed capital, particularly in the decades following 1815 in which the cotton kingdom rapidly expanded. It required funds to underwrite all the activities necessary to create millions of bales of cotton and then deliver them to distant markets: slave purchases, land sales, the clearing of woodlands in cotton producing regions, annual acquisitions of seeds and machinery, transportation of commodities from plantations to port cities. Southern planters engineered new commercial associations and financial instruments that opened to them the capital markets of the North, Britain, and continental Europe. Planters pooled their resources together into state-chartered associations that raised money in distant capital markets by selling securitized bonds backed by the collateral of land, or even slaves themselves. Louisiana was a particularly popular destination for foreign investors. The London firm of Baring Brothers loaned more capital to it than to any other state in the Union in the years between 1815 and 1860; indeed, 52 percent of the capital invested in the state's sixteen new banks was foreign, primarily British. The South's integration into the wider Atlantic financial system was far from an orderly and stable process, as the great financial panics of 1819 and 1837 attested, but it did provide the capital the booming cotton kingdom required.[7]

In other realms, however, the slaveholding class of the South pursued its interests not through integration but through appropriation and domination. Nowhere was this more the case than in politics. Southern slavers and theorists appropriated the symbols and history of the young nation in order to buttress the peculiar institution. Nationalism flourished in the antebellum South, but it was a peculiarly Southern variant that interpreted the nation's founding documents and ideals as endorsements of racial slavery. By the mid-nineteenth century, Northern critics were talking about the "slave power." They pointed to how Southern slavers exerted power disproportionate to their numbers, owing in large part to the three-fifths compromise. Slaveholders assumed leadership roles in key congressional committees, the military, the foreign service, and the judiciary. Today we tend to equate the Old South with states' rights. To be sure, the idea of states' rights existed in the antebellum South, particularly in regard to the compact theory of the Constitution that prioritized the state powers over those of the federal government. But states' rights were not the South's only political tradition. Southern statesmen were not uniformly opposed to central power. One of the secrets to their success was how they commandeered the power of the federal government to advance their interests. They created a proslavery foreign policy; they used the federal judiciary to their advantage; they sought to build up national military and naval power to insulate the South from foreign threats and abolitionism; they demanded a draconian federal fugitive slave bill that trampled upon the states' rights of the North; and they went so far as to make their allegiance to the Union conditional on a series of radical proslavery federal measures, not least governmental protection for them to carry their slaves into all federal territories of the West.[8]

The South's embrace of central power appears paradoxical when set against the constitutional tradition of states' rights, but it makes perfect sense when we look beyond the domestic scene to consider the South's heightened perception of foreign threats. Any Southern slaver who consulted a map of the Western Hemisphere by the 1830s had cause for alarm. The gradual end of slavery in the Northern states was not the only ominous development. Slavery was on the retreat outside of the Union. It had been violently demolished in the slave rebellion in Haiti. The new states of Spanish America were in the process of gradually phasing slavery out. Most significant was neighboring Mexico's acts in 1829 and 1837 that abolished slavery. Mexican abolition in time would shape the course of the US sectional conflict. By ending slavery in the territories that the United States would annex in 1848, Mexico helped to ignite the long fuse on the combustible issue that would bring down the Union in 1860–1861.[9]

The foreign antislavery measure that had the most immediate effect on the United States was Britain's Slavery Abolition Act of 1833. Once the engine behind the slave trade, the world's greatest power now committed itself to a plan of gradual emancipation in its Caribbean possessions. British abolition was a fillip to opponents of American slavery, encouraging radical abolitionists and African Americans to demand an immediate end to what they viewed as an immoral and un-Christian institution. "The English are the best friends the coloured people have upon earth," wrote black abolitionist David Walker even before Parliament acted. Britain's antislavery turn transformed the international politics of slavery, raising Southern perceptions of threat in the process. Britain threw her mighty naval power against the international slave trade. Southerners feared that their former colonial master might go further by containing the expansion of slavery, if not promoting abolitionism within the remaining proslavery holdouts of the Western Hemisphere. As one South Carolinian wrote in 1833, "The great Slave question has started in England, if realized [it] will transfer a great bearing on the United States: of course, the whole evil will fall on the Southern section."[10]

Of most concern to Southerners in the 1830s and 1840s were the precarious slaveholding polities of Texas and Cuba. Southern political elites feared that both territories were in the crosshairs of British abolitionism. Most urgent was the situation in Texas. American immigrants had poured into this province of Mexico in the 1820s at the invitation of Mexican officials. Many of these American settlers disregarded Mexican laws, including prohibitions on slavery and a ban on further immigration in the 1830s—thereafter, Anglo settlers were illegal immigrants. When Mexican officials moved to tighten their grip on the renegade province, the Anglo population responded by declaring its independence in 1836. Thus began Texas's brief period of independence. What most alarmed Southern elites was the possibility that the insecurity of Texas would lead it into the arms of antislavery Britain. Slaveholders deemed a free-labor Texas an unacceptable risk on the grounds that it would block the western expansion of slavery and destabilize it in neighboring states by becoming a magnet for runaway slaves. Acting through the national institution of the Democratic Party, proslavery Southerners, led by successive secretaries of state Abel Upshur and John C. Calhoun, who worked in the administration of President (and future Confederate) John Tyler, engineered the annexation of Texas in 1844–1845 to preempt the scenario of an antislavery, British satellite on the doorstep of the cotton kingdom.

British interest in "the emancipation of slaves in Texas," Tyler wrote Calhoun, "decided me on the question as it did…Mr. Upshur."[11]

With Southerners advocating annexation on proslavery grounds, sectional conflict ensued. Indeed, Texas had to be annexed by a congressional joint resolution, which required only a simple majority, after the attempt to ratify a treaty, which required a two-thirds majority, failed. The South's strategy for Cuba differed in that it did not see annexation as necessary to preserve slavery on the island. But by the 1850s, Southern statesmen, collaborating again with Northern Democrats, made it clear that they would take preemptive action if Cuban slavery came under threat. The vulnerability of slavery in an increasingly antislavery world led statesmen in the South to advocate an assertive diplomacy aimed at protecting their interests. "I think that this Government, upon all occasions," Calhoun declared in 1848, "ought to give encouragement and countenance, as far as it can with safety, to the ascendancy of the white race."[12]

The slaveholding South's increased assertiveness unleashed a morally charged debate within the United States. There had been factions for and against slavery since the founding era; what changed as the nineteenth century progressed was each side's intensity, institutional sophistication, and political reach. Central to this story was the emergence of a network of abolitionist and antislavery societies that spanned the Atlantic. Today, we most often remember the abolitionists for the passion and perseverance with which they advanced their moral arguments against the evils of slavery, but just as important as content was form. Those opposed to slavery created dynamic societies and networks capable of reaching mass audiences, as well penetrating into the corridors of political power. The antislavery movement had its internal factions and divisions, not least of which were the tensions between black abolitionists, who tended to demand immediate abolition, and antislavery whites, who often argued for incrementalism. But these divisions should not obscure from view the fact that abolitionists established a social movement capable of raising funds on both sides of the Atlantic, coordinating political action across vast distances, delivering emotive and intellectually cogent arguments against the institution of slavery, and assisting those slaves fortunate enough to escape the grip of their master.[13]

Meanwhile, back in the South, a parallel process consolidated support for slavery. Southern politicians and theorists developed the political and moral defense of the institution. Gone was the talk of slavery as a "necessary evil"; it was replaced in the 1830s by an affirmative—indeed, an aggressive—proslavery ideology that presented it as a "positive good." But support for slavery required more than an ideology. It required the almost universal backing of the Southern whites. Nonslaveholders totaled roughly three-quarters of the South's white population in 1860. There were signs that this group was beginning to develop a political consciousness that might be receptive to antislavery appeals. Yet antislavery whites within the South, like Hinton Rowan Helper, who tried to persuade his fellow nonslaveholding whites that they had a bad deal in the cotton kingdom, were the exceptions that proved the rule. Most nonslaveholding whites condoned slavery. Poor whites, for instance, often joined the slave patrols that rounded up runaways. The South's proslavery move had an international dimension as well. Just as antislavery groups drew power from their British counterparts, slavery's defenders plotted its expansion into the Caribbean, sought to protect it where it remained in the Western Hemisphere (particularly Cuba), and presented their labor system as one suited for exportation to foreign lands.[14]

The emergence of powerful political groupings and ideologies for and against slavery made the future of the peculiar institution an unavoidable issue in American public life. No gag order could make the slavery question disappear. What made the slavery question so dangerous to the Union was how it fractured institutions and social networks that tied the sections together. Indeed, some of the most significant battlegrounds and turning points on the road to disunion occurred in realms apart from that of formal politics.

None were more important than evangelical Christianity. As politicians grappled with the question of the expansion of slavery, a comparable struggle concerning the morality and theology of slavery took place within the powerful evangelical churches, particularly the Baptists, Methodists, and Presbyterians. These churches were the backbone of the early American nation, both as propagators of a shared belief system and in the more concrete terms of institutional reach and coordination. Churches unified people from all sections of the Union. "If the Churches divide on the subject of slavery," nationalist Henry Clay feared, "there will be nothing left to bind our people together but trade and commerce." It thus was an ominous portent of the storm to come when the Baptists and the Methodists fractured along sectional lines in the 1840s. "How little is to be expected from any other Union, if the union of Christians fail," wrote a reporter from the Southern Baptist Convention of 1845. The very beliefs and institutions that had been one of the primary engines of nationalism did an abrupt about-face, redirecting their power on behalf of sectionalism.[15]

The fissure within the evangelical churches was part of a broader pattern in which national institutions and networks fractured along sectional lines. Sometimes even families, particularly those in border states, such as Kentucky, found themselves divided on the morality of slavery. The question confronting the United States in the mid-nineteenth century was if any of its national institutions could withstand the onslaught of the slavery issue, absorbing the blows until that wrecking ball somehow lost its momentum.

II

The prime candidate to remain standing was the nation's economic pillars. As Henry Clay put it, if the churches failed, the economy would be the strongest thing binding Americans together. He had good reason to believe this. Of the many achievements of the founders, none were more visible by the mid-nineteenth century than the awesome material growth of the Union. A number of forces fueled America's development, including the integration of the national market, new systems of transport and communication, technological innovations, the Supreme Court's broad interpretation of the commerce clause, and the continuation of profitable economic relations with Great Britain. All of these and more greased the wheels of an economic juggernaut—prone to overheating, though it was—that raced across the bountiful lands of North America, reaching all the way to the gold mines of California by the midcentury.

The South was not alone in developing a dynamic and outward facing economy in the decades preceding the Civil War. In the new states of the West, agricultural output increased at a rate not unlike that of cotton in the Deep South. In the single decade of the 1850s in Illinois, for example, the production of corn doubled and that of wheat ballooned nearly threefold. This boom was made possible by new technologies that mechanized agricultural production. Just as the cotton gin revolutionized cotton production, the McCormick reaper expanded harvesting capacity in the emerging wheat belt of the new states of the West. New infrastructure, including roads, canals, and, by the 1850s, railroads, cut transportation costs and opened distant markets to American farmers. In Illinois, a catalyst of agricultural development in the 1850s was the opening of what was then the world's longest railroad, the Illinois Central Railroad (ICR). The funding of the ICR demonstrated that it wasn't just Southerners who found new ways to raise capital. The ICR received federal support in the form of land grants, the first of what would become many land grant lines in the United States. But equally important to the success of the ICR was its ability to attract foreign capital. Two-thirds of the company's shareholders were Britons who saw the railroad as a means of more efficiently transporting grains from the American wheat belt to England, where they were needed to feed the working classes—many of whose appetites came from working in mills fueled by Southern cotton. When renowned British liberal Richard Cobden visited Illinois in 1859, he did so not to observe American democracy firsthand but rather to inspect the railroad on behalf of its foreign shareholders.[16]

For all the success and expansion of the cotton kingdom, it should be remembered that far more British capital poured into the Northern states than into the slaveholding South. Before the Civil War, ten railroads had $1 million or more of their stock held abroad—but only one was located in the South, even though 35 percent of the nation's railroad mileage in 1860 ran through slaveholding states. This pattern of capital migration was, in part, a result of a downgrade in the South's credit rating that followed the Panic of 1837. Nine US states and territories defaulted on their debts during that crisis, but the three that took the further step of repudiating their obligations were all slaveholding (Mississippi, Florida, and Arkansas). Foreign capitalists took notice when slaveholding advocates of repudiation vowed that they would rather "slap John Bull in the face than to quail before his power." The result was that Northern states were able to attract foreign capital at lower rates than those of the South (and that during the Civil War the Confederacy would find it difficult to persuade foreign capitalists to lend it money). At the same time, British investors began to consider the morality of their investments. "The existence of even a minute fraction of the population in bondage places the government of that state at a serious disadvantage in the money market," the *Westminster Review* reported in 1850.[17]

The free and slave states might have competed on the London money market, but the economies of the North and South were not always in competition. Indeed, as Clay pointed out, the headline story of the first half of the nineteenth century was the

emergence of a national market. Northern industrialization and
the emergence of Wall Street helped to provide the manufactured
goods and financial services that were in demand in the South and
West. The development of the national economy was further advanced by the transportation revolution of new roads, canals, railroads, and steamship lines. By 1860, the United States possessed
more railroad track mileage than the rest of the world combined.
Communications pulsed through these circuits, stimulating the
integration of markets across the Union and spurring economic
growth and innovation. Contemporaries noted the change from
the late eighteenth century. "In the early days of the country, before we had railroads, telegraphs and steamboats—in a word, rapid
transit of any sort—the States were each almost a separate nation-
ality," Ulysses S. Grant later reflected. The federal government
played an important role in this process. Federal subsidies were
given to upstart steam transport systems, and federal agents sur-
veyed and organized new territories. The Post Office Department,
the largest federal bureaucracy of the era, facilitated the exchange
of information across the nation, particularly in the form of the
newspapers that constituted the largest item by bulk delivered by
the postal system. The Post Office also contributed to the creation
of national political parties by functioning as a patronage spoils
ground for the era's politicians.[18]

Commerce and infrastructure brought together the diverse markets and regions of the Union. Nineteenth-century Americans at-
tached such significance to these material bonds that they became
an important element of American nationalism itself. "Open up a
highway through your country from New York to San Francisco,"
declared New York Whig William H. Seward in 1853. "Put your domain under cultivation, your ten thousand wheels of manufacture in
motion. Multiply your ships, and send them forth to the East. The
nation that draws most materials and provisions from the earth, and
fabricates the most, and sells the most of productions and fabrics to

foreign nations, must be, and will be, the great Power of the earth."
Not surprisingly, some of the most powerful players and institutions
of the national economy resisted the march toward disunion. Most
of the business community in New York City, for example, fought
to the bitter end for sectional compromise, hoping to defuse the
combustible slavery debate. Business elites led the way in the frantic
and ultimately doomed attempts to avoid war during the secession
winter of 1860–1861, arguing that the benefits of national union
outweighed the differences of opinion on the slavery issue. These
actions reflected the success of national economic integration and
the profitable relationships that were imperiled by secession. As Lincoln declared in his inaugural address, "Physically speaking, we can
not separate. We can not remove our respective sections from each
other nor build an impassable wall between them."[19]

Yet, for all their strength, the material and economic bonds of
the Union could not withstand the advance of Southern separatism. In some regards, economic structures and policies contributed to rising sectionalism even as they fostered the emergence
of a national market. A key issue was the tariff, a federal tax on
imported goods. When the tariff is mentioned today in relation to
the origins of the Civil War, it is normally trotted out by apologists
of the Confederacy or dogmatic libertarians who make the case
that the real cause of disunion was not slavery but rather the emergence of a centralized state that trampled upon states' rights and
economic liberties. The tariff did not cause the Civil War, but that
does not mean it should be ignored when examining the origins
of the conflict. As the sectional crisis intensified, the tariff debate
became entangled in the broader question of how the divergent
economies of the free and slave states should engage with the international economy. The tariff issue was an extension of the debate over slavery, not separate from it.[20]

Tariffs were not always politically contentious in the United
States. In the tumultuous age and aftermath of the Napoleonic

Wars, American political elites—even the young South Carolinian John C. Calhoun—embraced protectionism on the grounds that it would foster national strength and independence in a volatile geopolitical order. But as the international position of the United States stabilized in the second quarter of the nineteenth century, this short-lived consensus unraveled. The tariff became a political lightening rod. The most famous of the great tariff showdowns was South Carolina's attempt to nullify the federal tariff in the 1830s during the administration of Andrew Jackson. The nullification crisis was a dress rehearsal for disunion. South Carolina radicals made the case for state sovereignty and the right to nullify federal legislation, shrewdly choosing the tariff issue as a first line of defense for slavery. The crisis helped lay the groundwork for many of the arguments for Southern unity and separatism that would later gain great traction—not least the "forty-bale theory" of South Carolinian George McDuffie, which posited that for every one hundred bales of cotton produced by the South, national tariffs redirected 40 percent of the profits to a parasitic class of Yankee merchants and protected laborers. But for all of the portentous features of the crisis, the Union survived it, and indeed, emerged stronger after South Carolina accepted the compromise tariff of 1833. Andrew Jackson's defense of the Union strengthened the national spirit and tethered it to the constitutional precedent that the federal government was supreme.[21]

The nullification crisis did not end controversy over the tariff, which evolved into one of the great wedge issues that divided Democrats (generally advocates of tariff reduction) and Whigs (most often proponents of tariffs). But overall, the tariff debates of the era buttressed the Union by sustaining political divisions that crossed sectional lines, despite the best efforts of South Carolina hotheads to make the tariff a sectional issue. Although opposition to tariffs was strongest in the staple exporting South, which had a material interest in dismantling barriers to trade, it had many

Northern advocates, not least Western farmers, port city merchants, and cosmopolitan reformers who viewed free trade in the moral terms advanced by Victorian free-trade advocates such as Richard Cobden, John Bright, and the British free-trade weekly *The Economist.* At the same time, there were proponents of the tariff in the slave South, particularly sugar planters and hemp producers, and a nascent protectionist lobby based primarily in New Orleans and the economically dynamic state of Virginia. Jacksonians fought over the tariff—with the gloves off and sucker punches not off limits—but doing so brought them into political alliances that crossed the sectional divide and transcended the slavery debate. It is worth pointing out, too, that the debate was never one of pure free trade versus unalloyed protectionism. Even the apostles of free trade from the mid-nineteenth century would be protectionists today—ad valorem rates of 20 percent were considered low in the mid-nineteenth century, whereas today, rates higher than 3 percent would be considered protectionist. In the end, the tariff question boiled down to disputes over how high specific rates should be.[22]

In the decades preceding the Civil War, there was an overall downward trend in US tariffs. The most important tariff reduction occurred in 1846. In an underappreciated moment of transatlantic integration, Britain repealed its protectionist Corn Laws in the same year that the Southern-dominated Democratic Party passed the reductionist Walker Tariff. Atlantic trade boomed, helping to end the depression years of the "hungry forties," as they were known in Britain, that followed the catastrophic Panic of 1837. The United States further reduced tariffs in the following decade. The trend of tariff reductionism was one reason the Atlantic economic order reached its heyday at the very moment the United States was unravelling. There was a corresponding surge in British investment in the United States, which was further fueled by capital's search for stable markets during the European revolutions of

1848. "Many persons are now looking to the American stocks as a means of profitable investment... [after] the shocks recently given to the public funds of the several national of Europe," *The Economist* reported.[23]

As the transatlantic economy entered a boom phase—which was further stimulated by the discovery of gold in California and Australia—the march of protectionism stalled. The language, ideas, and alliances of protectionism remained, but the push for tariff increases lost momentum. The politics of the tariff were not so much buried as they were reconfigured. In the fifteen years before the Civil War, the tariff issue played out within the sections as opposed to across them. As slavery conditioned Americans to think in starkly sectional terms, those on either side of the divide developed sectional conceptions of the policies that should govern their integration into what was starting to become, thanks to steam power and imperial expansion, a global economy. Like so much else in this period, the tariff morphed from a national issue into a sectional one.[24]

Low tariffs remained the cornerstone of Southern political economy. As an exporting economy that largely relied upon imported manufactured goods, it was natural for the South to embrace free trade, or something approaching it. The rise of Southern separatism was inseparable from the cotton kingdom's integration into the broader Atlantic economy. "England and the United States are bound together by a single thread of cotton," Friedrich Engels observed, "that which, weak and fragile as it may appear, is, nevertheless, stronger than an iron cable." The point cannot be emphasized enough. American slaveholders were economic internationalists whose connections to distant markets, particularly that of Britain, pulled them away from the Union. But the economic internationalism of the Southern master class was not without its limits, as it did not fully embrace the liberalism of the great British free traders—many of whom, not least Cobden and Bright, were fervently antislavery. When Southern politicians made the political case for tariff reduction, they emphasized not liberal ideology but Yankee exploitation of the slaveholding states. The South's gospel of free trade was not Cobdenite liberalism but rather the conspiracy theory that Yankee protectionists and merchants were grasping middlemen who sucked away the profits of the cotton trade even as they hypocritically sought to block the expansion of slavery.[25]

As Southerners increasingly viewed the tariff in relation to fears of Yankee domination, they began to develop their own version of economic nationalism. Here, once again, the innovative and dynamic nature of the slaveholding South is visible. The South's attitudes toward the tariff subtly evolved in the 1850s. As Southerners calculated the value of their position in the Union and contemplated the creation of an independent, slaveholding confederacy, they began to consider how best to promote the development of their infrastructure, commercial services, and nascent manufacturers. "Political independence is not worth a fig without commercial independence," Southern proslavery theorist George Fitzhugh wrote in 1854. A nascent entrepreneurial class coalesced in the South, working out ideas for promoting economic modernization in new commercial publications such as *Debow's Review*. The message propagated by *Debow's* was a powerful one: maximizing the profitability of slavery meant diversifying the South's economy to decrease dependence upon Yankee parasites. This Southern version of economic nationalism was rooted in its export economy that sought integration into a liberal international order, but it nonetheless acknowledged the need for some revenue-generating tariffs as well as coordinated and state-supported programs of economic diversification and development. It was ardently proslavery. Indeed, in the view of these Southern nationalists, slaves could provide a labor pool for future development projects and resource extraction. The economic vision that emerged in the South in the 1850s was a far more robust model for an independent South than the old one-dimensional railing against Yankee tariffs. Ultimately, this modernizing vision would help to broaden the appeal of the Confederate project to those outside the cotton belt, not least Virginia. Its legacy can be seen in the centralizing tendencies of the wartime Confederate state.[26]

The story in the North was more complex, but similarly one in which the old nationalist dimensions of the tariff gave way to a sectional organization of political economy. The key was the rising appeal of antislavery among Northern whites on the grounds of economic self-interest. Old divisions within the North over the tariff and other economic issues subsided as US politics came to be dominated by the question of whether the western territories would be open to slavery. This issue led many Northern whites to link antislavery to their own material well-being. The moral arguments of the abolitionists resonated with a relatively small constituency; in contrast, the critique of slavery that was grounded in free-labor ideology was more widespread. Advocates of free soil warned that if the territories were opened to slavery, as Southern slavers demanded, the North's free-labor economy would be imperiled. The slave power would come to dominate the territories, thus cutting off new land for migrants and for immigrants from abroad, leading to increased urbanization and industrialization in the existing free states, which in turn would destabilize Northern social relations and transform the republic into a class-ridden version of an Old World country. "The public lands," New York newspaperman Horace Greeley wrote, "are the great regulator of the relations of Labor and Capital, the safety valve of our industrial and social engine."[27]

This emerging free-labor ideology increasingly resonated with Northern voters as the sectional crisis progressed in the 1850s. The new political alliances and coalitions constructed upon the foundation of opposition to the expansion of slavery in the territories transcended the old battle lines on the tariff, inverting the Jacksonian-era formula. Of the many tightrope balancing acts managed by the new Republican Party in the 1850s, few were of greater significance than how the party brought into the fold both protectionists and tariff reductionists. This was a matter of electoral necessity: to win the presidency, the new party needed to win states with powerful protectionist lobbies, such as Pennsylvania, as well as those Midwestern agrarian states whose export economies led them to advocate tariff reductions. The party achieved this by fudging the tariff issue whenever possible, euphemistically speaking of protectionism in the terms of necessary revenue generation. Some Republicans even voted for the tariff reduction of 1857.

The 1857 financial panic, however, pumped new life into the old cause of the tariff in the North. This sharp downturn hit Northern cities and manufacturers particularly hard, leading many Yankees to embrace protection as a means of securing manufacturing jobs and economic prosperity. "The tariff looms up again," wrote one New York protectionist. "It is going to be the great question now and will enter largely I think into the canvass of 1860." As the South's export economy weathered the storm in 1857, many Northerners came to view low tariffs in a way similar to how Southerners viewed high ones—as a harmful imposition foisted upon them by a rival section with antagonistic economic interests. "Free Labor, Protection to American Industry, and death to the Free Trade, Pro Slavery, Sham Democratic Party," wrote one Yankee editor in the aftermath of the Panic of 1857. This revival of Northern protectionism in the late 1850s portended the high tariffs of the Civil War years and beyond.[28]

Back in the 1840s, Henry Clay had hoped that the material bonds of union would withstand the political crisis over slavery. But what had happened with the tariff was just the opposite. As the sectional conflict progressed, the tariff evolved from an issue that transcended divisions over slavery to one that reinforced and even deepened them.

III

The shifting course of America's tariff politics correlated to changes in its national security and foreign relations. Protectionism flourished in moments of crisis—most of all in the eras and aftermaths of the War of 1812 and the Civil War—while it receded in periods marked by a decrease of security threats. The tariff was not alone in being connected to changes in the broader international system. The fate of the Union itself was entwined with a dramatic shift in its national security that occurred in the 1840s and 1850s. In an underappreciated irony of its history, the increased power and security attained by the United States in this period had the effect of escalating its internal divisions. "All the armies of Europe, Asia and Africa combined," a young Abraham Lincoln noted as early as 1838, "could not by force, take a drink from the Ohio." Danger, Lincoln believed, "cannot come from abroad. If destruction be our lot, we must ourselves be its author and finisher."[29]

This newfound security stood in marked contrast to the republic's traditional state of fear and perceived vulnerability. From the start, security considerations had been one of—if not the—greatest drivers of national integration. Back in 1787, the founding fathers designed the union to solidify America's independence, fend off rival powers, and subjugate Native peoples. Later, the War of 1812 unleashed a powerful nationalist spirit that lived on after the conflict in annual social rituals of the Fourth of July and, perhaps most of all, the political celebrity of Andrew Jackson, the hero of the Battle of New Orleans and the architect of Indian removal. The Monroe Doctrine of 1823, which sought to insulate the fragile union from foreign threats by unilaterally proclaiming a prohibition on further European colonization in the Western Hemisphere, infused US foreign policy with a nationalist spirit.[30]

This nationalist ethos persisted in the aggressive ideology of Manifest Destiny, which helped to fuel the imperial expansion of the 1840s. The Democratic Party, now led by slaveholder James K. Polk (who bought and sold slaves while in the White House), had an answer for the sectional and partisan rancor triggered by the annexation of Texas in 1845: more expansion. When Mexico, the previous sovereign in Texas, refused to accept the new border, war was the predictable result. The United States here benefited from yet another stroke of good fortune: Mexico's hold on its northern provinces had been decimated by decades of Native raids. It was the mighty Comanche people, not Mexico, who called the shots in this borderland territory. The territory was highly vulnerable to conquest. With the powerful Comanche having cleared the way, the United States quickly wrested from Mexico its nominal northern provinces in the brief, but consequential, war of 1846–1848. It was a stunning victory that, in conjunction with the 1846 treaty with Britain that divided the Oregon Territory, made the United States a transcontinental power. The ultimate prize was the Pacific coast, particularly, California—the source of so much of America's future power.[31]

The United States continued to flex its newfound muscle in the years after 1848. Yankees gained control of strategic corridors in the Caribbean and Central America through which chugged new US steamships, including the famous wooden-hulled paddlewheelers that were built in the shipyards of New York and Philadelphia. In Panama, Wall Street financiers managed the world's first transcontinental railroad, which was completed in 1855. The track was only forty-seven miles long, but it revolutionized communications between the booming coastal hubs of New York and San Francisco. Indeed, more migrants arrived in California during the gold rush of this period via the isthmian route in Panama and its competitor in Nicaragua than in covered wagons crossing the overland South Pass. Panama became a de facto protectorate of the United

States in this period—indeed, the Marines landed to impose control over the passageway in 1856, an act that would be repeated time and again in the coming decades. Congressmen, statesmen, and private business interests drafted blueprints for further infrastructure projects, not least a transcontinental railroad across North America. Coal production soared as new markets for it appeared, even in hitherto distant outposts such as the fast-growing ports of California. The United States extended its reach across the Pacific, particularly in Hawaii, which was brought into its orbit by American missionaries and traders. The United States signed a commercial treaty with China in 1844 and, after the expedition of Commodore Matthew Perry, one with Japan in 1854. The fact that the homeland was fracturing did not stop outward-looking Americans from going about laying the foundations for what in time would become a global American empire.[32]

Now stretching from the Atlantic to the Pacific and with commercial interests around the world, the United States was no longer an insecure power. What had been demonstrated in the 1840s was that the powers of the Old World had acquiesced to a US continental dominion that neighboring states like Mexico and powerful, yet numerically small, Native tribes like the Comanche were unable to stop (the Comanche numbered only around 20,000 in the mid-nineteenth century and their population was fast diminishing). If anything, foreign powers facilitated the expansion of the United States. This was true not only of the Comanche, but also of the republic's old enemy, the British Empire. London financiers advanced some of the funds the United States used to pay the indemnity to Mexico as agreed in the Treaty of Guadalupe Hidalgo, which ended the war; the Royal Navy opened Chinese ports to Yankee traders; and the Clayton–Bulwer Treaty of 1850 pledged Anglo-American cooperation in the Central American isthmus. Southern slavers still feared British abolitionism but now could take comfort in the fact that antislavery Britain rolled over when the proslavery United States gobbled up Texas and California. Southerners concluded that British acquiescence to their expansion derived from the old country's dependence upon their cotton. Here were the roots of the confidence that would shape the ill-fated diplomacy of the future Confederacy.[33]

It was no coincidence that the Civil War occurred just as the United States was emerging as a world power. This newly attained security intensified the controversy between the slaveholding South and the free states of the North in two general ways. First, with foreign threats receding, there were fewer brakes on sectionalism. Foreign threats still lingered in American politics, but their greatest significance was how they now mapped onto and deepened sectional divisions. As with the tariff, what had once tied Americans together now pulled them apart. Most ominous was how both sides of the sectional debate over slavery came to see each other in light of the old British threat. Proslavery Southerners viewed the antislavery forces within and outside the Union as interlinked (not without reason); meanwhile, Northerners began to speak of the slave power as an aristocratic clique that mimicked the opponents of democracy in the Old World (again, with some justice). "An aristocracy has arisen here," Seward warned, and it "is already undermining the republic."[34]

Far from being a binding force of union, foreign policy issues now widened sectional divisions. Nowhere was this more the case than in US foreign policy in Central America and the Caribbean. Assertive Southerners called for annexationist policies in the region in order to expand their proslavery empire into the warm climes of the Caribbean. The potential annexation of the slaveholding island of Cuba became a wedge issue in the 1850s. Expansion into the Caribbean was not purely a sectional issue, as many Northern Democrats of the Manifest Destiny ilk, such as Illinoisan Stephen Douglas, continued to advocate the acquisition of new territories. "Whenever it becomes necessary, in our growth and progress to acquire more territory," he asserted in one of his famous

1858 debates with Abraham Lincoln, "I am in favor of it, without reference to the question of slavery." But the fact that Cuba was slaveholding meant it was impossible to sidestep the matter, particularly when Republicans couched their opposition to further expansion in antislavery terms. As suspicion of the slave power increased in the North, Democrats found that their traditional embrace of territorial expansion was becoming a political liability. As with so much else, many foreign policy matters morphed into referenda on the issue of slavery.[35]

There was a second way in which the increased security and power of the United States accelerated the descent toward civil war. Now left to their own devices on the continent, Americans were confronted with one of the basic facts of empire: establishing dominion is easier than consolidating and maintaining it. The experience of Britain after its triumph in the Seven Years' War provides a parallel. Just as Britain's victory over France and its Native allies set in motion the events that would lead to the imperial crisis in the 1760s and 1770s, the establishment of US continental dominion in 1848 thrust to the fore of domestic politics the contentious question of whether the federal territories of the West would be open to slavery. The federal lands in question included those taken in the war and in which slavery had been prohibited by Mexico as well as some of the old but still unorganized territories of the Louisiana Purchase. The status of slavery in the territories became the single greatest driver of US politics from the end of the war against Mexico to the election of Lincoln in 1860. That Mexico had abolished slavery in the 1830s gave a leg up to those who opposed the reintroduction of the peculiar institution, such as Pennsylvania Democrat David Wilmot, the sponsor of the famous proviso that sought to continue the Mexican prohibition on slavery. "Free it is now," Wilmot declared, "and free, with God's help, it shall remain." Before the conquest of northern Mexico was even complete, the United States had been thrown into political crisis over the future of slavery in its expanded continental realm. "Mexico will poison us," Ralph Waldo Emerson predicted.[36]

This phase of the crisis was momentarily put to bed with the Compromise of 1850, which mitigated immediate tensions without fundamentally resolving the issue in all of the territories (California, however, was admitted as a free state). The political crisis of 1850 brought to center stage for one last time the old generation of politicians, led by Henry Clay, Daniel Webster, and John C. Calhoun, who had come of age in the nationalist era of the War of 1812. These veteran politicians continued to argue that the Union was necessary to preserve national independence and sovereignty. Indeed, Webster exploited old fears of European monarchy during the political crisis of 1850 when he publicly denounced the Austrian government for quashing an insurrection in Hungary. Webster later confessed that his motive had less to do with Austria than it was to "touch the national pride, and make a man feel sheepish and look silly who should speak of disunion." But despite old timers like Webster reaching deep into their bag of political tricks, the legislation of 1850 was not achieved in a single, grand compromise as originally proposed by Clay, but—ominously—via separate votes on individual provisions, as orchestrated by the rising political star within the Democratic Party, Illinoisan Stephen Douglas. The nationalist spirit of those who came of age during the War of 1812 was giving way to rising sectionalism and the radical spirit embodied in the European revolutions of 1848. Events across the Atlantic set precedents for secessionist movements as well as for forcible attempts to quash them. Revolution was in the air—not least the word *revolution* itself, the frequent appearance of which in American politics portended what was to come.[37]

The question of slavery in the territories did not go away after 1850, because the colonization of the continent by Americans could not be stopped. There was no attempt to impose a version of the old British Proclamation Line of 1763 as a means of thwarting the danger. Far from suppressing the westward push, the competition between the sections to gain the upper hand accelerated the colonization of the West, which in turn intensified debate over the question of whether slavery should be allowed. The increased security and power of the United States had ended the old fear that settlers would detach from the Union and ally with the British or Spanish. The management of the vast continent was now a question of imperial administration, not geopolitics. Stephen Douglas once again took center stage, proposing what he deemed to be a compromise option in the infamous Kansas-Nebraska Act of 1854, which sought to find resolution to the territorial question so that a railroad to the Pacific coast could be constructed—with a terminus in his home state of Illinois. Douglas proposed passing the buck to the peoples of the territories, who would be empowered to decide the slavery question for themselves based on the principle of popular sovereignty.

The Kansas-Nebraska Act marked the point of no return in the sectional crisis. The bill deserves the condemnation it has received in history textbooks, but it bears pointing out that it was the best compromise on offer. There simply weren't better options for bridging the widening gulf between the Democratic Party's Northern wing, which housed a growing faction that opposed slavery in the territories or at least recognized the political imperative of so doing, and its traditional Southern core, which demanded slaveholder access to the West. The quality that made the Kansas-Nebraska Act most attractive—that it kicked the can down the road by empowering the inhabitants of the territories to decide the slavery question for themselves—was what led to its failure. Douglas's bill set off a violent scramble for influence in Kansas among the most ardent defenders and opponents of slavery. Compromise became increasingly difficult once blood had been spilled and the territory became known as "bleeding Kansas." The constitutional question of slavery in the territories had become tethered to violence in Kansas, which soon had rival territorial governments.

Intended to diffuse the slavery question, the Kansas-Nebraska Act set in motion a chain reaction that led to disunion and civil war.

When that civil war was just days from beginning in April 1861, the new secretary of state, William H. Seward, made one more desperate attempt to prevent disunion. With supplies running low at the federal Fort Sumter outside of Charleston, South Carolina, and as the powers of Europe began to take advantage of US weakness by reasserting themselves in the Caribbean, Seward hatched a plan to save the Union. In a confidential memo to President Lincoln, Seward urged the new president to convene Congress and declare war on Spain and France. Such a course, the secretary of state argued, would "change the question before the public from one upon slavery, or about slavery, for a question upon union or disunion." That Seward's scheme went nowhere revealed not only the soundness of Lincoln's political instincts—"one war at a time," he was purported to have said during the war—but also the extent to which foreign threats now paled in significance to the internal divisions between the slaveholding South and the free-labor North.[38]

IV

Of all the national institutions and practices that collapsed in this period, none did more to determine the course of disunion than political parties. The breakdown of the national Whig and Democratic political parties ushered in a new political era, one in which parties were more closely tethered to sectional interests and the slavery question. By the mid-1850s, the political landscape had been transformed: a new antislavery party in the North, the Republicans, vied for power with a Democratic Party that was itself on the road to fracturing into Northern and Southern wings in 1860.

Slavery was the principal driver of this political realignment. But it was not the only one. An unanticipated surge in immigration in the 1840s and 1850s destabilized national party politics. The decade after 1845 witnessed the largest increase in the percentage of the population that was foreign-born in a ten-year span in US history. Some three million immigrants arrived to a nation that in 1850 was estimated to be home to just over twenty-three million people. This immigration boom accounted for a remarkable 13 percent of the nation's population. Proportionately, this would be as if forty-two million immigrants arrived in a decade's span in the early twenty-first century (as a point of comparison, an estimated fourteen million immigrants arrived in the United States in the first decade of the twenty-first century). The principal cause was the great humanitarian crisis of the mid-Victorian era, the potato famine in Ireland. Deprived of a core source of sustenance, and with the British state failing to provide adequate relief, desperate Irish boarded vessels bound for the other side of the Atlantic. Joining them were unprecedented numbers of Germans, who sought higher wages and better prospects than were on offer in Europe, as well as refugees from the failed European revolutions of 1848. What made this burst of immigration politically significant in the United States was not only its suddenness but also its ethnic and religious composition. Some two-thirds of the migrants in this period—including both Germans and Irish—were Catholic. They arrived into the world's most dynamic and market-driven evangelical Protestant culture.[39]

The result was social and political confrontation. Ethnic and religious tensions already were running high in the mid-1840s, evident, for instance, in the Philadelphia riots of 1844, which pitted Protestants against Catholics. Each vessel that arrived from the Old World with more migrants increased the ire of "native" white Protestants. Fueling their discontent was increased labor competition as well as religious sectarianism. It is no coincidence that many of those who joined the nativist American Party, popularly known as the Know-Nothing Party, were young men of modest means. Adding further fuel to the fire were the attempts of Catholic leaders, particularly in New York, to claim public funds for their parochial schools. New wedge issues appeared on the political landscape, including the wait period for the naturalization of immigrants, as well as the prohibition of alcohol, which many Protestants associated with Catholic immigrants—indeed, Maine passed a bill restricting alcohol sales in 1851 that was strongly supported by nativists. New York and Massachusetts took matters into their own hands in other ways, passing laws that restricted indigent arrivals and empowered state authorities to deport those deemed to be immigrant paupers.[40]

The rising nativism of this period intensified as the perception spread among native Protestants that the political establishment was unresponsive to their concerns. The Democratic Party, which cultivated votes from the expanding Irish population, certainly was not about to kowtow to the nativist lobby. The Whigs were generally more sympathetic to nativist critiques of Catholicism, but they were of two minds on the issue when it came to political strategy. To fully commit to nativism risked undermining economic growth and the party's future electoral prospects in states with large immigrant populations, not least New York, the great swing state of nineteenth-century politics. It was New York that had cost Whig candidate Henry Clay the presidency in 1844 (thus handing the election to James K. Polk, who interpreted his narrow victory as a mandate to launch the war of conquest against Mexico). The emerging politics of nativism destabilized the Whigs, eroding their party's foundation and legitimacy just as Douglas pulled the pin from the grenade of the Kansas-Nebraska bill. The Whigs likely would have imploded under the pressure of one crisis; there was no way they would survive the furore of both immigration and slavery. Indeed, the two issues had a way of feeding off one another. Many of the angry Northern voters and politicians who denounced the slave power of the South also took aim at the "papal power" that allegedly ruled over Catholic immigrants.

The sheer political energy unleashed by these two emotive and divisive issues overwhelmed the Whig Party, ripping it apart on two separate axes: a sectional one as well as an ethnocultural one. The Whig Party did not die—it was killed. It was killed by innovative political start-ups that seized the opportunity provided by the political crisis of the mid-1850s. The Know-Nothing Party, whose name came from the response members were to give when asked about their political association, creatively exploited the power of anti-Catholicism and nativism. It brought new voters and candidates into the political process. It swept onto the scene at the local as well as national level. The Know-Nothings' bigotry, antiestablishment agenda, and harnessing of evangelical energy now looks less like a distant curiosity than a portent of the nationalist populism of more recent times.[41]

But for all their potential strength, the Know-Nothings were weak compared to another party that rose from the political rubble of the collapse of the Whigs—the Republicans, whose primary objective was to restrict the expansion of slavery into the Western territories. The rapid ascent of the party in 1854–1856 was a result of not only its ideological coherence on the issue of slavery in the territories but also its inclusiveness. Republicans encouraged negotiation and compromise among different and often competing interests; they fostered connections between local, state, and national organizations; they developed elastic frameworks that allowed, indeed encouraged, local and regional variation on a number of policy issues. Like the Know-Nothings, they drew power from evangelical churches, but they did so without fully embracing the nativism that limited electoral possibilities. Some of their future leaders, including Lincoln and Seward, distanced themselves from nativism. "I am not a Know-Nothing," Lincoln wrote in 1855. "How can any one who abhors the oppression of negroes, be in favor of degrading classes of white people?" Indeed, one of the key demographic groups that swung elections during this period in the Republicans' favor were German Protestants.[42]

Such political balancing acts typified the Republican Party. In Massachusetts, the Republicans fused with the Know-Nothings; in New

York, they stood against them. In the long term, internal divisions over immigration, tariffs, and currency would rip through the Republican Party. But in the near term, the new party's decentralized and pluralistic approach gave it the flexibility it needed in the political realignment of the mid-1850s. By 1856, America's political landscape had been transformed. The once-great Whig Party was on its way toward extinction as the Republicans rapidly assembled a diverse coalition that included former Whigs, Know-Nothings, and Democrats who were fed up with the South's increasingly radical demands regarding slavery in the territories. The Republicans came surprisingly close to capturing the White House in 1856. Four years later, the Republican Party found a leader who personified its powerful combination of political pluralism and moral clarity on the key issue of slavery.

The collapse of the Whig Party reverberated through the South. Sleeper cells of Whigs remained, particularly in the Upper South and the sugar and commercial state of Louisiana. But overall, the Deep South became a place of de facto single-party rule. The dominance of Democrats radicalized the politics of the Deep South in the 1850s, creating a self-perpetuating dynamic of proslavery extremism. Candidates for office raced to establish themselves as the most ardent defender of Southern institutions and honor. There was little political incentive for Southern statesmen to pursue compromise with the North when it would imperil their electoral prospects in the next election. This dynamic helps to explain why the South's position on slavery in the territories morphed into a hardline policy that left no room for compromise with Northern Democrats. Slaveholders, Southern Democrats contended after the notorious proslavery *Dred Scott* decision, should receive the support of the federal government when they took their slaves into any federal territory that they so desired.

The immigration surge destabilized the system of Whigs and Democrats that tied the sections of the Union together. Would the United States have avoided civil war had there been no Irish

potato famine? It is an old question worth consideration. The case
for an affirmative answer would go something like this: Absent the
social and political conflict surrounding the influx of Catholic immigrants (from Germany as well as Ireland), the Whigs could have
weathered the storm during the Kansas-Nebraska Act—which, after all, was a Democratic bill. If the Whigs survived, there would
have been no new, Northern party opposed to the expansion of
slavery in the territories of the West, no election of Lincoln—and
thus no rational case for secessionists to use in their bid to con-
vince their fellow Southerners that disunion was an urgent priority.

It is a seductive line of thought but one with a weak first link in
the counterfactual chain: the Whigs would not have survived the
strain of the slavery question. They would have divided at some point
into Northern and Southern wings, just as the other parties did (the
Know-Nothings split over the question of slavery in the territories in
1855, as did the Democrats at their fiery party convention in Charleston in 1860). But if the burst of immigration in 1845–1855 no more
caused the Civil War than did the tariff, it nonetheless demands our
attention because it conditioned how and when the Union collapsed
by accelerating the process of political realignment along sectional
lines. The quick ascent of nativist politics was the jab that left the old
Whig versus Democratic party system stunned just before the knock-
out blow was delivered in the form of the Kansas-Nebraska Act.

V

The secession of the Southern states in the months following the
election of Lincoln in 1860 was a rational and calculated action.
The goal was to create a new nation committed to insulating slavery
from outside pressures while at the same time leveraging its export
economy to its advantage. Much like the US Constitution of 1787,
the 1861 Confederate Constitution sought to establish the international legitimacy of the new state. Although the new constitution

explicitly mentioned slavery ten times, Confederates did not emphasize their peculiar institution when they approached foreign nations to recognize their independence. Instead, Southerners presented their new nation as an exemplar of self-determination, social order, and liberal economics. A month before the war started, the Confederate leadership dispatched emissaries to Britain and Europe to hand deliver their new constitution—"the best proof which you can afford of the wisdom, moderation, and justice" of the new slaveholding nation. Additional agents crossed the Atlantic in search of foreign loans. Thus began the slaveholding South's diplomatic gambit that would do as much as any army or domestic policy to determine the Confederacy's fate.[43]

But for as much as secession and the creation of the Confederacy were the products of carefully calibrated statecraft, also underlying these political moves were emotions—above all, fears and anxieties about the stability of the Old South's racial hierarchy. Southerners remained terrified of not only the external forces of antislavery but also the slaves themselves, whom they publicly depicted as content and subservient. As secessionist conventions formed in the critical winter of 1860–1861, rumors spread throughout the South of imminent plots hatched by slaves and their "black Republican" allies in the North. Advocates of secession in Mississippi in 1860 circulated fears that the abolitionists had already distributed "poison, knives and pistols" as part of a scheme to "emancipate the Slaves of the South." Such fears had long been a feature of the Old South. What gave them newfound force during the mid-nineteenth century was the erosion of Southern confidence in the Union. It was this broader national situation that slaves became masters at exploiting.[44]

The significance of such fears might seem counterintuitive given that one of the most striking features of American slavery in the high antebellum period was its relative stability. In the opening three decades of the nineteenth century, there had been at least four major slave revolts or conspiracies: Gabriel's conspiracy (Virginia, 1800); the Deslondes revolt (Louisiana, 1811); the Denmark Vesey plot (South Carolina, 1822); and Nat Turner's insurrection (Virginia, 1831). The years between Nat Turner's insurrection and John Brown's raid in 1859, in contrast, lacked a rebellion or plot on the same scale. There were acts of organized slave resistance, to be sure, but the master class's fear of an American version of the Haitian rebellion never came to pass.[45]

Slaves found more practical and viable ways to resist. They honed their skills of resistance in the unending power struggles that took place on the plantations. The daily friction and conflict led them to understand that the deck was stacked against them when it came to a full-on, Caribbean-style rebellion. They were a minority population in the South, whereas they had been an overwhelming majority population in Haiti; they understood that their masters could call in insurmountable power if the occasion arose; and they took note of the list of failed attempts at revolt. So, instead of engaging in an act that would be tantamount to suicide, they resisted in a more effective manner: they ran away.[46]

There were two forms of running away, which were largely determined by geographic location. The first was common in the cotton states of the Deep South, where the densest concentration of slaves was to be found. Slaves here knew that there was almost no chance of making it to freedom. Imagine trying to survive a journey on foot from the Gulf South all the way to Ohio with no provisions and while being hunted down by slave patrols. "No man who has never been placed in such a situation," wrote African American abolitionist Solomon Northup, "can comprehend the thousand obstacles thrown in the way of the flying slave. Every white man's hand is raised against him—the patrollers are watching for him—the hounds are ready to follow on his track, and the nature of the country is such as renders it impossible to pass through it with any safety." Slaves might attempt to melt into the free black communities of cities such as New Orleans, or those with light skin might try to "pass" for being white and travel in the open among the racial class that kept them bonded. Such escape attempts required untold nerve, social versatility, and self-confidence. They were rare.[47]

Most runaways in the Deep South did not seek a freedom that was nearly impossible to attain; rather, they sought to protest specific terms of their enslavement. The two most common triggers of running away are revealing: whipping and family separation. Many who took to the woods did so preemptively, before the master raised the lash or placed a slave family on the auction block. "They didn't do something and run," one ex-slave remembered. "They run before they did it...in them days they run to keep from doing something." Running away deprived the master of labor, the very purpose of the institution. The master might have to take out an escaped-slave ad in the local paper or hire a patrol of poor whites to do the dirty work of tracking the slave down. And the costs went beyond the master's pocketbook. In a society that fancied itself as the embodiment of civilized gentility, a master whose slaves ran away became stigmatized as one who had abnegated his paternalist responsibilities. For all these reasons, running away was an effective mode of resistance that, although mostly undertaken by individuals, sought to achieve the collective aim of protesting the most unbearable aspects of slavery. The goal was not only to make the master pay in some form for his abuse of power but also to make him think twice before resorting to the lash or breaking up a family in the future. Running away in the Deep South thus echoed the working class's use of the strike to improve labor conditions in other capitalist societies of the Victorian era.[48]

The other path taken by runaway slaves is the one more commonly remembered today—the underground railroad. These runaways might better be called "run-towards," for they raced toward free soil just as much as they ran away from their enslavers. They

were often based in the Upper South, the borderlands of slavery—
Missouri, Kentucky, Maryland, Virginia—and fled to free territory,
usually with the assistance of the "conductors" who managed abolitionist "stations" on the underground railroad, a loose network established by those prepared to risk their own lives to help those who
sought freedom. About one thousand or so slaves reached freedom
in this way each year in the decade preceding the Civil War. The numbers were proportionately small, but the political impact was great. If
there was one social group that did more than any other to make the
slavery question so dominant in public life in mid-nineteenth-century
America, it was the slaves who ran for their freedom. They destabilized slavery not only by disrupting the operations of individual planters but more so by making it clear to every master that slaves were not
content with their bondage. Runaways further challenged slavery by
giving abolitionist societies a popular issue with which to attract public support. The narratives written by escaped slaves, most famously
that of Frederick Douglass, revealed the horrors of slavery while at
the same time empowering readers with the knowledge that the odds
could be overcome through heroic action.[49]

Perhaps most important was how runaways ensured that the
sectional conflict remained on the national political stage. Because
the race to freedom entailed crossing state lines, the act of running
away forced white Americans to grapple with the contentious issue
of slavery and the powers of the federal government. The advocates
of slavery pointed to the Constitution's fugitive slave provision as
well as legislation from the early republic; meanwhile, Northern
states advocated states' rights when it came to which layer of government should determine the legal rights of those suspected of being
fugitives. The resulting Fugitive Slave Act, part of the broader Compromise of 1850, came down on the proslavery side. Its egregious
provisions diminished the legal rights of fugitives, who were denied
habeas corpus and the right to testify in their own defense, while it
empowered federal officials to enforce the compliance of Northern

whites. "This vile, infernal law," Frederick Douglass thundered, is "a degradation and a scandalous outrage on religious liberty." In the tug-of-war that was the sectional crisis, the harder the South pulled, the more resistance it met; the more antislavery sympathies manifested themselves in the North, the harder the South pulled.[50]

For all their political and economic triumphs, for all their talk about the sustainability of the peculiar institution, Southern white elites were haunted by the specter of runaway slaves and the free blacks and abolitionists who aided them. The ultimate fear was that a nexus of slaves and outside agitators were plotting insurrections. John Brown's attempt to incite a slave rebellion by commandeering the federal arsenal at Harper's Ferry, Virginia, in 1859 was more than just another episode on the road to disunion. From the white South's perspective, it was a harbinger of a future of terror. It didn't matter that Brown's attempted rebellion was a failure. Southern elites might have interpreted it as a demonstration of the power of their proslavery firewall. But they didn't. They saw it as the beginning of a new era in which the region would be gripped by the terror of slave rebellion and Yankee infiltration. We should listen to the slaveholders' terrified reaction and hysteric predictions of other such plots, for it reveals a point of fundamental importance: the master class's persistent fear of slave rebellion might well have been an accurate assessment of threat.

It certainly appears as such when one considers what unfolded as soon as the Civil War began. Slaves did what they long had done, but now in previously unimaginable numbers and with previously unimaginable results. They ran toward freedom, thus setting in motion a chain of events that would lead to the ratification of the Thirteenth Amendment in 1865 that forever ended slavery in the United States. The Civil War did not start as a war of liberation, but the actions of the slaves quickly made it into one. The Union Army was the magnet; wherever it went, it attracted slaves who seized the opportunity to liberate themselves. By late 1862, Union policy caught up with what was happening on the ground. Congressional acts and, most of all, Lincoln's Emancipation Proclamation provided legislative and constitutional backing for the Union's turn toward emancipation, while incentivizing more slaves to run toward Union lines. Events on the war's various fronts and in Washington began to move in sync. The climax came in early 1863, when the Union formally took the previously unimaginable step of harnessing the power of the African Americans to the military effort. This policy shift occurred as Grant marched his powerful western army through the Mississippi Valley, the core of the cotton kingdom that soon turned into a deep well of military manpower for the North. "The colored population is the great *available* and yet *unavailed* of, force for restoring the Union," Lincoln wrote in March 1863. "The bare sight of fifty thousand armed, and drilled black soldiers on the banks of the Mississippi, would end the rebellion."[51]

Armed ex-slaves in blue coats marching through the heart of the Old South—this was surely the most revolutionary moment in US history. A shifting international scene had intensified and accelerated a political crisis in America, which in turn had evolved into what deserves to be called a social revolution, incomplete though it would be. Here emerged a new swing pattern of that wrecking ball, which no longer oscillated between the sections but instead focused its destructive force within one of them, delivering the crushing blows that brought down the world's mightiest slave empire. What is so remarkable about this is how quickly it happened. Just before the war erupted in March 1861, Lincoln signaled that he was prepared to accept an amendment to the Constitution that would forever forbid the federal government from abolishing slavery from within the states in which it existed. Less than two years later, his administration enlisted escaped slaves into the Union Army. The speed of transformative change was not limited to emancipation and black military service. The Civil War set off a series of shock waves that rippled throughout the world.

CHAPTER 3

The Last Best Hope of Earth

ON THE FOURTH of July 1861, less than three months after South Carolina unleashed its guns on Fort Sumter, Abraham Lincoln attempted to give meaning to the Civil War in an address to a special session of Congress. What was at stake, Lincoln asserted, was "more than the fate of these United States. It presents to the whole family of man the question whether a constitutional republic, or democracy—a government of the people by the same people—can or can not maintain its territorial integrity against its own domestic foes." The United States, Lincoln declared the following year, was "the last best hope of earth" for those who wanted to see republican self-government succeed. In late 1863, Lincoln returned to this theme when revising what would become the most famous line of the most famous presidential speech in American history, the Gettysburg Address. He deleted the qualifying "this" in front of "government" and spoke of "the earth" rather than just "North America" in words that have circulated around the globe ever since: "We here highly resolve...that government of the people, by the people, for the people, shall not perish from the earth."[1]

America was not alone in facing a great national crisis in the 1860s, as Lincoln was well aware. That decade witnessed conflicts around the world that stemmed from contestations over nationhood and sovereignty. In Mexico, an internal civil war morphed into a French imperial venture that installed Austrian archduke Maximilian upon a newly created throne in Mexico City; in Santo Domingo, Spain intervened with the aim of reestablishing its colonial rule; in Ireland, radical separatists unsuccessfully fought for liberation from British rule; both Germany and Italy endured contested phases of national unification; Tsar Alexander II initiated a series of reforms aimed at updating Russia's inefficient political economy, including the emancipation of the serfs in 1861; and in Japan, Meiji modernizers implemented far-reaching social and political changes in order to counter encroaching European imperialism. The list could go on. The American Civil War was a variation on this international theme of nation making and economic modernization. It was further connected to these global processes in that its course and outcome hinged upon the actions of foreign powers and people. The Civil War was a global event, albeit one whose international course was perhaps most notable for what did not happen—foreign intervention.[2]

The implosion of the Union in 1860–1861 was a jolt to the movement of capital and people across the Atlantic. Its effects might be likened to the New Madrid, Missouri, earthquake of 1812, which temporarily reversed the current of the mighty Mississippi River. The inflow of foreign capital, especially from Britain, that had been a feature of the Atlantic economy since 1815 suddenly ceased—indeed, anxious capital fled the war-torn republic in a wave of financial repatriation in 1860–1862. "The anticipation of a bloody conflict between the North and the South," London-based American financier George Peabody observed during the secession crisis, "has already destroyed confidence in the U.S. Government and States securities." The unprecedented immigration of the 1840s and 1850s was reduced to the lowest levels recorded in the period between 1844 and 1931. The war led to an almost complete cessation of the cotton trade thanks to an ill-conceived embargo that Confederates implemented to hasten British intervention on their behalf. Perhaps most striking, the security realized by the Union after the Mexican War was all of a sudden in grave jeopardy as European powers, particularly the British, contemplated options, including supporting the Confederacy.[3]

New possibilities opened up in this upended international context. The outcome of America's greatest crisis hinged upon not only the battles of the Civil War but also the actions of foreign powers and peoples. Like the imperial crisis of the late eighteenth century, its result was far from predetermined. As we will see, the Civil War had a Saratoga moment, but it played out differently than that of 1777–1778. The eventual destruction of Southern slavery and separatism marked a victory for the liberal political ideology Lincoln had seen as "the last best hope of earth." Furthermore, the political stabilization of the United States catalyzed unprecedented booms in immigration and foreign investment in the postwar decades. But the Union victory did not point in a uniformly liberal direction, for the war effort extended momentum to economic nationalism, the concentration of wealth and political power, and, in time, racialized imperialism. The ends to which the United States would project its newfound power were not immediately apparent. What was clear, however, was that the outcome of the Civil War had not only saved the Union and destroyed slavery but also positioned the United States to take full advantage of the late nineteenth-century version of what we now call globalization.

I

When the Union collapsed in the months following the election of Abraham Lincoln in 1860, many observers around the world expected that it would be the first act of a much larger drama.

Southern secession, in this view, was more than a domestic crisis; it was a harbinger of a broader political transformation in North America, the Caribbean, and possibly even further afield.

It did not take much imagination for contemporaries to envision how the fracturing of the United States could set in motion a chain of events that would radically alter the region's configurations of power. "Revolutions are epidemical," wrote Secretary of State William H. Seward, who feared that the South's bid for independence would "threaten the stability of society throughout the world." An independent, slaveholding Confederacy might be sucked into the orbit of the British Empire, not least because of the powerful bonds of the cotton trade. The Southern master class would model itself even more than it already did upon the aristocracies of Europe, possibly rolling back democratic practices at home in order to consolidate its grip on power. But that would not be all. The slaveholding republic would aggressively protect its labor system, its reason for being, thus putting it on a collision course with its prospective ally of Britain, the world's most committed antislavery power. It was within the realm of possibility that an independent Confederacy would seek to acquire new slave territories in the Caribbean and even reopen the banned international slave trade. The slaveholding nation would do everything in its power to preserve slavery where it existed in the hemisphere, particularly Cuba and Brazil. Compounding matters would be the tense relations between the Confederacy and the free states of the North, which themselves would be in danger of fragmentation were Southern secession successful. The implosion of the union, in sum, threatened to destabilize North America in ways reminiscent of the predictions made by the founding fathers back in the late eighteenth century. Seward feared that the "success of the revolution" would constitute "not only a practical overthrow of the entire system of government, but the first stage by each confederacy in the road to anarchy, such as so widely prevails in Spanish America."[4]

It wasn't just the state of affairs in the United States that suggested a broader political reconfiguration was in the works. Elsewhere in North America and the Caribbean, the status quo was unraveling. The vision of a happy family of independent republics across the New World that had been widely held by advocates of republican government in the Western Hemisphere in the early nineteenth century was turning into a nightmare of internal instability and foreign intervention. "The Powers of the Old World are flocking to the feast from which the scream of our eagle has hitherto scared them," the *New York Times* warned in March 1861. "We are just beginning to suffer the penalties of being a weak and despised power." Long running turmoil and ballooning foreign debts in Santo Domingo prompted Spanish intervention in 1861. The goal was the restoration of Spain's power in the troubled Caribbean state that shared a border with Haiti. Unrest in Panama, which was now of global strategic significance thanks to the US-built railroad, threatened to provide the pretext for a similar act of foreign imperialism.[5]

Most ominous of all was the situation in Mexico, which had been ravaged since 1857 by a civil war between liberals, intent on economic and political reform, and conservatives, who sought to fortify the Catholic Church and establish a strong central government modeled after the monarchies of the Old World. When the beleaguered liberal government of Benito Juarez suspended payment on its foreign debt in 1861, warships from Britain, Spain, and France arrived at the port of Veracruz. The French had their eye on more than just debt repayment. French emperor Napoleon III seized on the debt issue to justify a full-scale intervention aimed at establishing a puppet monarchy in Mexico, the centerpiece of France's "grand design" for reestablishing its imperial grandeur in the New World. With the collaboration of Mexican conservatives, French forces (now operating without Britain and Spain) eventually overran the liberal resistance, occupying Mexico City in 1863 and installing Austrian archduke Maximilian on the newly created throne of Mexico the following year.

Though these conflicts had their own distinctive features, their simultaneity was no accident. Each of these postcolonial societies had long been the site of internal power struggles. What was new was how these internal conflicts intensified at the very moment when they became entangled within the global economy and resurgent European imperialism. Outward flows of European investment tightened economic connections and, crucially, increased the likelihood of intervention, which often was precipitated by default. The mid-nineteenth-century's revolution in steam power tied together transatlantic markets and enabled European powers to more efficiently exploit distant economies and rule over foreign peoples. Resurgent ideas of imperial grandeur fueled Old World aggression, including Napoleon III's "grand design" for French expansion in the Americas and Spain's dream of recolonizing territories it had lost earlier in the century.[6]

Advocates of republican government and national independence across the New World interpreted events in ideological terms. They detected an Old World plot to turn back the clock to the days when European empires ruled over the peoples of the Western Hemisphere. They saw a climactic battle between republicanism and monarchy, self-government and foreign rule, liberal progress and reactionary conservatism. Old anti-imperial symbols gained new leases on life, not least the Monroe Doctrine, which was fleetingly embraced by Yankee and Latino alike. "The French invasion of Mexico," Union general Phillip Sheridan asserted, "was so closely related to the Rebellion as to be essentially part of it." Mexican minister to the United States Matias Romero sounded a similar note when he labeled the French intervention and Southern secession as "parts of one grand conspiracy" intended to "strike a united blow against republican liberty on the American continent."[7]

But for all the similarities among the crises of the 1860s, there was a fundamental difference between what happened in the United States and what happened elsewhere: the European powers forcibly intervened in Mexico and Santo Domingo but not in the United States. The American Civil War stands as one of the most significant civil wars in modern history that did not precipitate foreign intervention. The closest parallel in this regard was the 1868 Meiji restoration in Japan, which also unfolded without foreign intervention and similarly culminated in the emergence of a new global power. But the case of the American Civil War is even more peculiar than that of Japan, given the depth of the connections between the United States and the great powers of Europe. In an underappreciated stroke of geopolitical good fortune, Americans were left to settle their differences in the 1860s with surprisingly little foreign assistance given to either side. Even foreign financial support to the warring parties was minimal, at least relative to the flows of capital in the antebellum period.

What explains this peculiar feature of the American Civil War? The question becomes even more of a riddle when one considers the remarkable interest the conflict generated abroad, particularly in Britain, the most interested European party in the conflict as well as the nation whose diplomatic response to the conflict conditioned that of the other great powers. The Civil War fractured public opinion in Britain along lines of political orientation, religion, and class. Where Britons stood on the American question often depended upon their views on domestic issues. Those who advocated political reform at home and the expansion of the franchise gravitated toward the democratic and free-labor North. Devout Anglicans who supported social hierarchy tended to support the Confederacy. Social class was another loose indicator of British sympathies. The working classes generally identified with the Union, whereas blue-blooded aristocrats tended to sympathize with their imagined aristocratic brethren in the Old South, whose bid for independence would discredit the democratic forms of government that threatened social hierarchy at home. But British sympathies were not always so easily accounted for. British middle-class liberals, for example, were fervently antislavery and hence inclined to support the North. But they also viewed free trade in ideological—indeed, in moral—terms. Confusion and uncertainty thus prevailed among liberals when Republicans hiked tariffs early in 1861 and proclaimed they had no desire to pursue emancipation as a war aim. "The protectionists say they do not seek to put down slavery," wrote British liberal Richard Cobden. "The slave-owners say they want Free Trade. Need you wonder at the confusion in John Bull's poor head?"[8]

Confederate diplomats and propagandists attempted to tip public and ministerial opinion in their favor. The foundation of Confederate diplomacy was economic. Southerners calculated that Britain's dependence upon their cotton would translate into diplomatic support; the British, Southerners believed, would come to their aid just as the French had done back in 1778. The Confederacy's "king cotton diplomacy" sought to hasten this inevitability by withholding cotton exports and dangling the prospect of a low tariff in front of the free-trading British. The strategy played out according to plan in that it helped trigger a "cotton famine" in Britain's mill towns of Lancashire by 1862. Thousands of textile workers lost their jobs, which threatened to overwhelm the Victorian era's ad hoc relief system. British elites feared social unrest if the cotton famine continued. "The distress among the Poor here and in the Manufacturing districts is great, and I fear on the increase," wrote Liverpool merchant William Rathbone.[9]

Here we arrive at the Civil War's Saratoga moment. In September 1862, Robert E. Lee's army advanced into Maryland in search of a victory on Union soil. Meanwhile, Lincoln had in his desk drawer a draft of the Emancipation Proclamation but waited for a military victory to make it public. Taking the advice of Secretary of State Seward, he did not want it to appear to foreign powers as a desperate gambit to incite a slave rebellion. Across the Atlantic, the powers of Europe looked to the British cabinet of Prime Minister Viscount Palmerston for diplomatic direction; the Palmerston government awaited the outcome of the ensuing battle. "If the Federals sustain a great defeat," Palmerston wrote to Foreign Secretary Lord John Russell on September 23, 1862, "they may be at once ready for mediation, and the iron should be struck while it is hot." But Palmerston was unaware when he wrote that note that the Union had won a victory at Antietam a few days earlier, in the bloodiest day of American history. He was also yet to learn that the previous day Lincoln had issued the preliminary Emancipation Proclamation that linked the fortunes of the Union to the destruction of slavery.[10]

If Antietam was the Civil War's Saratoga moment, it was so in reverse: a critical battle thwarted, rather than hastened, the internationalization of a North American civil war. The outcome of Antietam led the Palmerston government to shelve proposals to recognize Confederate independence and extend an offer of mediation to the warring Americans. Secretary of War Sir George Cornwall Lewis made the case against intervention most forcefully, arguing that such courses of action entailed great risks, not least a war with the North. "Better to endure the ills we have," Lewis wrote to his colleagues, quoting Shakespeare's Hamlet, "than fly to others which we know not of." The British decision not to intervene in the Civil War was a triumph of hardheaded realpolitik. British statesmen carefully calculated risks and rewards, concluding that there was more to be lost than gained through diplomatic intervention in the American war.[11]

British nonintervention also was the result of the South's poorly conceived "king cotton strategy." As the British understood, there was no guarantee that recognition of the Confederacy would reopen the flow of cotton from Southern ports that were blockaded by the Union navy. Furthermore, the profitable Atlantic economy was built around more than just Southern cotton. Northern grains, investments in Yankee railroads, partnerships with Northern businesses, the enormous export market of the free states—all of these interests counterbalanced those of the cotton trade and would be imperiled by a diplomatic move in favor of the South. Union statesmen, above all Secretary of State Seward, shrewdly

played upon British fears of a third Anglo-American war to deter
any pro-Confederate move. As the London *Times* put it, "it would
be cheaper to keep all Lancashire on turtle and venison than to
plunge into a desperate war with the Northern States of America."
In the end, the South's king cotton diplomacy paradoxically led
Britons to understand the importance of their economic relations
with the North. But the damage went further. By depriving the
South's treasury of its principal source of foreign exchange, the
cotton embargo exacerbated the Confederacy's financial difficulties. "It is true that cotton is almost a necessity to us," wrote British
minister to Washington, Lord Lyons, "but it is still more necessary
for them to sell it than it is for us to buy it."[12]

The Confederacy's political appeals for foreign support proved
as self-defeating as their economic ones. The South claimed the
right to self-determination. "Every people," one Confederate wrote
to London *Times* correspondent William Howard Russell, has "a
right to judge of the kind of government, (whether monarchical,
autocratic or republican) which could best advance their happiness
and progress." But self-determination sat uneasily beside the South's
unapologetic embrace of slavery. The Emancipation Proclamation
changed how Britons viewed the war. Although initial press reports
in Britain emphasized the danger that the American war was spi-
raling out of control—thus bolstering the argument for humanitarian intervention advanced by Chancellor of the Exchequer William
Gladstone—the Union's embrace of emancipation as a war aim ultimately turned the tide of British opinion in its favor. The antislavery
Victorian British state and people would not act on behalf of the
slaveholding Confederacy once the implications of the Emancipation Proclamation had become clear. "In my opinion," British Foreign Secretary Lord John Russell wrote, "the men of England would
have been forever infamous if, for the sake of their own interest,
they had violated the law of nations, and made war, *in conjunction
with these slaveholding States of America,* against the Federal States."[13]

Beyond economic, political, and moral concerns, the cause of Southern separatism challenged the very stability of Old World empires. Any move by Britain on behalf of the Confederacy risked extending legitimacy to secessionist movements within its own domains, not least in Ireland, where separatist political movements sought to dissolve the 1800 act of union, as well as in India, where there had been a bloody uprising against British rule in 1857. As the British realized, separatism and self-determination were threats to the stability of their empire. Furthermore, Britain's diplomatic tradition, going back to 1815, of nonintervention in North America had a proven track record of fueling the growth of the profitable Atlantic economy. The British understood that the only certain result of any intervention would be the disruption of the booming Atlantic economy. Indeed, Britain's policy toward both the United States and Canada followed a similar script in the 1860s. The British North America Act of 1867, the "founding" document of Canadian history, fostered Canadian unification and home rule. This act of imperial devolution also brought the newly federated Canadian provinces into the British imperial system in ways reminiscent of Canada's southern neighbor in the decades after 1815: British investment, immigration, and trade with Canada increased after 1867. Taken as a whole, British policy in North America in the 1860s was less a resurgence of imperial interventionism than a self-interested political withdrawal that facilitated the growth of the transatlantic economy. The benefits of this policy would become apparent in the coming decades, when North America's centrality to the Victorian economic order steadily grew. In the 1865–1914 period as a whole, North America received 34.3 percent of Britain's foreign investment, dwarfing the percentages of the next closest continents: South America (16.8 percent); Asia, including India (14 percent); and Europe (12 percent).[14]

The French and Spanish took a different approach and paid a high price. The interventions in Mexico and Santo Domingo became quagmires that sucked up resources, manpower, and political will. Spain ignominiously slinked out of Santo Domingo in 1865, and Maximillian's reign in Mexico dramatically ended in front of a republican firing squad in 1867. The lesson European powers took from these disasters was that attempts to impose imperial rule in the New World were fraught with risks, not least after 1865 when a newly powerful, Yankee-dominated United States emerged from the rubble of its civil war. Better to turn to Asia, the Near East, and Africa for targets for imperial expansion. There would be no colonial scramble in the Americas as there was in Africa and Asia. In the coming decades, the European powers entered these territories, bringing with them some of the innovations that they had pioneered in North America in the 1860s: new technologies of transport and warfare; creative forms of proxy rule as well direct control; racialized ideologies of colonialism. The redirecting of imperial energies from North America to Asia and Africa was further fueled by the disruption to the cotton trade during the American Civil War. Deprived of their traditional source of white gold, British officials and merchants turned to alternative producers, particularly India and Egypt, where forms of coerced labor emerged to satisfy the market's insatiable appetite. Thus, even as the US Civil War confirmed the sovereignty and free labor of most of greater North America, it also indirectly resulted in exploitative labor regimes and European imperial expansion elsewhere. Soon enough, the reunified United States would participate in this sort of imperial adventurism.[15]

II

When the war erupted in the United States in 1861, most European observers anticipated that Southern independence would be the end result. After all, as 1776 and the Latin American revolutions of the early nineteenth century had shown, when a large, organized body of people in the New World were prepared to fight for their independence—particularly one that could draw on outsiders for support as the South then appeared likely to do—it was incredibly difficult to stop them. If the mighty British Empire had been unable to maintain its grip on the American colonies, how could the Yankees impose their will upon the recalcitrant Southern states, which spanned an even larger territory than had the thirteen colonies?

The challenge confronting the North was not simply that of defeating Confederate forces in the field of battle. In many ways, that was a secondary concern. The more immediate hurdles were how to raise the necessary resources, capital, manpower, and political will. There were grounds for bullishness. The Northern states held many inherent advantages over those of the South: the Yankees possessed 90 percent of the old Union's industrial output and 85 percent of America's banks were located in the free states, as was 65 percent of the nation's railroad mileage. The Union states enjoyed a population advantage of more than 2 to 1—and that figure includes slaves in the South's population. But wars are never determined by such figures alone. The Civil War was won by the side that better exploited its advantages. The North performed the unimaginable, or at least what was unimaginable to many in 1861: it realized its potential power.[16]

The United States had not been designed to engage in a protracted domestic war of conquest—at least not one targeting white citizens. Judged by European standards, it lacked a sizable professional army; its political system and culture were notoriously populist and opposed to the centralization of state powers; and its citizens abhorred taxation. There wasn't even a national currency or banking system in 1861. No wonder many Old World observers doubted the Union's ability to crush Southern separatism. Even a British liberal friend of the North like Isabella Bird resigned herself in 1861 to watching "the Union itself falling to pieces...the vaulted Federal tie no stronger in an emergency than a rope of sand, and the Federal Government a symbol of confusion, humiliation, and contempt, in the sight of the armed despotisms and constitutional monarchies of Europe."[17]

To prove such predictions wrong, the decentralized Union would need to generate and then sustain the power required to defeat a highly motivated adversary. The Union war effort was improvised, ad hoc, and with no shortage of internal tensions and contradictions. Its closest historical parallel might be the New Deal, a similar patchwork effort stitched together under great duress. Like the Great Depression of the 1930s, the crisis of the Union in the 1860s catalyzed political adaptation and innovation. The central state grew in new and often unexpected ways. But the Civil War was not won by the side with the biggest state. There was no Yankee version of what would become known in Britain in the First World War as "wartime socialism." Indeed, by most metrics, the Confederacy was more politically centralized and command-control than the Union.[18]

The secret to the Union's success was how it co-opted power from sources other than the central state: its civil society; its dynamic market economy; its patriotism; its highly literate and educated society, including its female population; and, often forgotten, its ability to attract immigrants. The growth of the wartime state harnessed, rather than created, this patriotic energy. A revealing example was the US Sanitary Commission, a volunteer society on the Northern home front devoted to assisting the Union's sick and wounded troops. The "sanitary fairs" organized by the commission, particularly its women, did more than assist wounded troops; they generated enthusiasm for the war effort. "One might as well try to dam up the Niagara as to stem the succession of 'Fairs'," wrote one Sanitary Commission official. The Union cause was at its most potent when its central state collaborated with volunteer organizations such as the Sanitary Commission.[19]

One of the greatest challenges facing the Union was in the material world of public finance. The outlays of the US Treasury the year before the war totaled $63 million. By 1865 the federal government was spending this amount every twenty days. Raising this unprecedented amount of money was every bit as important to the war effort as was military strategy, political leadership, and public support. The Union was fortunate not to have to operate from a blank slate. The fiscal regime established in the founding era had proven to be up to the task in 1812 and had risen to the challenge in the war against Mexico. But the Civil War was a conflict on an altogether different scale. When Lincoln asked Congress for funds in July 1861, he requested an amount—even at this early stage of the war—that would have covered the War of 1812 four times over and no less than five Mexican-American wars.[20]

As the Union confronted this colossal financial challenge, one important point soon became clear: the capital markets of London were not betting on a Union victory. The world's greatest financial market—and the chief funnel of foreign investment into the United States since 1815—provided minimal support for the Union (nor did it do so for the Confederacy, it should be said) during its moment of greatest need. Indeed, London financiers did more than turn away from America; they started to call in their American loans and investments, leading to the repatriation of roughly half of all foreign investments in the United States. "I doubt whether we are not as deeply interested in the matter as the parties themselves," remarked Lord Overstone, one of the largest British holders of American securities. The repatriation of foreign capital depleted the nation's gold reserves, setting the stage for the suspension of specie payments in late 1861, which was precipitated by the Trent affair, a diplomatic crisis with Britain precipitated by a Union naval commander's unlawful seizure of Confederate diplomats en route to Europe. When news of the crisis hit the floor of the London Stock Exchange, the London *Times* reported, "after a few moments, during which it was deemed almost incredible," Union bonds crashed by a devastating 10 percent. Throughout the coming years, Union military setbacks triggered similar panics on European financial markets, ultimately leading US treasury bonds to bottom out at forty cents on the dollar in the bleak summer of 1864 when Grant's army was taking huge casualties and it looked like Lincoln might not win reelection. "Federations at a crisis of revolutionary disunion cannot hope to have credit abroad," *The Economist* explained.[21]

With foreign capitalists keeping their distance, the Union had no choice but to self-fund its war effort. It started by reviving the tariff. In the waning days of the Buchanan administration in early 1861, Congress passed the Morrill Tariff, which ended the era of relative free trade that began back in 1846. The measure was presented as a means of revenue generation and was only possible because the Deep South's representatives had left Washington when their states seceded. Today's neo-Confederate libertarians have got the sequence all wrong: the tariff did not cause the Civil War so much as the Civil War precipitated tariff hikes. By 1865, average tariff rates were more than double what they had been in 1857. Reborn in the Civil War, the tariff was more than a revenue-raising measure; it was an expression of nationalism and sovereignty. The implementation of a protective tariff, protectionist Henry Carey wrote to Lincoln in June 1861, would "secure the maintenance of the Union," but if the "British free trade system be readopted—the Union must, before the lapse of many years, be rent into number fragments, mere instruments in the hands of foreign powers." The tariff opened the door to other tax increases during the war, including a progressive income tax, the first of its kind in American history. "Congress has passed a tax law, and a tariff," *Harpers Weekly* declared in 1862. "The two are co-ordinate parts of one integral system."[22]

As important as taxation and tariffs were to the Union war effort, they lagged far behind war loans in terms of overall revenue generation. Roughly two-thirds of the North's war effort was financed with borrowed money. The federal debt ballooned from $90 million in 1861 to $2.7 billion four years later. What was most remarkable was that the overwhelming majority of this debt was contracted at home. This was in sharp contrast to the 1850s, when roughly half of the national debt had been held abroad, chiefly in Britain. Raising this amount of money necessitated the integration and regulation of the North's decentralized system of banking and finance. These innovations did not nationalize banking; rather, they synchronized and regulated the nation's private banks and financial markets so that they could better assist the war effort. An important, early step was the Legal Tender Act of 1862, which established a national currency of "greenbacks," known for the green ink used on the paper bills, which were legal tender for all transactions except customs revenues and interest payments on the national debt. Financiers purchased bonds in depreciated currency, knowing that the Treasury would pay the interest in increasingly valuable specie coin, which would be generated by tariff revenues. A similar story can be told of the National Banking Acts of 1863–1864. Rather than creating a central bank along the lines of the Bank of England, this legislation established the conditions through which private business associations of five or more people could establish a nationally chartered bank anywhere in the Union. These "national banks" were given the privilege of circulating new national bank notes, printed by the Treasury, as well as the previously issued greenbacks. The National Banking Acts stimulated private investment in Union war bonds, thanks to a regulation linking the quantity of national bank notes allotted to a member bank to the value of US bonds it held in reserve.

The Civil War made Wall Street the epicenter of US finance. The increased activity on the bond markets necessitated the construction of a new building in 1863, the New York Stock Exchange. When Herman Melville set his short story "Bartleby, the Scrivener" on Wall Street in the 1850s, one of his characters took long, alcohol-fueled lunch breaks. A decade later, the nonstop bustle of Wall Street led to the innovation of the lunch counter, which enabled bond traders to quickly refuel before racing back to the trading floor. And the new culture of national finance extended beyond Wall Street. One of the most significant features of Union war bonds was that they were sold in various denominations, including one as low as fifty dollars. This enabled citizens of modest means to commit their own funds to the Union cause, thus linking their personal fortunes to the war effort. The Treasury outsourced the job of selling bonds to the Philadelphia financier Jay Cooke, who developed a shrewd marketing strategy. Churches, newspapers, political networks, and immigrant communities became de facto partners in Cooke's enterprise. Patriotic citizens, many of whom had never before entered the securities market, invested their savings in war bonds to the profit of bankers like Cooke, who worked on commission, and to the benefit of the larger Union cause. Finance and the shared interests of profit fused together government, capital, and citizen in the Union war effort.[23]

Cooke pioneered tactics for marketing war bonds to the masses that would be used again in the world wars of the following century. But for as much as Cooke democratized war finance, the most significant legacy of the finance capitalism that emerged during the war was the creation of a new class of American financiers who would amass immense fortunes and, as a result, political power. The Union was mortgaged to a new group of capitalists and industrialists whose future was as bright as the gold in which their interest payments from the US government were received. The Civil War set the stage for the emergence of a financial elite that would come to dominate the politics of what became known as the Gilded Age. Financiers like Cooke and J. P. Morgan as well as upstart industrialists like Andrew Carnegie consolidated their wealth and power by reinvesting the profits from Civil War loans and contracts into the rail network that rapidly expanded after 1865. They further profited from federal policies, including generous subsidies and protective tariffs, which triggered a boom in American iron and steel. That the Union relied on domestic financial markets, rather than those abroad, to cover the war's costs would have a lasting legacy. The war destroyed slavery and advanced individual freedoms, but it did not destroy social inequality. Indeed, it made the

United States a more economically stratified nation, both socially and geographically. Increasing inequality, in turn, transformed the way in which the postwar United States related to the wider world. American foreign policy had been set by the slave power before the war; after 1865 it was the product of a Republican Party increasingly dominated by high finance and industry.[24]

III

Money was not the only thing the Union needed to raise to crush Southern secession. It also needed men. All told, around 2.25 million men served in the Union army and navy during the four years of conflict. This was more than double the roughly one million who served in the Confederate forces. Raising this amount of manpower required every bit as much political innovation and patriotic energy as had financing the war effort.

The Union's methods of military recruitment resembled how it raised funds in that the central state collaborated with and harnessed the energies of the North's civil society. The Union implemented conscription in 1863, a year after the numerically disadvantaged Confederacy had done so. But only a small number of recruits—some fifty thousand—came into the Union military machine this way. The Union's conscription policy included many exemptions as well as provisions for the hiring of substitutes and an opt-out commutation fee that functioned like a form of progressive taxation in that the wealthy could buy their way out of military service. The real significance of conscription was how it incentivized voluntary enlistment. It did so through a combination of social stigmatization—preachers, community leaders, and even family members urged young men in the direction of the recruitment office rather than risk the ignoble fate of being drafted—and personal self-interest, which came in the form of federal, state, and local bounties that were offered to those who answered the nation's call to arms. The "bounty jumpers" who serially collected these payouts without ever donning a blue coat gamed a new system to their advantage in ways not unlike the emerging robber baron financial elite on Wall Street.

Even this relatively light-touch method of conscription raised the political temperature on the Northern home front. The largest and deadliest social disturbance in US history was the New York draft riots of 1863, in which working-class and Irish-immigrant anger over the new conscription policy boiled over into a full-on riot targeting African Americans and the city elite alike. The draft riots were the most dramatic sign that an anxious home front teetered on the edge of social conflict. It is notable that these social tensions simmered during a Union war effort that mobilized less than half of the nation's manpower. Whereas the Confederacy enrolled around 80 percent of its military-age male population, the Union mustered only about 33 percent of its own. The North did not put its economy on hold during the war—it even promoted western settlement and development during the conflict—and its lower enlistment rates are the proof.[25]

Here we arrive at one of the least appreciated factors in the equation that led to the Union victory: the military service of immigrants. Foreign-born recruits provided the Union army with the advantage it needed over its Confederate rival. An estimated 25 percent of the soldiers in the Union army (some 543,000) and more than 40 percent of the seamen in the navy (84,000) were foreign-born. If one includes soldiers with at least one immigrant parent, the overall figure climbs to 43 percent of the Union army. Almost all of the immigrant soldiers were volunteers; they were greatly underrepresented among those who entered the army through conscription. Most had been in the United States for a decade or less, having arrived in that burst of immigration in the 1845–1855 period. Many landed on American shores during the conflict itself. Their motives varied. Some were ideologically committed to saving the Union, the exemplar of republican self-government; some viewed service as a form of employment and upward mobility. Others signed up because the local elite or their church, family, or peer group encouraged them to do so; and a small number appear to have been duped into service by deceitful recruiting agencies. The largest number, some 190,000, were German, followed by the Irish, who were underrepresented proportionate to their population but still provided the Union with 144,000 soldiers—more than Robert E. Lee's famed Army of Northern Virginia. The Germans and Irish were joined by smaller numbers of soldiers who came from Britain, Europe, Canada, and Latin America.[26]

The demands of war meant that Union officials needed to appeal to immigrants. Military recruitment placards were printed in foreign languages; Union officials presented the war as part of a transnational struggle for republican government, thereby decoupling the idea of the nation from Anglo-Saxon Protestantism; and positions of authority within the Union army were opened to leaders of immigrant communities. There is a story that as Lincoln thumbed through a list of German candidates for a generalship, he stopped at the name of Alexander Schimmelfennig. When an advisor told the president that there were better options, Lincoln dug in: "His name will make up for any difference there may be."[27]

The Lincoln administration went further, seeking to increase immigration during the war years. Although neutrality laws prevented US consulates from recruiting soldiers overseas, there was no prohibition against the recruitment of immigrant laborers who might choose to join the army once they arrived. One of the most assertive proponents of immigration was Secretary of State Seward, who circulated around the world the news of the 1862 Homestead Act, which offered immigrants (as well as US citizens) 160 acres of land each in the western territories. "I am always for bringing men and States *into* the Union, never for taking any *out*," Seward once declared. The platform of the 1864 Union Party, as the Republicans rebranded themselves, gave a full-throated endorsement of immigration, resolving "that foreign immigration, which in the past has added so much to the wealth, development of resources and increase of power to the nation, the asylum of the oppressed of all nations, should be fostered and encouraged by a liberal and just policy." Lincoln signed into law an act on July 4, 1864, creating a federal immigrant office in New York that supported business and civic organizations seeking to attract foreign arrivals. The flow of peoples to the United States plummeted in 1861–1862 but returned to prewar levels in the following years. An estimated 800,000 immigrants arrived in the North during the war, of which about 180,000 joined the Union army.[28]

The military service of the foreign-born did more than enhance the Union's advantage in the field. It also transformed the politics of nativism in the United States. From the nativism of the 1850s, exemplified by Know-Nothingism and bigoted anti-Catholicism, the Union now moved in the direction of welcoming—indeed, encouraging—foreign arrivals. In the 1850s, immigrants had been depicted in American culture as aliens, if not threats: revolutionary exiles from Europe in 1848; stooges of the pope in Rome; even ape-like, subhuman creatures. The Civil War did much to change this. Immigrants commanded respect, even those who lagged behind in the enlistment rate tables. The image of the Irish during the war was not simply that of the marauding mobs of the draft riots but also that of the courageous Irish Brigade, whose five thousand original recruits numbered only 520 after the slaughter at the 1863 Battle of Chancellorsville. Such sacrifices demolished old stereotypes of the Irish as an indigent, troublesome minority beholden to the antirepublican Catholic Church. "Let the nativist bigot think and say what he will," one Northern newspaper declared, "the Irish element in America is giving conclusive evidence of devoted attachment to the Union."[29]

Immigrant troops did not dissolve into a cultural melting pot during the war. Indeed, many came out of the conflict with a more thoroughgoing ethnic consciousness. When Thomas Francis Meagher raised troops for what would become his famous Irish Brigade, he appealed to both Irish and American nationalism: "It is not only our duty to America but also to Ireland." German and Irish volunteers formed their own regiments that marched under their own colors and to tunes from their homeland, and Catholic units used priests rather than chaplains. "There are those damned green flags again," muttered Confederate General George Pickett after seeing an Irish unit prepare for an assault. Military service provided immigrants with newfound cultural and political power. The Irish draft rioters in New York in 1863 were the most extreme manifestation of a wider trend in which immigrant communities made clear that they would act in their own interests, regardless of the political needs of the Union. Indeed, Irish enthusiasm and enlistment dried up after the massacres endured by the Irish Brigade and the draft riots of later that year. The increasing unpopularity of the war put Democratic-voting, Catholic immigrants at odds with their old rivals in the Republican Party. They were not alone. German Catholics staged a draft riot in Wisconsin. The pressures of the war also pitted immigrant and racial groups against each other: Protestants against Catholics, Irish versus African Americans. The Union home front as well as the army's encampments were by no means forerunners of multiculturalism. Ethnic tensions ran high, portending future social and political conflict.[30]

The Civil War's legacy for the foreign-born, as well as future immigrants, thus had two sides. On the one hand, the idea that America was open to laborers from around the world witnessed a revival. On the last full day of his life, Lincoln informed an Indiana congressman of his desire to encourage immigration "from overcrowded Europe. I intend to point them to the gold and silver that waits for them in the West...I shall promote their interests...because their prosperity is the prosperity of the nation, and we shall prove in a very few years, that we are indeed the treasury of the world." This embrace of immigration also can be seen in the enshrinement of birthright citizenship during Reconstruction. The Fourteenth Amendment declared that all born in the United States and subject to its jurisdiction—including

African Americans and the children of immigrants (although not Native Americans)—were automatically citizens. On the other hand, although the war propped open America's door for immigrants and offered citizenship to their heirs, it at the same time underscored the ethnic and religious identities of the foreign-born in the United States. For as much as the Civil War promoted a civic definition of national citizenship, it also reinforced the idea that ethnicity, religion, and race were fundamental social building blocks, embraced by immigrants themselves. Nativism was in hibernation, not buried in a grave.[31]

IV

There were many parallels between the wartime experiences of immigrants and those of African Americans. As with immigrants, the military service of African Americans was instrumental to the Union effort. If one adds the number of African Americans who wore blue coats (180,000) to the total number of soldiers born overseas or to one foreign-born parent, the sum comprises a majority of the Union army. "The war for freedom and the Union has been carried on by the whites and negroes born on this continent, by the Irish and the Germans, and indeed by representatives of every European race," acknowledged Massachusetts Republican George Boutwell in 1865.[32]

The military service of African Americans during the war provided a powerful rejoinder to racist myths of black subservience and inferiority. "You can say of the colored man," African American soldier Henry Harmon wrote in 1863, "we too have borne our share of the burden." Although African Americans continued to face discrimination and racism—including within the Union army, where they received lower pay than white soldiers—their sacrifices to the nation eventually commanded respect from whites. There was no small amount of self-interest in white America's embrace of black military service. Northern states could meet their enlistment quotas (and hence avoid the politically controversial draft) by sending recruiters into occupied regions of the South to raise regiments of former slaves. But self-interest alone does not account for white Northerners' acceptance of black troops. As with immigrants, it became increasingly untenable to deny the basic humanity of peoples who were prepared to fight and die for the cause of the Union. And black troops went into battle facing graver risks—if captured, they could be executed. The shift toward granting rights to blacks during the war appears frustratingly slow and incomplete to us today. But in broad historical terms, it was remarkably quick. Black troops weren't given full federal support until the beginning of 1863. Just a little more than two years later, Lincoln, in his last public address, became the first president to endorse the right of some African Americans to vote. "I would myself prefer that [the vote] were now conferred on the very intelligent, and on those who serve our cause as soldiers," Lincoln asserted days before his assassination.[33]

Like other moderate Republicans, Lincoln hoped to advance the rights of the freedmen after the war without relying on force. Conquest had destroyed secession, but political collaboration would bring the South back into the Union as well as guide the modernization of the economy and culture of the Old South. "To send a parcel of Northern men [to Washington], as representatives, elected as would be understood, (and perhaps really so,) at the point of the bayonet, would be disgusting and outrageous," Lincoln asserted during the war. Rather than conceiving of Reconstruction as a nation-building project directed from Washington, Lincoln more likely had in mind a model resembling the flexible and ad hoc construction of the Republican Party in the 1850s, in which compromise and negotiation had created a durable political coalition.[34]

But this view of Reconstruction was not shared by all within Lincoln's party. The Radical Republican alternative, first outlined in the Wade-Davis bill of 1864 and then implemented during the phase of congressional Reconstruction in 1866–1869, aimed to use federal power to transform the "conquered provinces," as

Pennsylvania Republican Thaddeus Stevens called the states of the Old South. What the South needed, Indiana Republican George Julian argued, was "the strong arm of power, outstretched from the central authority here in Washington, making it safe for the freedman of the South, safe for her loyal white men…safe for Northern capital and labor, Northern energy and enterprise, and Northern ideas to set up their habitation in peace, and thus found a Christian civilization and a living democracy amid the ruins of the past." The notion that central power ought to play a larger role than it previously had underlay the key achievements of Reconstruction, particularly the passage and ratification of the Fourteenth Amendment, whose first section prevents states from denying "to any person within its jurisdiction the equal protection of the laws."[35]

This brief and consequential phase of radical Reconstruction was made possible by a unique set of conditions that drew Republicans together. The resurgence of white supremacy and racial violence in the South, most notably in Memphis and New Orleans in 1866, and the politics of President Andrew Johnson, a former Democrat from the South who opposed extending federal assistance to the freedmen, helped to close the differences among Republicans. Once relatively united, they crafted legislation that empowered the federal government to assist African Americans and set the terms of the reentry of the formerly rebellious states into the Union. New institutions such as the Freedman's Bureau pointed toward an expanded role for the central state. It is revealing to contrast the 1867 Reconstruction Acts, which divided the South into five districts under military control, to the British North American Act of the same year, which signaled Britain's strategic withdrawal from North America and united its provinces into the new dominion of Canada that exercised its home rule. Radical Reconstruction, in short, was a unique moment in America's nineteenth-century history.

Yet the very novelty of the Republican conception of the federal government limited its accomplishments in the longer term. White

Southern Democrats soon coupled the reinvigorated language of home rule with the force of white supremacist paramilitary organizations to oppose the dictates of the Republican Party. Old Confederate leaders like Alexander Stephens rose again to denounce the new "centralized empire" that the Union had become. Opposition from the South comes as little surprise. But even within the ranks of Northern Republicans lurked a powerful group of moderates who narrowly interpreted the federal government's newfound role as guardian of individual rights and equal protection under the law. These moderate Republicans viewed the Reconstruction amendments and legislation as necessary to address the specific problems confronted in the postwar South, not as harbingers of a revolutionary change in the role of the federal government. They rejected radical proposals for the redistribution of land to African Americans, for instance. Their limited conception of federal power can be seen elsewhere too, particularly in late nineteenth-century Supreme Court rulings that shrank the scope of the Fourteenth Amendment.[36]

"The political system of this Republic rests upon the right of the people to control their local concerns in their several states," declared the moderate Republican Carl Schurz in support of the Fourteenth Amendment. "This system was not to be changed in the work of reconstruction." Similar arguments were advanced on behalf of the Fifteenth Amendment, which was presented as inaugurating the federal government's withdrawal from the Southern states on the grounds that it nominally gave African American men the right to vote. Such logic led Republicans in the years of the Ulysses S. Grant administration (1869–1877), particularly after an economic downturn began in 1873, to backpedal from commitments in the South. Federal power had subdued the rebellion and, during congressional Reconstruction, established a Republican bridgehead within the South in the form of the tenuous political alliance composed of African Americans, "carpetbagger" Northern migrants, and "scalawag" Southern whites. With these accomplishments in hand, the majority of Republicans in Washington bid adieu to their counterparts in the South.

The fate of Reconstruction thereafter hinged upon the ability of the fragile coalition of Southern Republicans to secure and extend their vulnerable bridgehead in the face of attacks from the Southern white majority. The power that came to call the shots in the postwar South was not that of the federal government but that of a resurgent white South, which rolled back the civil rights and economic possibilities of the freedmen. The late nineteenth century would be marked by the institutionalization of Jim Crow segregation; by the practice of lynching; and by the ongoing exploitation of the labor of the majority of the former slaves on the cotton fields—now in sharecropping arrangements that set a low ceiling on black advancement, thus depriving African Americans of the social and economic foundations required to exercise their new political rights. In a sense, the restoration of white rule in the Jim Crow South was an American variation of the late nineteenth-century's global theme of the hardening of racial divisions and of European colonial expansion into Africa.[37]

The North's conquest of the South, in short, was partial and unfinished. The Union crushed secession and destroyed slavery, but apart from the brief experiment of radical Reconstruction, it did not impose its will upon Southern society. It laid the constitutional foundations for later civil rights movements, but it did not upend white supremacy in the near term. It launched economic modernization and infrastructure development in the South, but the former Confederacy remained an agrarian society. It crushed the old Southern slave power but did not bury it—indeed, ex-Confederate leaders soon were elected to congressional seats and returned to Washington, DC. The new forms of national power that the Union war effort created had proven up to the task during the war, but they were not geared toward the ends of refashioning the ex-Confederacy in the image of the North. Reconstruction demanded a protracted military occupation of the South overseen by a powerful imperial state capable of overcoming both ex-Confederate resistance and flagging support on the Yankee home front, where white voters were quick to ask why they had to continue to sacrifice after the Union had been restored. "The whole public are tired out with these annual autumnal outbreaks in the South... [and] are ready now to condemn any interference on the part of the Government," President Ulysses S. Grant wrote in 1875 when asked to dispatch troops to ensure that African Americans could vote in an election in Mississippi.[38]

There was an imperial project to which the kind of national power that the United States wielded after 1865 was better suited: the conquest and colonization of the West. The federal government was primed for the tasks that it confronted in its vast western territories, where it sought to facilitate voluntary settlement, infrastructure development, exploitation of natural resources, and subjugation of powerful but relatively small numbers of indigenous peoples.

The key legislation that unleashed the conquest of the West came in the Thirty-Seventh United States Congress, elected at the beginning of the Civil War. This Congress has a claim to the title of the most productive in US history alongside the Congress of the first term of the New Deal. In addition to the financial legislation that transformed the nation's political economy, the Congress passed regionally specific bills aimed at accelerating the settlement and development of the West. These included the Homestead Act, which offered 160 acres of federal land to settlers and immigrants who had not taken up arms against the Union; the Pacific Railroad Act, which paved the way for the construction of the transcontinental railroad; the Morrill Land Grant Act, which offered federal lands to states for the use of institutions of higher education; and a bill that established the Department of Agriculture, initially tasked with assisting farmers and promoting agricultural science in the new land grant universities. These bills gave federal land to settlers, states, and railroad companies. In the case of the transcontinental railroad, Congress lent bonds to private corporations, even guaranteeing the principal and covering the annual interest payments for thirty years. These were not the actions of a traditional imperial state so much as those of a state conditioned to incentivizing its citizens toward certain ends. In time, as power consolidated within fewer and fewer hands, the state would come to take its marching orders from a financial elite.[39]

The colonization of the West was not an orderly, well-conceived process. It was a frenetic race. The objective of the legislation was not simply to promote the settlement and development of the West but to supercharge it. Its roots can be located in the antebellum years of the sectional crisis and the fight over the future of the West. The side that gained the early advantage would place its hands on the levers of political power in those territories, hence the imperative of bursting out of the gates. The legislative giveaways had that effect. After 1865, the rivals were no longer the North and the South but rather a plethora of groups: settlers and immigrants vying for the best lands, capitalists constructing rival investment empires, miners jostling for mineral access. At the center of the postwar boom in the West was the railroad. One of the most remarkable statistics in American history is this: the nation's railroad mileage, which already was without equal in the world, doubled in the eight years following the Civil War. Ultimately, the pace of development was not sustainable. The implosion came in the global Panic of 1873. The local trigger was the failure of the banking house of the old Civil War hero, Jay Cooke, which collapsed under the weight of the failing Northern Pacific Railroad, an unnecessary transcontinental rival of the Union Pacific line. The failure of the house of Cooke was but the first of many failures and unfinished projects produced by the frenzy of westward colonization. Less than half of the new homesteaders remained on the same land five years later.[40]

The colonization of the West spelled doom for Native peoples. By unleashing a turbocharged process of settlement, the legislation of the war years triggered conflict with the powerful tribes of the continental interior, particularly the mighty Sioux of the northern plains. By the mid-1870s, the contrast between US policy in the South and the West had become crystal clear. At the very moment the federal government ended its occupation of the South, it dispatched military forces to crush the resistance of Native peoples. The federal government paired this stick with the carrot of Grant's so-called peace policy, which outsourced aspects of the administration of Indian reservations to Christian missionary organizations. As in the founding period of the early republic, the hard power of the United States was most evident in its dealings with Native Americans. Native peoples and culture, of course, survived the frenetic colonization of the late nineteenth century. What was lost was their ability to mount an effective military resistance to the onslaught.

V

The "winning of the West" in the decades after the Civil War was a particularly intense version of a set of trends that could be seen around the late nineteenth-century world: imperial expansion, volatile economic growth, and the contested integration of previously distant peoples and markets. Late nineteenth-century globalization further witnessed a surge in cross-border trade, investment, and migration. New technologies of communication and transportation brought hitherto distant people into contact with one another as never before. In the span of a few short years, for example, world travel was revolutionized by the inauguration in 1867 of the first transpacific steam line (from San Francisco to Yokohama, Shanghai, and Hong Kong), the completion of the American transcontinental railroad in 1869, and the opening of the Suez Canal later that year. "The world *has* grown smaller," declared one of the characters in Jules Verne's 1873 *Around the World in Eighty Days*, a novel that introduced readers to these new global connections. Upon returning from a world tour in late 1871, William Seward commented that "you can buy your 'through ticket' in New York and go from steamer to railway, and railway to steamer, stopping at ports occasionally, where you will find hotels and tourists, merchants and missionaries, people talking English, and dinners and tea parties, like what you see at home."[41]

The American Civil War, of course, did not cause this wave of globalization, whose roots can be traced to long-running trends in the world economy and short-term bursts of technological innovation and imperial expansion. Regardless of what happened on the battlefields of America in the 1860s, there was going to be a revolutionary reconfiguration of the world's demography, economy, and distribution of power in the late nineteenth century. Even if Lee's army had vanquished McClellan's at Antietam, there still would have been tens of millions of people pushed out of their homelands in the Old World as a result of the increase in global agricultural production. There still would have been a surplus of capital, particularly in Britain, that searched for opportunity abroad. One can go further. Even if it had been Grant who surrendered to Lee at Appomattox, there still would have been victories elsewhere for advocates of self-government. After all, Mexican liberals received little assistance from their Yankee allies and still managed to kick out Maximillian and his French enablers, and British liberals would have at some point in this period achieved the expansion of the franchise that was secured in the Second Reform Act of 1867.

The Union victory did not save democracy around the world, at least not in the immediate term. But it did achieve something of cardinal international significance. The political stabilization of the United States positioned it to take full advantage of the late nineteenth-century version of what we now call globalization. The United States emerged as the most attractive and profitable developing economy in an age in which there were many, not least Canada and Argentina.

It could have been different. The crisis of the Union, as we have seen, disrupted the economic and demographic flows of the international system in 1860–1862. The capital flight, trade disruption, low immigration, and geopolitical instability of this period offer a glimpse into what the history of North America might have looked like had the conclusion of the Civil War been different. A Confederate victory, or even just an indecisive outcome, might well have produced further conflicts waged for continental supremacy between rival sectional confederacies and their foreign supporters, just as the founders had feared back in the 1780s. We will never know what that alternative history might have looked like, for the Union victory settled the political questions that had plagued the republic since its founding, stabilizing the nation's international position in the process. The results were immediately apparent. Just as the current of the mighty Mississippi returned to its normal direction of travel after the New Madrid earthquake, the Union victory opened the sluice gates to an unprecedented inflow of peoples and capital. Post-1865 America sucked up power from abroad like a thirsty sponge.[42]

The draw of the United States in part came from how the war's outcome enhanced its reputation as a liberal and socially open nation. With the stain of slavery and the quasi-aristocratic slave power now removed, the Union reemerged as the world's leading light of political freedom and economic opportunity. "Under a strain such as no aristocracy, no monarchy, no empire could have supported," wrote one British supporter of the North at war's end, "Republican institutions have stood firm." In death, Abraham Lincoln became a global celebrity, one who personified the opportunities available to the common man in America. Parents in Britain and Europe named their children "Lincoln"; his speeches, particularly the Gettysburg Address's embrace of "government of the people, by the people, for the people," reached into even the most remote corners of the world. At the turn of the century, the Russian author Leo Tolstoy encountered a Circassian tribal chief deep in the Caucasus Mountains who considered Lincoln "the greatest general and greatest ruler of the world...a Christ in miniature."[43]

What Lincoln embodied about America was not only the benefits to the common man of its political system of republican self-government but also its material riches and bountiful economic prospects. Lincoln was the archetypal self-made man in economic, as well as political, regards. Foreign observers found in his ascent from a Kentucky log cabin to the White House an illustration of the opportunities available for a self-made man in a democratic political system paired with a market-based economy. Here was another dimension of the United States as "the last best hope of earth": America as a land of economic opportunity, a place where immigrants had a fighting chance to move up the social ladder—certainly when compared to their current prospects. More than anything, it was the relative economic prospects on offer that sucked in peoples in the decades after the Civil War. Immigrants were further attracted to the United States by the low fares and the frequent departures of steamers that serviced American ports. Bolstered by tales of economic opportunity and channeled to New York and San Francisco by the transport networks of a globalizing economy, immigration to the United States became a self-perpetuating phenomenon in the half century that followed the Civil War.

The immigration in the half century after the Civil War transformed America, particularly the states of the North and West, which attracted the overwhelming majority of arrivals. The sheer number of arrivals was without precedent. The decade of the 1860s saw 2.3 million immigrants arrive in the United States, most of whom came after the Civil War concluded. The inflows dipped during the economic downturn that followed 1873 but surged once again in the 1880s, during which 5.2 million immigrants arrived. As early as 1870, the percentage of the nation's population that was foreign-born surpassed 14 percent. It would remain around this level until 1920, peaking at 14.8 percent in 1890. These immigrants were distinguished from previous arrivals by their ethnic and religious diversity. They came from all corners of Europe, particularly the southern and eastern regions of the continent, as well as from across the Pacific. They diversified American culture and religious practices; of particular note was the growth and transformation of American Judaism. Many of the immigrants hailed from rural areas and became homesteaders in the West. A notable example is the German Russians, religiously persecuted people who had moved from Germany to Russia in the eighteenth century, only to flee the tsar's rule a century later. These people settled in the Great Plains, transforming the harsh prairies into centers of wheat production. The majority of immigrants, however, settled in urban areas, particularly the booming cities of the Northern industrial core that stretched from New York through Philadelphia, Pittsburgh, Cleveland, and Chicago. These immigrants provided the United States with the labor that made it the world's largest industrial power by the end of the century. In time, the immigrants who arrived after the Civil War, and their children, would change not only the nation's economy but also its culture and, during the New Deal era, its politics.[44]

Foreign capital poured in at similarly unprecedented levels. The conclusion of the war led to the improvement in the credit rating of the United States on Europe's money markets, particularly after the Grant administration committed the United States to a return to the gold standard. Already by 1869 nearly half of the US national debt was held abroad, particularly in London. The majority of America's capital development came from internal sources. But this was nonetheless an age that saw an unparalleled surge of foreign investment in the booming American economy. More than a quarter of the nation's net capital growth in the peak year of 1869 came from overseas. The improved credit of the United States kept down interest rates on the Civil War debt and brought specie back into the United States, advancing the Republican Party's agenda of returning to the gold standard (achieved in 1879). But for as important as was foreign investment to the Treasury, most of the incoming capital in this period was attracted to private enterprises,

such as mining companies and—above all—railroads. By the eve
of the First World War in 1914, foreign investment in the United
States totaled $7.1 billion, making America the world's greatest
debtor nation. Far from a sign of economic dependence, the inflow
of foreign capital signaled the unrivalled growth and opportunity of
the American market. Foreign capitalists wanted in on the profits.[45]

The danger of foreign investment in this period was not that it
imperiled US sovereignty but rather that its volatility produced devastating downturns. As with immigration, foreign investment came
in cycles of boom and bust. The postwar bubble burst in the global
financial crisis of 1873. The failure of Jay Cooke's bank most immediately stemmed from his inability to place a loan in London on behalf of the Northern Pacific Railroad. The collapse of the banking
house of this Civil War hero sent shockwaves throughout the financial system, triggering a sharp economic downturn that lasted until
1878. When the economy started to recover at the end of the decade,
new financiers emerged to fill the void left by Cooke. None were of
more significance than J. P. Morgan, whose rise reveals much about
the continued significance of foreign capital to American economic
growth. Before the war, Morgan had been an apprentice to his father's investment bank in London. Morgan returned to the United
States in time to make his initial fortune from government contracts
he secured during the Civil War. Throughout the late nineteenth
century, he worked to channel British investment to the United
States, amassing profits in the process that would lead to a personal
financial empire. In time, Morgan would begin to redirect the flow
of capital across the Atlantic.[46]

The quantity, composition, and volatility of the incoming traffic of
immigrants and foreign investment thrust those issues to the fore of
late nineteenth-century politics. Opposition to immigration emerged
within labor organizations, who blamed low wages and poor working
conditions on new arrivals; racist xenophobes targeted Chinese immigrants, ensuring that they were denied the right of naturalization;

and populists denounced foreign bankers and capitalists, blaming them for economic downturns and falling grain prices. But for as widespread as such nationalist sentiments were, they met with limited results when it came to restricting incoming flows of peoples and capital. To be sure, this period witnessed new federal restrictions on immigration, most notoriously in the 1882 Chinese Exclusion Act that marked a reversal from the 1868 Burlingame Treaty with Qing China that had sought to attract Chinese labor to construct the West's burgeoning railroad network. Chinese exclusion portended the race-based immigration restriction legislation of the 1920s. But the Chinese Exclusion Act did not slam the door completely shut. Ingenious Chinese arrivals found ways of exploiting loopholes in the restrictions, which were poorly enforced by US consulates in Asia and private shipping companies in the era before the federal facility at Angel Island in San Francisco Bay was established in 1910. For all the portents of future restrictions, the half century after the Civil War remained one of unprecedented immigration.[47]

Where the United States most succeeded in walling off incoming traffic was with the tariff, that persistently powerful symbol of Civil War nationalism. The Gilded Age was the apogee of protectionism. Here was the United States at its most coldblooded in exploiting its position within an international system presided over by a free-trading British Empire that had a vested interest in maintaining peaceful Anglo-American relations. The high tariffs of this period sheltered America's developing industries from foreign competition at the same time that the nation sucked in British capital and low-wage labor from around the globe. Few nations have enjoyed such a fortuitous position within the international economy. It wasn't just industry that benefited from protectionism. There were rural claimants for the spoils of the tariff, as well. Wool, hemp, and sugar producers were notorious players in the protectionist politics of this era. Protectionists had to earn their political victories, owing to a well-organized free-trade lobby comprising a transatlantic chain of "Cobden clubs," named after the Victorian liberal. The domestic politics of the tariff were complex, scrambling partisan affiliations and leading to party defections in 1872 and 1884 when many liberals bolted the protectionist Republicans for the Democrats. The overall trend in this period, however, was an increase in duties. The climax came with the 1890 McKinley Tariff, which raised duties to an all-time high. This tariff bill also contained a clause that empowered Secretary of State James B. Blaine to promote exports to Latin America through reciprocal trade agreements. Like other rising powers, such as Germany and Japan, the United States used trade policy to expand its power and influence against the free-trade British Empire. US economic nationalism flourished in this competitive environment of imperial rivalry, one in which the self-proclaimed anti-imperial power would soon take part. In the War of 1898, the United States burst onto the global colonial scene when it annexed Hawaii and seized from Spain the Philippines, Guam, Cuba, and Puerto Rico.[48]

Here was the other global legacy of the Civil War: the projection of US power beyond its borders. The foundation of the rising power of the United States was its immense and now secure continental domain. The Yankee victors were not bashful when it came to stating their ambitions. "This North American continent belongs to us and ours it must be," Michigan Republican Zachariah Chandler declared shortly after the war. Many forward-looking statesmen, particularly those of the Republican Party, such as Seward and Blaine, looked for opportunities beyond the nation's borders. After 1865, the United States increased its economic presence in foreign markets, particularly in the Western Hemisphere. "While the great powers of Europe are steadily enlarging their colonial domination in Asia and Africa," Blaine declared in 1884, "it is the especial province of this country to improve and expand its trade with the nations of America." One of the most important markets for the United States in this period was Mexico—"one magnificent but undeveloped mine—our India in commercial importance," as one Yankee booster put it. Mexico became a chief destination of a new and portentous phenomenon: the exportation of US capital.[49]

But for all its ambitions, the post–Civil War United States did not consistently or even effectively project its power outward. This remained an era of US history dominated by the incoming traffic of peoples and capital. The drive to annex new territories was as notable for its failures, such as President Grant's unsuccessful bid to acquire Santo Domingo in 1870, as it was for its successes, such as the 1867 annexation of Alaska. Many of the overseas business ventures of the era fizzled out. A revealing example was the Pacific Mail Steamship Company, an American company and one of the world's largest shipping conglomerates in 1870. Thanks to a generous federal subsidy from the Civil War–era Congress, it was Pacific Mail that opened the world's first transpacific steamship line in 1867. The company operated services to twenty-five ports in the Americas and the Pacific, most of which (including its signature transpacific route) were serviced by the last fleet of the great wooden-hulled side-wheelers, the largest of which burned through fifty tons of coal each day. The insatiable appetites of these steamers prompted Pacific Mail to successfully lobby for the US annexation of a coaling station at Midway Island in 1867—the future site of one of the pivotal battles of the Second World War. The company's shipyard in Benicia, which serviced its San Francisco hub, marked the beginning of the industrialization of California. This was a steam company of remarkable size and sophistication. But it was built upon a political house of cards. When a corruption scandal in the 1870s led Congress to terminate its subsidy and brought it under the thumb of hostile railroad interests who gutted its management, it nearly went bankrupt. Pacific Mail continued operating many of its services but fell far behind its foreign rivals, including the Japanese, whose upstart Mitsubishi conglomerate bought the American company's lucrative Shanghai–Yokohama route in the 1870s. The

Mitsubishi enterprise centered its shipyard and heavy industry in the port of Nagasaki, making that city an industrial center of the rising Japanese empire. Already in the 1870s there were portents of the US-Japanese rivalry that would not end until the atomic age.[50]

The demise of the briefly dominant Pacific Mail was testament to the haphazard and inconsistent manner in which the United States projected its power overseas in the decades after the Civil War. For all the dynamism of its capitalist economy, for all the ambitions of its statesmen, the United States did not yet systematically assert itself abroad. This was not because it was isolationist—no nation whose economy was so internationally integrated and that attracted so many immigrants can be considered as such. Nor was it a product of some tradition of anti-imperialism—"we have a record of conquest, colonization, and territorial expansion unequalled by any people in the nineteenth century," Henry Cabot Lodge accurately observed at century's end. Rather, it was because the international interests of the United States were well served by the global order structured by the British Empire. America did not need to construct a vast colonial apparatus or global system of transport and finance; the British had done that work for them.

Late nineteenth-century America was one of modern history's great freeloaders. It did not matter if Americans shipping companies went bankrupt because British-subsidized lines serviced the ports used by US traders and travelers, not least the world's densest transoceanic steam route of Liverpool to New York. The US foreign service could be downsized when public finances were tightened after 1873 because Americans in need of assistance abroad could knock on the door of the nearest British consulate. The American missionaries who sought to spread the gospel to foreign lands did not need their own empire in which to work because they had access to a massive market of souls, without the overhead expenses, within the vast realms of the British Empire. "For the first time the students of the Anglo-Saxon world are united in a mighty enterprise," exulted one

American missionary leader in the 1880s. Most of all, the United States could avoid the costs of maintaining a large army because of the relatively secure position it enjoyed in an international order presided over by its former colonial master.[51]

There were, of course, lingering tensions and the occasional diplomatic crisis between the two English-speaking powers during this period. Anglophobia remained a staple of US domestic politics, particularly in the Democratic Party with its large Irish American constituency. "It is no doubt unpleasant," *The Nation* reported of the collapse of US bond prices in London during one moment of diplomatic tension, "to be thus obliged to count in advance the cost of every shift in our foreign policy." But this was on balance a price worth paying in exchange for the advantageous international position the United States occupied in this era of Victorian globalization. As Americans rode the coattails of the powerful British Empire, they took on board lessons for their own imperial future. Racial theorists in America, as well as Britain, came to embrace the duty of "Anglo-Saxons" to shoulder the "white-man's burden." Alfred Thayer Mahan's treatises on sea power examined the history of the Royal Navy, noting how Britain had captured Manilla and Havana during the Seven Years' War—two port cities that would find themselves occupied by the United States in 1898. The new American empire of the early twentieth century continued to take cues from the British. The US protectorate in Cuba established by the 1901 Platt Amendment was modeled after Britain's 1882 arrangement in Egypt. "It was a good thing for Egypt...and for the world, when England took Egypt," Theodore Roosevelt wrote. "And so it is a good thing, a very good thing, for Cuba...and for the world that the United States has acted as it has actually done."[52]

THE LINE FROM 1865 to the imperialism of 1898 and beyond was not a straight one, but there can be little question that the

outcome of the Civil War placed the United States on a path toward world power. But just as the war's domestic legacies were
far from straightforward—slavery was destroyed, but racism and
the exploitation of black labor persisted; republican government was saved, but social inequality deepened and ethnic tensions persisted—its international implications also were not
one-dimensional. The Union cause ignited passion among liberals
and republicans in the United States and beyond, but it also empowered those in favor of protectionism, racialized nationalism,
and imperial expansion. The 1860s demonstrated the ability of the
United States to mobilize its immense power on behalf of the objectives crushing secession and conquering the West. But the Civil
War era also revealed the limits of US power when it came to transforming the postwar South and in projecting its power overseas.
One of the most significant legacies of the war is one that is most
often overlooked today: by stabilizing the politics of the United
States, the outcome of 1865 ignited a surge of immigration and
foreign investment that would enhance the population, economy,
and power of the nation.

But for as much as the roots of future power can be located
in the Civil War era, America's global ascendance was not preor-
dained. The nation that emerged from the rubble in 1865 carried with it traditions of political decentralization that inhibited
the efficient projection of power beyond its borders. Its growing
socioeconomic divisions, as well as its simmering racial and ethnic tensions, compounded its vulnerability to the sharp economic
downturns of this volatile age of globalization. The United States
would not realize its potential world power until it was rustled into
a period of further political innovation during a new crisis—one
that witnessed the collapse of the international political and economic order from which it had so greatly benefited.

CHAPTER 4
Zigzagging through Global Crisis

AN EXHAUSTED FRANKLIN Delano Roosevelt knew he was far from the finish line when he accepted the Democratic nomination in 1940 for an unprecedented third term in the White House. "Eight years in the Presidency, following a period of bleak depression, and covering one world crisis after another would normally entitle any man to the relaxation that comes from honorable retirement," Roosevelt mused. But the greatest worldwide crisis of all loomed on the horizon. Imperial Japan aggressively expanded in Asia. In Europe, Hitler's Nazi war machine had overwhelmed France in a matter of weeks. The mighty British Empire was now in danger of collapse as Germany prepared plans for an invasion of the British Isles. When prompted by a reporter to reflect on how this crisis compared to the economic one that had greeted him on his entry into the White House eight years earlier, Roosevelt confessed that "it is probably more serious than the one eight years ago. I think we might let it go at that."[1]

The mid-twentieth century was indeed marked by "one world crisis after another," as Roosevelt put it. In a span of three decades, the world was convulsed by two world wars, a devastating global economic depression in the 1930s that empowered extreme ideologies, and a reordering of the distribution of power in the international system in the aftermath of the Second World War. The United States was not insulated from these crises. Far from just being sucked into the maelstrom, America did its part to destabilize the international order. It, too, was a colonial power whose imperial expansion and relentless search for economic advantage triggered competition and instability, not least in its traditional sphere of influence where Mexico underwent one of the century's great social revolutions. After the Wall Street crash of 1929, America's colossal economy became a deadweight that pulled the world into the depths of depression and national protectionism.[2]

In this era of global crisis, the international policies of the United States were volatile and inconsistent. A presidential commission of the 1930s described US policy as oscillating "between isolation and independence, between sharply marked economic nationalism and notable international initiative in cooperation moving in a highly unstable zigzag course." Nowhere was the shift from a zig to a zag sharper than in immigration policy. The "nation of nations" that had long been the most popular destination for European immigrants moved to restrict further arrivals in the 1920s. The result was a historic decrease in the percentage of the population that was foreign-born—and, perhaps unexpectedly, the emergence of a more unified and politically powerful working class. But this was not all. US foreign policy swung from traditional aloofness in the European-dominated world order to military intervention in the First World War in 1917. Then, America reversed course again, attempting to disentangle itself from international politics while still pursuing national interests in the 1920s and 1930s. Next came the greatest crisis of all—the rise of fascist and imperialist regimes in the 1930s—which prompted another change of course, now toward a global conception of national security that revolutionized American statecraft and changed the course of world history. This time there was no going back.[3]

In economics, too, the United States dizzyingly veered between the poles of internationalism and nationalism. The world's greatest debtor nation became, almost overnight during the First World War, its greatest creditor. "We are down on our knees to the Americans," the London newspaper magnate Lord Northcliffe wrote in 1917 of this remarkable change on the global capital markets. America's industrial output and cultural exports similarly surged past its rivals as though they were in slow motion. But then came the implosion of the global capitalist system after 1929, which prompted a dramatic turn toward US economic nationalism: tariff walls shot up, the international gold standard was abandoned, overseas colonies were left to fend for themselves, and US-dominated international capital markets froze. The politics of nationalism predominated at home. Roosevelt's New Deal was the ultimate expression of the era's nationalism. It renovated and rationalized the nation's political economy, setting in motion processes of consolidation that went into hyperdrive during the Second World War. Here came the biggest reversal of all: the greatest economic depression of the twentieth century was immediately followed by its greatest economic boom.[4]

Like the imperial crisis of the eighteenth century and the Civil War of the nineteenth, the American nation that emerged on the other side of this great crisis of the twentieth century bore the imprint of the foreign threats, international pressures, and demographic changes that had been placed upon it. The peculiar postwar form the new American superpower took—it was a proponent of liberal internationalism whose political culture was nevertheless dominated by a powerful and self-referential nationalism—was as much the creation of its zigzagging course through this era of international crisis as it was the culmination of long-standing policies and political ideas. The newly refurbished nation that would do so much to define the second half of the twentieth century was itself the product of a worldwide crisis.

I

The story of America's course through the crises of the mid-twentieth century begins with the Great War, or the First World War as Americans came to call it. The epochal conflict of 1914–1919 deranged and unsettled the European-dominated international order that had come into being in the nineteenth century. As the traditional powers of Europe destroyed one another, the United States, after years of neutrality, burst across the Atlantic in 1917–1918, deploying more than a million "doughboys" to the front lines. Even before America's entry into the war gave the allies the boost they needed, President Woodrow Wilson had announced that American principles would govern a new world order. "I am proposing, as it were," Wilson declared in 1917, "that the nations should with one accord adopt the doctrine of President Monroe as the doctrine of the world." Wilson's subsequent "Fourteen Points," which outlined a vision for a world composed of sovereign, self-determined states, found an audience around the globe, particularly in the colonial world. "It is impossible that the noble truths uttered by President Wilson in his War Message, could be limited in their application," the Indian nationalist Lajpat Rai predicted. "He has conferred a new charter of democracy and liberty on the latter and the people of Asia are going to make as much use of this charter, if not even more, as are those of America and Europe."[5]

That the United States was on the cusp of global power also could be seen in the realms of culture, transportation, and economy. New forms of American culture penetrated global markets. Hollywood movies—which often cast foreigners, such as Englishman Charlie

Chaplin and Canadian Mary Pickford, in lead roles—dominated European cinemas. Enclaves of Americans around the world, particularly in major European cities like London and Paris, became the face of the nation's power abroad. Cultural exports were but part of a broader trend of outflows from the United States. One of the manifestations of the rising power of the United States in this period was Pan American airlines, which opened services to Latin America and, beginning in 1935, across the Pacific. The largest American export of the 1920s remained what it long had been— cotton, which totaled some 15 percent of all exports. But the war created new demands and markets for US industrial products: the next two largest exports were machinery (12 percent) and—that most American of products—the automobile (10 percent). By 1929 the United States produced a remarkable 42 percent of the globe's industrial output, outpacing by some distance the combined productivity of Britain, France, and Germany.[6]

The most dramatic economic shift occasioned by the war was on global financial markets. The world's greatest debtor of the preceding century quickly metamorphosed into its greatest creditor. The escalating costs of the war first led the great powers to liquidate their overseas assets, before compelling them—particularly the British, hitherto the world's greatest lender—to resort to the cap-in-hand financial diplomacy that Americans themselves had perfected in the nineteenth century. "It almost looks as if they took a satisfaction in reducing us to a position of complete financial helplessness and dependence," wrote the British economist John Maynard Keynes. The US state supported the rise of American finance through deregulation, exempting American businesses engaged in overseas activities from antitrust laws and allowing American banks to set up foreign investment corporations to stimulate and guide the flow of capital across the Atlantic. In the decade after the First World War, the United States became the center of a global financial system in which US loans to Germany enabled that nation's reparation payments to Britain and France, who then used the funds to repay their war debts to Wall Street.[7]

The First World War, in short, accelerated the international rise of the United States. But there were countervailing forces to American ascendance. As the coming decades would illustrate, the world needed the American economy—specifically, access to its markets and capital—more than the United States needed the world. As had been the case in the nineteenth century, American financial and business interests focused on domestic opportunities, of which there were no shortage. The amount of US capital that went abroad was but 6 percent of total American investments for the first three decades of the twentieth century, roughly equivalent to the capital invested in the booming domestic market of California alone. The 1910s and 1920s offered the new American exporters of capital a series of lessons concerning the perils of foreign investment. The Mexican Revolution and political instability in the Caribbean and Central America endangered US investments, leading to costly and unpopular interventions in the first third of the twentieth century to impose order in the region. Critics of US imperialism, both at home and abroad, condemned the use of force to collect debts. "The United States cannot go on destroying with impunity the sovereignty of other peoples, however weak, cutting across the principles for which our fathers fought," wrote one American opponent of imperialism in the Caribbean. With profits to be made at home, there was less incentive to engage in risky and unpopular ventures abroad.[8]

For all the portents of US global power, the dominant trend of its diplomacy after the First World War was the attempt to advance its national interests while limiting commitments to an international order still managed by the imperial powers of Europe. The prospect of membership in the League of Nations spooked the majority of the US Senate, which failed to ratify the Treaty of Versailles in 1920 on the grounds that it constituted an entangling alliance that would commit the United States to uphold the old European imperial order that it had long denounced. Although some of the treaty's opponents were against any such international agreement, the majority of the no votes came from nationalist statesmen such as Henry Cabot Lodge who favored the assertion of US power abroad, just not in the form of the League of Nations. The United States was certainly no isolationist power, for the decade after the First World War marked the high tide of US colonialism in the territories it had seized from Spain back in 1898. In the Philippines, Governor-General Leonard Wood sought to forestall the islands' independence and increase their economic reliance on US markets. The international policy of the United States in this period was largely unilateralist, not isolationist. It also prioritized the promotion of private economic interests overseas, thus mirroring the 1920s revival of deregulation at home—"the business of America is business," as Republican President Calvin Coolidge proclaimed. "If the federal government were to go out of existence," muttered Coolidge on another occasion, "the common run of people would not detect the difference."[9]

But for all the talk of a laissez-faire "return to normalcy" in the 1920s, as President Warren Harding, Coolidge's predecessor, dubbed it, the United States imposed a series of sweeping new regulations to restrict the inflow of people and goods. The most striking new policy was immigration restriction. A combination of racial anxieties and national security considerations lay behind the creation of a new national quota system to guide US immigration policy. The Johnson-Reed Act of 1924 restricted the further arrivals of eastern Europeans, Italians, Greeks, Jews, and Asians. The act carefully tabulated the numbers of immigrants allotted to foreign nations, using as a baseline the 1890 census—referred to at the time as the "Anglo-Saxon census" for pre-dating the largest inflows from southern and eastern Europe. "The day of indiscriminate acceptance of all races has definitely ended," thundered the bill's cosponsor, Republican Albert Johnson. It was no coincidence that immigration restriction came in the same decade that saw the Ku Klux Klan reach the peak of its national power. Accompanying the racialized motive for immigration restriction were security anxieties. Indeed, such was the fear that Congress passed the Emergency Quota Act of 1921 to restrict immigration while it went to work on what became the Johnson-Reed Act. The concern was that immigrants exposed the United States to the radicalism that had toppled regimes elsewhere, particularly the Bolshevik communism of the new Soviet Union. In the background of immigration restriction was the "red scare" of 1919–1920. Attorney General A. Mitchell Palmer cracked down on suspected communists and anarchists, deporting immigrants suspected of radical political orientation. The episode revealed that US officials continued to connect immigration policy to national security. Some even saw immigration restriction as a means of advancing national independence, in that it would insulate the United States from radical ideas from abroad, particularly international communism. It harkened back to the debates in the founding era about how to limit the infiltration of foreign political ideologies. Immigration restriction, Johnson declared, was "America's Second Declaration of Independence."[10]

The turn toward immigration restriction was not total. The national origins quotas of the 1921 and 1924 legislation did not apply to the Western Hemisphere, thus enabling an increase in immigration from Canada and Mexico. In the first decade of the twentieth century, arrivals from Mexico had accounted for less than 1 percent of all immigrants, but in the 1920s the figure increased to 11.2 percent. Nor was the new legislation without precedent: it drew from nineteenth-century models, especially the 1882 Chinese Exclusion Act. But the precedents and limits of the legislation of the 1920s should not obscure the fact that it represented a monumental reversal for a nation that had been the most popular destination for European laborers and persecuted religious and political minorities. The numbers told the tale. In the decade before the First World War, just under 10 million immigrants arrived in the United States, the largest gross figure of immigration in a ten-year span to that point in US history. By the 1930s, the average annual net inflow to the United States amounted to less than seven thousand—a mere two days total back in the pre-1914 period.[11]

Immigration restriction was not the only way the United States restricted incoming traffic in the years after the First World War. This period saw a ferocious resurgence of economic nationalism. The Democratic Wilson administration and its congressional allies had begun to dismantle protectionism, most notably in the reductionist Underwood Tariff of 1913. The nation changed direction after the war, first in another emergency act of Congress, the Emergency Tariff of 1921, which primarily protected American farmers from revived foreign competition. The following year the Republican Fordney-McCumber Tariff extended protections to American industries, harkening back to the high tariffs of the post–Civil War era. "I believe in the protection of American industry," President William Harding announced, "and it is our purpose to prosper America first."[12]

The erection of new tariffs and related policies of economic nationalism were part of an international trend that stemmed from the nationalizing impulses of the war years. It was given further momentum by the renewal of international economic competition in an unstable postwar environment. The stage was thus set for a surge of economic nationalism when the Wall Street crash destabilized the global economy in 1929. The United States led the way with the infamous Smoot-Hawley Tariff of 1930, one of the most protectionist tariffs in US history and certainly the one with the highest duties of the twentieth century. Meanwhile, France increased the barriers it already had constructed around its imperial markets, and Britain followed suit in the 1932 Ottawa Agreements, which promoted trade within the British Empire but constructed tariff walls around it. World trade plummeted by 60 percent between 1929 and 1932. The story was even more dramatic on international financial markets. The American credit that had sustained the Versailles Treaty system of German reparations and Allied debt repayments dried up, wreaking havoc on both sides of the Atlantic. International lending shriveled by 90 percent between 1929 and 1933. As depression descended upon the global economy, nations turned inward, hoping to insulate themselves from the contagion of crisis.[13]

II

This nationalist turn toward protectionism, immigration restriction, and unilateralism is the backstory to the most transformative moment in twentieth-century US politics—the New Deal. To be sure, the New Deal had global horizons. It just did not always look up to see them. In the words of the British philosopher Sir Isaiah Berlin, who was among the most ardent of Roosevelt's foreign admirers, the United States of the 1930s was where a "great social experiment was conducted with an isolationist disregard of the outside world."[14]

Berlin was referring, of course, to the New Deal, the priorities of which—"relief, recovery, and reform"—were domestic. President Franklin Roosevelt possessed internationalist instincts, in both economic and political regards. But these did not prevent him at the beginning of his presidency from turning away from the World Economic Conference in London in 1933, which would have committed the United States to international efforts of currency stabilization. Instead, Roosevelt joined Britain, Canada, and

Scandinavia in going off the gold standard so as to retain control of national monetary policy. "The sound internal economic system of a nation," Roosevelt wrote in what became known as his "bombshell message" to the London conference, "is a greater factor in its well-being than the price of its currency in changing terms of the currencies of other nations." The inward focus of economic policy could be seen elsewhere. Tariffs remained high despite the Democratic Party's traditional opposition to protectionism. Indeed, provisions of the 1933 Agricultural Adjustment Act placed import levies on foreign farm goods, particularly cotton products.[15]

Many of the New Deal's policy innovations—including Roosevelt's monetary views, which can be traced to British economist John Maynard Keynes—drew from foreign models. But the New Deal was, nevertheless, first and foremost a national project. "It is clear we have to do this in an American way," New Dealer Harry Hopkins declared. "Instead of copying foreign schemes we will have to devise our own." The New Deal created new national institutions, it was infused with the language and symbolism of nationalism, and it fostered new relationships between citizens and the state—and to Franklin Delano Roosevelt himself—that changed how the public viewed the federal government. In this regard, the New Deal was an American variation on the international theme of a decade that saw the great powers adapt their economic and political systems in response to depression and international rivalry. Germany and Italy generated fascism, Stalinism dominated the Soviet Union, and Japan formed a powerful imperial state with expansionist objectives. The United States produced the New Deal.[16]

The New Deal was an untidy hodge-podge of reforms. In so being, it reflected the diverse and pluralistic nation from which it came. Above all, the New Deal was the product of crisis: it was less a coherent vision of political development than it was a frenetic and multifaceted response to a depression that brought the American economy to its knees. To understand it, we must recover the acute sense of crisis that prevailed when members of the Roosevelt administration took their oaths in 1933. The nadir of the financial collapse was not the 1929 Wall Street crash but rather the dark winter of 1932–1933, during which 6,500 banks across the nation failed and one thousand overstretched municipalities defaulted on their debts. Unemployment stood at 25 percent. Homeowners were foreclosed upon; family farms were lost; bread lines formed on main streets across the country. As the nation's economy took on water, the prospect that depression might bring down the broader social and political order became real. Americans feared that worse was to come. "Only a foolish optimist can deny the dark realities of the moment," Roosevelt bluntly put it in his inaugural address.[17]

Moments of crisis open the door to new political possibilities. The 1930s were no exception. The New Deal was not only a race to save the capitalist order; it was also part of a competition between upstart political alternatives. There were no Hitlers, nor Hirohitos, in the United States. But there were radical alternatives to the New Deal: the populist demagoguery of Louisianan strong man Huey Long and Catholic radio celebrity Father Charles Coughlin; the folk socialism of Upton Sinclair and the popular, if unworkable, redistribution scheme of Francis Townsend; and the resistance of the unapologetic and still powerful conservative right, which insisted that the relatively moderate New Deal was a grave threat to national life. Even within the emerging New Deal coalition, there was political competition, particularly between advocates of racial segregation and white supremacy on the one hand and those who strove for racial equality on the other.[18]

The New Deal sought to ward off the twin perils of economic collapse and political radicalization. It sprayed solutions at the problems confronting the United States. Its political calculus was premised not on ideological purity or even coherence but rather on pragmatic experimentation and trial and error. Roosevelt and his allies calculated that it was better to do something—anything— than to run the risks of inaction. "The country demands bold, persistent experimentation," Roosevelt declared in 1932. "It is common sense to take a method and try it: If it fails, admit it frankly and try another. But above all, try something." Unsurprisingly, the New Deal was full of contradictions. It embraced the growth of the central state in some domains, particularly political economy and social welfare, even as it repudiated federal power when it ended Prohibition and deferred to the states' rights of the Jim Crow South. Roosevelt's Democrats engaged in deficit spending, only to then lurch back to balanced budgeting with disastrous results in the "Roosevelt recession" of 1937. The New Deal sought to reinvigorate the national economy through the creation of corporatist cartels while at the same time empowering opponents of big business and facilitating the historic expansion of organized labor. The architects of the New Deal were well aware of these and other contradictions. Upon being asked how he would describe the Tennessee Valley Authority, one of the more radical measures of the early New Deal that experimented with federally led economic development projects in the South, Roosevelt responded: "I'll tell them it's neither *fish nor fowl*. But whatever it is, it will taste awfully good to the people of the Tennessee Valley."[19]

If the New Deal was not the product of a clearly defined political ideology or blueprint, its various programs and policies did have common denominators. For all its divergent trajectories, the New Deal sought to mitigate the risks inherent in the era's capitalism. The aim was not to destroy capitalism—far from it. Rather it was to smooth off its roughest edges. The New Deal created an array of new government agencies and powers, but some of its most significant policies reformed and buttressed existing institutions and practices. For example, the New Dealers eschewed heavy-handed control or nationalization of America's volatile financial markets and banking system in favor of lighter-touch reforms and regulations, most notably the creation of the Securities and Exchange Commission and the Federal Deposit Insurance Corporation. Although labeled "a traitor to his class" for being an aristocrat who worked on behalf of the common man, Roosevelt and his administration should be remembered as saviors of capitalism whose reforms breathed new life into the nation's failing financial system. "We socialists are trying to save capitalism," declared one New Dealer in the Department of Agriculture, "and the damned capitalists won't let us."[20]

The New Deal was more than a set of policies aimed at stabilizing capitalism; it was a new method of politics that recognized changes in the distribution of power within the United States. The radicalism of the New Deal is not to be found in its piecemeal and (mostly) moderate legislation but rather in its inclusive political methodology, whose closest parallel might be the creation of the Republican Party back in the 1850s. It brought social groups to the political table that hitherto had been marginalized, if not kept on the outside looking in. The Depression revealed the extent to which the nation's political system had not kept up with demographic and social change. The power of certain groups— Wall Street, Southern whites—was overrepresented in political institutions, while that of other groups—African Americans, women, "white ethnic" workers—was strikingly underrepresented. Although built upon the foundation of the old Democratic Party, the New Deal created a new political coalition, one whose hallmark was its diversity.

The New Deal coalition, as it came to be called, was broad enough to accommodate both Southern white segregationists and African Americans who began to leave the party of Lincoln; urban machines and rural farmers; progressives from the Republican

Party as well as die-hard Democrats; elite reformers and agrarian populists; immigrants and the "native" born; Catholics, Jews, Protestants, and agnostics. Managing this crew of strange bedfellows presented untold challenges. Much of the policy incoherence of the New Deal can be explained by the attempt to give something— even if just the promise of crumbs in the future—to its diverse constituents. Viewed from the perspective of political coalition building, the New Deal appears far more coherent, even strategic, than when assessed solely on the grounds of policy and legislation. This political process was not always pretty, and it perpetuated inequalities even as it redressed them. Nowhere was this more the case than in the realm of race relations. Southern Democrats relentlessly leveraged their political power within the Party on behalf of upholding segregation, infamously scuttling attempts to pass a federal antilynching bill. The dismantling of Jim Crow would not occur until after the Second World War.[21]

The most significant social adjustments of the New Deal are to be found in its class politics. At the heart of the New Deal coalition was a working class that was fast developing the bargaining power it hitherto had lacked. Previously, old lines of ethnic division had prevented the diverse American working class from realizing its political power. But the xenophobia behind the immigration restriction of the 1920s paradoxically allowed American workers and organized labor to find a home within the emerging New Deal coalition. The story here was in part demographic. With the stream of new immigrants reduced to a trickle, and with the gradual transition from first to second generation, ethnic divisions gave way to an emerging collective consciousness. New technologies of mass culture—above all, the radio and cinema—provided common reference points for peoples of all backgrounds. But the most significant driver of the newfound collective consciousness of the working class was the economic crisis whose devastating effects exposed the limits of traditional relief organizations within ethnic communities. With the Depression wreaking havoc, workers turned to trade unions and the central state for relief.[22]

Those previously divided along ethnic and racial lines found themselves standing side by side in the swelling ranks of organized labor. The early New Deal only tentatively embraced this new constituency, offering federal support for the right of labor to organize into unions with section 7(a) of the National Industrial Recovery Act of 1933, although without the measures to guarantee it. But like so much else in the New Deal, the initial policy was the thin end of the wedge for further reform. For all its deficiencies, this early measure solidified labor's position within the Democratic coalition, helping to fuel the landslide midterm victory of 1934, which in turn gave birth to the more reformist "second New Deal" of the mid-1930s. The payoff came in 1935 with the Wagner Act, which established new federal mechanisms to bolster the rights of organized labor, and also that year's creation of a federal "social security" system of old age pensions, unemployment insurance, and assistance for dependent mothers and children. By facilitating the growth of organized labor, which in turn helped lay the foundations of a welfare state, the immigration restrictions of the 1920s had the unintended consequence of making the class politics of the United States look more, rather than less, like those of the nations of Europe.[23]

The complexity of the New Deal—the coalition building, the scramble to fend off rivals, the technical nature of the legislation—all reinforced the tendency to look inward, to focus energy and resources on domestic recovery and reform. The imagery of the New Deal was strikingly nationalist, no individual image more so than the ubiquitous blue eagle of the National Recovery Administration. There was more than a hint of the martial language of wartime in this moment of economic crisis. "I shall not evade the clear course of duty," Roosevelt declared in his inaugural address.

"I shall ask the Congress for the one remaining instrument to meet the crisis—broad Executive power to wage a war against the emergency, as great as the power that would be given to me if we were in fact invaded by a foreign foe." The New Deal created new bonds between the citizenry and the government. New programs like the Civilian Conservation Corps and the Works Progress Administration turned the federal government into a provider of jobs for the young and the unemployed. Roosevelt's radio "fireside chats" brought the president into sitting rooms across the nation. It was said that on a summer evening in which windows were open, one wouldn't miss a word of his radio addresses during a walk down a neighborhood street. Even the excesses and failures of the New Deal had the effect of strengthening the constitutional order. Roosevelt's aggressive attempt to pack the Supreme Court with supporters functioned to rally critics who reinforced the principle of the separation of powers in an era of executive branch growth.[24]

For all of the failings of the New Deal—not least that it did not solve the persistent problem of unemployment—it deserves credit for stabilizing the nation. The New Deal fortified and reformed the nation's liberal political system during a global crisis that elsewhere fostered the illiberal alternatives of fascism and communism. At a time when many around the world believed "that the choice now lay between two bleak extremes, Communism and Fascism," Sir Isaiah Berlin later remembered, "the only light that was left in the darkness was the administration of Roosevelt and the New Deal in the United States." Over time, as the United States confronted these ideological rivals, the inward tendencies of the New Deal gave way to a more internationalist and outward-looking politics. In 1933, the Roosevelt administration turned away from the World Economic Conference; yet just over a decade later it would lead the way in constructing the new international monetary and financial institutions established at the Bretton Woods Conference. The inclusive and creative politics that characterized the domestic coalition building of the New Deal also came to mark America's global leadership in a new era of internationalism. The corporatist military-industrial complex that harnessed and projected US power abroad bore the imprint of the New Deal, as did ill-fated exports, such as the attempt to remake Vietnam's Mekong River Delta in the image of the Tennessee Valley Authority in the 1960s. For better and for worse, in time the New Deal would reverberate around the world.[25]

III

Only the most optimistic of foreign observers envisioned a global future for the New Deal as America remained plunged in the depths of the Depression in the 1930s. Foreign observers were more likely to comment upon how the internal focus of American politics made it ill suited for confronting the dark forces of fascism that gathered strength as the 1930s unfolded. In the index to the book on the origins of the Second World War written by the British historian A. J. P. Taylor, who lived through the tumult of that decade, there is a revealing heading under the entry for the United States: "useless."[26]

Remarkably, a decade that began with the United States doing all that it could to insulate itself from international instability ended with a new conception of American national security that was global in scope. In the future, the United States would be criticized by foreign observers for being too globalist and interventionist rather than for its disregard for what happened abroad, as it had been in the 1930s. This reversal was the result of the international crisis of the 1930s, which prompted a domestic debate that changed how Americans perceived their security and broader role in the world.

It is obvious to us today who the good guys and bad guys were in the 1930s. But for many Americans at the time, it was not so

clear cut. There was more diversity of opinion—more confusion
and uncertainty—on foreign affairs in this period than the binary
categories of isolationists and internationalists suggests. Many
Americans believed that Germany had been harshly treated in the
punitive Versailles Treaty of 1919. It should come as little surprise
that many citizens of Irish and German ancestry remained suspicious of the British, even demanding that the Roosevelt administration pursue a policy of strict neutrality as the price for their
support of New Deal legislation. Such views emerged not only
from lingering ethnic solidarities but also from a popular interpretation of America's entry into the First World War, which held
that the United States had been duped into a European conflict
in which it had no direct interest by scheming British diplomats
and profit-hungry munitions producers and financiers. "War is
a racket. It always has been," wrote the critic of US intervention
Smedley Butler.[27]

The foreign policy of the United States in the 1930s resembled the ad hoc New Deal in that its defining characteristic was
the pragmatic, if haphazard, effort to insulate the nation from
risk. In the Neutrality Acts of this period, the United States actually ceded its neutral trading rights through self-imposed regulations on trade with foreign belligerents. The Johnson Act of 1934
similarly restricted American economic involvement with foreign
powers by prohibiting nations that had defaulted on debt obliga-
tions from raising capital on US financial markets. This legislation
aimed to avoid a repeat of the run-up to the First World War, when
American financial and commercial engagement with warring European powers had sucked the United States into the conflict. This
spirit of retrenchment and disengagement from an increasingly
volatile world can be seen elsewhere too: in the Tydings-McDuffie
Act (1934) that outlined America's withdrawal from its colonial
possession of the Philippines while setting strict limits upon Fili-
pino immigration and erecting new barriers to its export trade to

the United States; in the end of US occupations and interventions in the Caribbean and Central America as well as the elimination of tariff concessions for sugar producers in Cuba, which wrecked the island's export economy; and in the rigid enforcement of the immigration restriction legislation from the 1920s that denied entry to persecuted refugees, particularly European Jews. The foreign policies of the United States outsourced risk and economic dislocation. It is a testament to the nationalist ethos of the period that one the most internationalist policies of the day—Secretary of State Cordell Hull's efforts to negotiate bilateral, reciprocal trade agreements with Latin American nations—ended up looking less like the free-trade globalism that Hull so admired than the beginnings of a US-led trading bloc in the Western Hemisphere. "We must sell abroad more of these surpluses," Hull informed a group of newsmen at the 1933 Montevideo conference.[28]

This trend line of US retrenchment from the international system was reversed in 1938–1941, a period as critical to the development of the United States as were the 1780s and 1860s. The cascade of fascist aggression and imperial expansion—Japan's ruthless invasion of China in 1937 and Hitler's annexation of Czechoslovakia's Sudetenland in 1938 and invasion of Poland a year later—overwhelmed the world order that been predicated on balances of power in Europe and Asia within an international economic system presided over by the British Empire. The collapse of this order unfolded with the unforeseen speed of the Nazi blitzkrieg. The greatest shock of all was the sudden implosion of France, the presumed firewall to contain the spread of Nazism in Europe, in June 1940. The fall of France raised an alarming prospect. "If Great Britain goes down," Roosevelt explained in late 1940, "the Axis powers will control the continents of Europe, Asia, Africa, Australasia, and the high seas—and they will be in a position to bring enormous military and naval resources against this hemisphere. It is no exaggeration to say that all of us, in all the Americas, would be living at the point of a gun."[29]

The United States faced a clear choice: adapt to the emerging geopolitical order characterized by regional empires with closed economies and extreme political ideologies or buy time to prepare to join the fight by assisting the allies that remained standing against Germany and Japan. The first option was championed by so-called isolationists, who in truth were advocates of an American version of the power politics of the day. They sought not isolation from the world but a regional empire in the Western Hemisphere that would nurture US power and insulate the nation from the distant threats of fascism, communism, and Japanese imperialism. The political association called America First argued that sending material aid to allies would only increase the foreign threat, given the possibility such aid would end up in German hands. Due to this risk, it was best to construct a "fortress America" whose defensive strength and geographic distance would deter foreign aggression. "Even in our present condition of unpreparedness, no foreign power is in a position to invade us today," declared the famed aviator and America First leader Charles Lindbergh. "If we concentrate on our own and build the strength that this nation should maintain, no foreign army will ever attempt to land on American shores."[30]

Internationalists, including President Roosevelt, disagreed. When they looked out at the world—particularly after the fall of France—they saw liberal democracy imperiled everywhere. The domination of Eurasia by fascist and autarkic powers, they argued, would pose a grave threat to the United States even if it were not directly attacked. With the natural resources and productive capacities of most of the Eurasian landmass under their control, the illiberal axis of Germany and Japan would force the United States to change in undesirable ways. America would be cut off from its traditional markets across the Atlantic as well as those that it long had tried to develop in East Asia. In such a menacing environment, the United States would have no choice but to follow suit: expanding the powers of the central government, creating a large standing army, and increasing taxes to pay for it all. These changes would run counter to national traditions. They would be far more centralizing than the piecemeal reforms of the New Deal. Strategists and academics, such as the Yale political scientist Harold Lasswell, highlighted the dangerous global trend in which nation-states were evolving into militarized "garrison states—a world in which the specialists on violence are the most powerful group in society." It was not hard to see how the America First vision of a fortress America could lead in that direction. The United States was in danger of becoming a twentieth-century version of a centralized empire from which the colonists of 1776 had revolted. This emerging internationalist vision of national security, in short, was as concerned with protecting domestic liberalism as it was with countering foreign threats.[31]

The strategic coherence of this viewpoint, however, should not be overstated. The Roosevelt administration and its political allies formulated their ideas in response to fast-moving and disorienting developments abroad. The internationalists' conception of national security was also a product of the complexities of domestic politics. Indeed, it is hard to separate the hard-headed calculations behind this newly expansive conception of national security from the domestic salesmanship required to win popular support for it. That internationalists presented their policies as defensive measures can be seen in the name of their leading organization, the Committee to Defend America by Aiding the Allies. Groups such as these redeployed traditional symbols and rhetoric, engaging in a battle of appropriation with American First opponents. The establishment of a US protectorate in Greenland in 1940, for example, was presented as a logical extension of the hoary Monroe Doctrine of 1823. The Lend Lease Act of 1941, which increased US support to foreign allies, especially Britain, was entitled a Bill to Promote the Defense of the United States and numbered HR 1776. Roosevelt's fireside chats and public addresses presented the new threats facing the United States in ways that resonated with a public audience traditionally suspicious of foreign entanglements. In Roosevelt's memorable telling, foreign aggression was part of an "epidemic of world lawlessness," the solution to which was to "quarantine" expansionist powers; Nazi Germany was akin to a "rattlesnake" that was poised to strike at any moment; and sending material support to Britain was nothing more than lending a hose to a neighbor whose house was on fire.[32]

Of all the rhetorical devices used by Roosevelt and his support-ers to drum up support for assisting allies and projecting US power beyond its borders, none were of more long-term significance than the term *national security* itself. The term had appeared sporadically before the late 1930s, but it had not been tethered to a particular vision or strategy. In the years between the 1938 Munich agree-ment and the attack upon Pearl Harbor in 1941, Roosevelt used it more than all previous presidents combined. In Roosevelt's hands, the term was a means of countering America First opponents. Ap-propriating their nationalist language, he argued for an agenda of assisting Britain (and later the Soviet Union) in the struggle against Germany, imposing economic sanctions on Japan to deter its expansion in the Far East, and jump-starting war preparations at home. Just as the New Deal had been presented to the public as the means of enhancing social security, assisting Allies—particularly Britain—was depicted as the best way of securing the United States from foreign threats. "This is not a fireside chat on war," Roosevelt informed his listeners in December 1940 in his famous "arsenal of democracy" address. "It is a talk on national security."[33]

The domestic politics of national security went deeper than rhetoric. The rush to place the nation upon a war footing necessitated innovations in government power. Like the New Deal, this was a frenetic process in the midst of an acute international crisis. Even so, the effort to position the nation for the looming conflict had a distinctive trajectory, most evident in the consolidation of power in the executive branch. The 1940 destroyers-for-bases deal that exchanged American warships for British naval bases in the Caribbean was the product of an executive agreement, not an international treaty that required the consent of the Senate. The Roosevelt administration did not seek congressional approval when it implemented provocative economic sanctions against the Japanese and engaged in an undeclared war on the high seas against the Germans in 1941. The new powers of the executive were exercised internally as well. The FBI closely monitored those suspected to be fifth columnists at home. It was through the authority of an executive order that more than one hundred thousand Japanese Americans were rounded up and forced into internment camps in the frantic months following Pearl Harbor. The anticipated scale of war mobilization necessitated the construction of a massive, five-sided administrative complex for the War Department in Arlington—the building that would come to be known as the Pentagon.

Yet for all of these developments, the United States remained on the sidelines. As German bombers devastated British cities in the second half of 1940, the United States looked on with horror but did not enter the conflict. The Saratoga moment of the Second World War occurred before America was even in the war. As had been the case in 1777–1778 and 1862, the United States was the beneficiary of decisions and actions taken outside of its borders. This time, it had even less influence on the outcome. The resistance of "The Few" pilots of the Royal Air Force—and, in the bigger picture, the steely perseverance of the British people during the devastating German blitz—prevented what would have been the doomsday scenario of the fall of Britain, a calamity that could have extended Hitler's reach throughout the British Empire. The Battle of Britain was but the first phase of this Saratoga moment. The next was Hitler's decision to shelve plans to invade Britain in favor of going on the offensive against the Nazis' greatest ideological enemy, Soviet communism. The German invasion of the Soviet Union, authorized in late 1940 and executed the following June, gave the United States the time it so desperately needed to mobilize its immense, but still unrealized, power. It also ensured that Britain would live to fight another day, providing the United States in the process with a powerful ally and secure staging post from which to prepare a future invasion of Europe.

Most of all, the brutal German offensive in Russia became a quagmire that sucked up the resources and power of the Nazi regime—as well as those of the Soviet Union. As American industrial production picked up steam, the Germans and Soviets inflicted untold destruction upon one another. The turning point came in 1942–1943 with the Soviet victories at Stalingrad and in the great tank battle at Kursk, which shattered Germany's offensive capabilities on the Eastern front. Of all the many breaks that have fallen America's way in its curiously fortuitous history, perhaps none were of more significance than that the nation's greatest twentieth-century ideological rivals inflicted untold destruction upon one another, providing the United States with the time required to gather its power and pool it with the global networks and alliances of its former colonial master. Soviet communism was in this regard as much a savior of democratic capitalism as was the New Deal.[34]

After the Japanese attack on Pearl Harbor on December 7, 1941, and the German declaration of war four days later—another fortuitous break in that it spared Roosevelt political difficulties persuading Congress to declare war on Germany after a Japanese attack—the United States found itself in the position of managing two war efforts on opposite sides of the globe. This required more than just the mobilization of manpower and resources; it required an unprecedented flurry of diplomacy and alliance building. The nation that had long been suspicious of what it viewed as entangling alliances now raced to forge them with countries across the world. This compressed process of wartime internationalization had two notable features. The first was the truly global expansion of US hard power; the tentacles of US military and economic power reached to nearly all corners of the globe. The US armed forces, intelligence agencies, and foreign service did more than fight: they brokered new agreements with foreign partners as well as created new supply chains and transport networks. One of the most visible manifestations was the creation of the largest global network of military bases and installations that the world had ever seen. The first bases appeared along the old nodes of US empire and commerce. These were followed by ones established within the British and French empires. As the war progressed, US bases popped up in South America and Australia, throughout the Pacific, across the Middle East, deep within India, and even in Africa. By the war's end, US bases were being built at the astonishing clip of more than 100 per month, leading to the 1945 total of more than two thousand bases and thirty thousand military installations.[35]

The second feature of the international turn of the United States was the perhaps surprising support for it at home. Old prejudices against cooperating with foreign allies quickly faded. Most striking of all was the rapid acceptance of a close alliance with Britain, long the bogeyman in US political culture. When the United States entered the First World War in 1917, the Wilson administration did so as what it called an "associate" power. This euphemism spared the United States from labeling itself a formal ally of its old rival. But in the 1940s, Americans began to celebrate what Winston Churchill cannily called the "special relationship" between "the English-speaking peoples." Recognizing that the United States was now the premier power, the British grudgingly nodded in agreement when Americans proclaimed their devotion to self-determination and freedom of the seas. It is notable that the signature political document of this era—the 1941 Atlantic Charter that proclaimed America's liberal principles to the world—differed from the Declaration of Independence, Monroe Doctrine, Gettysburg Address, and Fourteen Points statement in that it was jointly authored by the United States president and the British prime minister. Churchill deserves no small credit for cultivating American public opinion. "The English-speaking democracies, the British Empire and the United States," Churchill declared during the Battle of Britain, "will have to be somewhat mixed up together in some of their affairs for mutual and general advantage. For my part, looking out upon the future, I do not view the process with any misgivings. I could not stop it if I wished; no one can stop it. Like the Mississippi it just keeps rolling along. Let it roll. Let it roll on full flood, inexorable, irresistible, benignant, to broader lands and better days."[36]

Underlying the American embrace of foreign alliances was a shift in the international distribution of power. The United States was no longer an ally; it now had allies. The Second World War became America's war in a way that the First World War had not. With national security at stake, this was not someone else's conflict; it was a struggle for core national values, even if mainland America was not under immediate threat of attack. *Time* and *Life* founder Henry Luce captured the mood in his 1941 essay "The American Century": "We are *not* in a war to defend American territory. We are in a war to defend and even to promote, encourage and incite so-called democratic principles throughout the world." Americans stopped thinking of allies as secret rivals out to exploit them and instead conceived of their foreign partners as extensions of themselves. The London broadcasts of CBS radio correspondent

Edward Murrow during the Battle of Britain in 1940 depicted Britons as a democratic populace united in defense of liberal values. The German blitz did much to change American views of Britain from a monarchical empire to a fellow democracy, thus preparing the ground for the special relationship. Even Stalin became "Uncle Joe," a public relations ploy that effectively Americanized this indispensable ally and future rival.[37]

The Second World War revolutionized how the United States engaged with the world. Indeed, many characteristics of US policy in the Cold War can be traced to the 1938–1941 period: the global conception of national security; the newfound reach of the US military; the growth of executive power and the central state; the birth of the military-industrial complex; the emergence of a fervently nationalist political culture that was liberal and tolerant when compared to its foreign rivals but nonetheless exhibited suppressive tendencies, particularly toward racial minorities; and the embrace of international leadership and alliance building. The terms upon which the United States entered the Second World War made it highly unlikely that it would reprise its stance at the end of the First World War, when America sought to limit its new international commitments. This time, there would be no going back.[38]

IV

The United States experienced a different Second World War than did the other principal belligerents. The US mainland was never seriously endangered. There was no aerial assault on New York or Washington, no siege of New Orleans, no firebombing of San Francisco. No enemy tank battalions rolled across the wheat fields of the Midwest; no enemy soldiers beat down farmhouse doors, raping and plundering their way through the American heartland. The Soviet Union lost an estimated twenty-seven million people during the war; the United States lost 418,500. The savage war on the Eastern front brought devastation to the Soviet Union. Some 1,700 Soviet cities were destroyed, as were 70,000 villages and hamlets, 31,000 industrial centers, 40,000 miles of railroad, and 90,000 bridges. The US experience of war was not unimaginable destruction but its complete opposite: unprecedented production.[39]

The war unleashed the most productive industrial economy the world had ever seen. If the Soviet's chief contribution to the fight against Nazi Germany was the tenacious persistence of its population in the face of invasion, the United States' was its herculean industrial output. When Churchill looked to America, he saw not only fellow "English-speaking peoples" but also a "gigantic industrial boiler." The US economy did more than support its own immense war effort; it also provided 60 percent of the Allies' munitions and was responsible for 40 percent of the arms produced in the world by 1944. The numbers were almost unbelievable to contemporaries who had grown accustomed to the bleak economic reports of the Depression years. The US industrial machine churned out 2,383,311 trucks, 299,293 aircraft, 88,410 tanks, 6.5 million rifles, 40 billion bullets, and, not to be forgotten, 2 atomic weapons. A new merchant marine—an immense armada of 5,777 "liberty ships"—departed fully loaded with war material from American ports on the Atlantic and Pacific coasts. The nature and geography of the war gave the United States a fortuitous head start on its future nemesis. The Soviet Union ended the war confronting a colossal reconstruction project; the United States emerged from the conflict primed to exploit its economic dominance on the world stage.[40]

Of all the zigzags in this era of global crisis, none was sharper than the Great Depression of the 1930s being followed by America's greatest economic boom. The previously intractable problem of high unemployment melted away as the engines of this economic juggernaut heated up. Networks of commerce and credit that had been frozen during the Depression surged back to life, powering new industries, supply chains, and conglomerations of economic might. The roaring economy not only fueled the Allied war effort but also laid the foundation for the postwar age. The labor market's insatiable appetite powered demographic transformation, leading African Americans from the South as well as poor whites to migrate to the industrial core of the North and the booming economy of California. The war economy empowered African American labor leaders such as A. Philip Randolph, who successfully campaigned for the creation in 1941 of a federal Fair Employment Practices Committee charged with rooting out discrimination within defense industries. Women entered the workforce—and armed services—in unprecedented numbers, challenging gender hierarchies and prefiguring the feminist advances of the coming decades.

The wartime economy was new in its industrial output and scale, but it contained echoes of the wild west capitalism of the Civil War era, not least in the pace of economic activity. The parallels between the 1860s and 1940s go deeper than speed. In both periods, the surge of economic activity was most transformative in the American West. As the 1860s unleashed the colonization of the West, the 1940s accelerated its industrialization. The war gave birth to some four thousand defense plants in Los Angeles County, whose combined output in 1945 stood second in the nation only to Detroit. Early tech industries like aviation drew from the intellectual power of Cal Tech, a research hub of the expanding Pacific military-industrial complex. It wasn't just Los Angeles. New industries, corporate conglomerations, and military entrepots appeared along the route of the recently constructed Pacific Coast Highway, as well as in the shipyards and refineries of the greater Bay Area. The New Deal, which had funneled federal dollars into the region, anticipated this war boom. But the government spending in the 1940s was on an altogether different level: the $7.6 billion in federal dollars the West received in the 1930s was but a tenth of the $70 billion sent its way during the war.[41]

Indeed, as in the 1860s, in the 1940s the federal government played an important role in the booming wartime economy. A constellation of new government agencies and boards sprouted up during the Second World War, frantically trying to keep up with the breakneck pace of economic activity. The government's presence could be seen not only in new regulatory bodies but also in escalating tax rates; taxes covered some 45 percent of the war effort (up from the roughly 33 percent of the Civil War). Yet the wartime state was defined not only by the powers it assumed but also by its strategies of incentivizing and co-opting the nation's economy. As in the Civil War, the federal government of the 1940s outsourced production rather than nationalizing it, channeling private enterprise toward ends of its own design through the seductive mechanisms of subsidies, tax shelters, and low-interest loans. The result—again echoing the 1860s—was a resurgence of big business, which was best positioned to capitalize on the opportunities presented by wartime mobilization. "If you are going to... go to war...in a capitalist country," Secretary of War Henry Stimson wrote, "you have to let business make money out of the process or business won't work." War industry and manufacturing consolidated. In 1940, 70 percent of federal contracts for war production was diffused among 175,000 companies; but by 1943, just one hundred firms held 70 percent of the contracts.[42]

The war economy reset US politics and society. The exigencies of war prioritized production, thus pushing to the margins the New Deal's emphasis on economic security, political reform, and support of organized labor. Although sharing the New Deal's spirit of pragmatic improvisation and experimentation, the politics of the war differed from it in its avoidance—indeed, denigration—of class politics. A 1943 Gallup poll found that labor leader John L. Lewis, who led a coal miners' strike in that year, was as unpopular as Hitler and Hirohito. To be sure, the heyday of trade unionism was far from over—indeed, union membership nearly doubled as the labor force swelled between 1939 and 1945. The inflation-adjusted 27 percent increase in wages generated by the war economy did not end strikes, which proliferated in the war's final years. Nor did it defuse racial conflict that arose from labor tensions, as the deadly Detroit riots of 1943 made clear. But the dominant trend of the 1940s, at least when compared to the preceding decade, was how wartime mobilization resulted in a turn away from the prolabor politics and political reforms of the New Deal.[43]

The war economy not only pumped new life into American capitalism but also brought ordinary Americans into the national war effort. This was particularly the case with the European immigrant population. The white-ethnic working class that had arrived in the United States from southern and eastern Europe in the late nineteenth and early twentieth centuries had endured great inequity and discrimination in their new home, but now, in the 1940s, they provided much-needed labor and military muscle for the fight against fascism. White ethnics further supported the war effort by purchasing war bonds and founding civic organizations devoted to the cause. The 1940s witnessed a burst of voluntary naturalization, with more immigrants taking up US citizenship during the war than in any five-year period of American history. One reason for this was that the prospect of return migration diminished as the war continued to ravage immigrants' homelands. And with improving job prospects in America, there was now ample reason to "buy in" to the United States. At the same time, government propaganda and mass culture celebrated America's multiethnic character and inclusive civic ideals. Cinema newsreels highlighted ethnically diverse army units. One revealing measure of the newfound acceptance of white ethnics can be found in the government publication *Selective Service and Victory*, which provided statistical information about military service. In contrast to the 1920s immigration restriction legislation that so meticulously concerned itself with the national origins of new arrivals from southern and eastern

Europe, the tabulations of the US military made no distinction among those of European origin.[44]

None of this is to say that wartime America was a social utopia. It certainly was not, as was illustrated by the internment of loyal Japanese Americans. The increased acceptance of immigrants from Europe during the war did not characterize the experience of other ethnic and racial groups. *Selective Service and Victory* might not have made distinctions among service people of European origin, but it did concern itself with recording African Americans and Native Americans as well as those from Asia, Mexico, and US territories and colonies. If wartime mobilization offered new opportunities, particularly economic ones, for workers of all races, it nonetheless emboldened conservatives who sought to block social change. Southern whites in Congress fought their Democratic colleagues during the war on issues of civil rights and new federal powers that might threaten state-level segregation. "The South isn't joking anymore," one legislator warned during the war. "Back them into the corner a little further and see what they do." Southern white opposition to civil rights during the war portended the "Dixiecrat" revolt in which some defenders of segregation broke from the Democratic Party in 1948. The conservative resurgence of the era was not limited to racial issues. The opportunities for economic and social improvement that the war provided to women dried up once male GIs returned. "From a humanitarian point of view," declared head of the National Association of Manufacturers Frederick Crawford, "too many women should not stay in the labor force. The home is the basic American institution."[45]

The war, in short, did not magically dissolve old social barriers and hierarchies. What it did, however, was to change the economic and ideological terms upon which the nation's social and racial politics played out. The ideological extremism of America's wartime enemies reinvigorated the old ideas and languages of American civic nationalism. The promise of America had seemed incongruous with the realities of the Depression-plagued 1930s. But the specter of Nazi brutality and Japanese imperialism revived the old "American creed," as the Swedish social scientist Gunnar Myrdal called it in his famous 1944 study of race relations, *An American Dilemma.* "Americans of all national origins, classes, regions, creeds, and colors," Myrdal wrote, "have something in common: a social *ethos*, a political creed." This was an overstatement. But even those who had ample reason to doubt that the American creed applied to them were aware of the possibilities opened by the war, hence the Double V campaign championed by the black press to win the fights against Nazism abroad and racism at home. "The very fact of [African Americans'] separation from any past or present national existence—German, English, Welsh, Scotch, Irish, Swedish, Italian, Polish, Finnish, Hungarian, or what have you— guarantees the purity of his national allegiance to the American ideal," wrote black educator Horace Mann Bond in 1942.[46]

So, too, did the sustained economic growth, rising consumption, and falling unemployment of the war years and beyond pave the way for social change, albeit of a certain type. The economic boom reduced old class frictions, thus diminishing the appeal of the more radical political alternatives that had sprouted up in the 1930s. It also dangled new consumer opportunities before all who saw the proliferating advertisements generated by the booming field of marketing. And it offered unprecedented opportunities for geographic and social mobility, not least to those who benefited from the GI Bill (which expanded higher education and business opportunities for veterans) and the employment options within the military-industrial complex. The prospects on offer emboldened those who remained marginalized during the post-1945 boom. Of particular note was a dynamic cohort of African American civil rights campaigners, not only Christian preachers like Martin Luther King Jr. but also labor leaders and female activists who fought for the civil rights victories of the 1950s and 1960s.[47]

The postwar context of stable economic growth and protracted ideological rivalry with Soviet communism fostered particular kinds of social and political movements, those that, like the civil rights movement, advanced incrementally, attracted wide support by appealing to national creeds, and could be presented as a means of advancing Cold War aims by demonstrating social progress and racial unity to diverse global audiences. "I think it is quite obvious," Acting Secretary of State Dean Acheson wrote to the Fair Employment Practices Commission as early as 1946, "that the existence of discriminations against minority groups in the United States is a handicap in our relations with other countries. The Department of State, therefore, has good reasons to hope for the continued and increased effectiveness of public and private efforts to do away with these discriminations." But if the Cold War environment facilitated some advances in civil rights, it nonetheless proved inhospitable to radical politics, which were snuffed out with missionary zeal in this age of anticommunism. Even trade unionism would find its growth halted amid the ensuing age of affluence, consumption, and runaway fears of socialism. In the 1930s, the economic crisis produced a wide range of political possibilities; the postwar boom narrowed them.[48]

V

There was no precedent for the global commitments the United States shouldered in the aftermath of the Second World War. The nation that had long railed against entangling alliances suddenly took the lead in creating new institutions of international economy (the International Monetary Fund, the World Bank, and the General Agreement on Trade and Tariffs), governance (the United Nations), and collective security (the North Atlantic Treaty Organization). The country that for much of its existence had been one of the world's foremost advocates of protective tariffs now promoted a liberal economic world order premised on the free exchange of goods and capital. United States internationalism went even further. The nation assumed global naval commitments and responsibility for the economic recovery of Western Europe, and it oversaw the massive occupations and reconstructions of its two wartime nemeses, Japan and (West) Germany. These global commitments had no parallel in world history, let alone in America's past.[49]

As important as was America's new security strategy and economic dynamism to understanding these changes, the key development was external. The Second World War brought down the century-old international order dominated by European colonialism. Global politics transitioned from the empires of the past to the postcolonial world of the nation-state. The two decades following 1941 witnessed a burst of nation making, with twenty-one new polities issuing declarations of independence, many modeled on the original of 1776. The collapse of the old order destabilized the international system, particularly within Europe's old colonial realms in Africa, Asia, and the Caribbean. The dissolution of the US empire followed this global trend, with the Philippines gaining independence in 1946 and Hawaii being incorporated as a state in 1959. Revolutionary Cuba paralleled the more radical alternatives that could be found in this anti-imperial age. Decolonization, or the transition of political organization from European empires into sovereign nation-states, created a constellation of crises around the world in the decades after 1945.[50]

The Cold War grew out of the antagonistic visions of the United States and the Soviet Union for what would replace the old world order of European empires. Leaders in Washington and Moscow looked out at this new global landscape through prisms tinted by their respective interests, ideologies, and—perhaps most of all—their experiences in the 1930s and 1940s. What most terrified the US foreign-policy establishment was that the implosion of the old world order would fuel a leftward turn that would play into the Soviets' hands. "They have suffered so much," Dean Acheson said of the inhabitants of Europe, "and they believe so deeply that governments can take some action which will alleviate their sufferings, that they will demand that the whole business of state control and state interference shall be pushed further and further."[51]

The lesson that US policymakers took on from the preceding decades of turmoil was simple. The United States required an open, liberal world order, a postcolonial version of the British-led system of the nineteenth century that had done so much to foster America's development and growth. "We have learned that we cannot live alone, at peace; that our own well-being is dependent on the well-being of other Nations, far away," Roosevelt declared in early 1945. Such thinking led to a historic reversal of US trade policy. The apostle of protectionism transformed itself into the world's leading proponent of free trade, dismantling its old tariff walls in a bid to stimulate commercial exchange and thereby pump life back into international capitalism. The new institutions and policies of the era—the Bretton Woods monetary and financial system, the Marshall Plan's material assistance to Europe, the integration of West Germany's currency—had the same aim. "Our deepest concern with European recovery," Harry Truman asserted in 1947, "is that it is essential to the maintenance of the civilization in which the American way of life is rooted." America's allies in Western Europe reciprocated by encouraging the traditionally unilateral United States to forge binding agreements with them. "The treaties that are being proposed cannot be fully effective nor be relied upon when a crisis arises unless there is assurance of American support for the defense of Western Europe," British Foreign Secretary Ernest Bevin wrote in 1947. "The plain truth is that Western Europe cannot yet stand on its own feet without assurance of support."[52]

The global policies required to contain the Soviet Union presented challenges at home as well as abroad. The United States

remained a nation whose electorate was suspicious of foreign entanglements, despite the alliance building of the war years. The
mid-term elections of 1946, in which Republicans took control of
both houses of Congress for the first time since before the New
Deal, brought in a new class of Republicans, such as Joseph Mc-
Carthy and John Bricker, who blended fervent anticommunist nationalism, advocacy of budget cuts, and lingering concerns about
international commitments. Truman faced the prospect of being
attacked both for being soft on communism and for committing
the nation to costly foreign policies. Stuck between a rock and
a hard place, the Truman administration sought a way forward
by framing the rivalry with the Soviet Union in the ideologically
charged terms of a struggle "between alternative ways of life." Truman raised the stakes when asking the new Republican Congress
for funds to assist anticommunist allies in Greece and Turkey in
1947. "If we falter in our leadership," Truman predicted, "we may
endanger the peace of the world—and we shall surely endanger
the welfare of our own nation." As Republican Arthur Vandenberg
put it, this approach worked "to scare the hell out of the American people." The Truman Doctrine, as it became known, applied
the national security thinking of the Second World War to the new
context of the struggle against the Soviet Union, which seamlessly
transitioned into the totalitarian role hitherto occupied by Nazi
Germany and Imperial Japan.[53]

The Truman Doctrine was one of many examples in the post-
1945 period in which ideologically charged nationalism was used
to leverage domestic support for the internationalist policies pursued in the struggle against the Soviet Union. The "American way
of life" became more than a slogan during the Cold War. It was
institutionalized in American politics and culture. The National
Security Act of 1947 restructured the nation's defense and intelligence bureaucracies. Politicians invented new national traditions.
As Truman became the first president since James Monroe to have

a foreign policy doctrine in his name, Vandenberg declared that "partisan politics stops at the water's edge," a slogan that was as untrue in the post-1945 period as it was in those that preceded it, but it has stuck ever since. A culture of anticommunism seeped into the daily lives of Americans. Loyalty and anticommunist pledges were imposed not only by the Truman administration but also by state governments and local institutions. It was in the 1940s that schoolchildren began starting their day with the recitation of the Pledge of Allegiance.[54]

This steroidal nationalism—as much a cultural creation from the bottom up as it was a political construct imposed from the top down—gave US Cold Warriors the muscle they needed to counter the Soviet Union. The United States projected its nationalist creed outward, selling its way of life to foreign audiences with the entrepreneurial vigor that characterized its booming professions of advertising and marketing. The radio service "Voice of America" literally broadcast this creed abroad in the bid to counter the messaging of the Soviet Union. The Hollywood western introduced cinemagoers around the world to an imagined frontier past. The United States supported American studies programs at foreign universities, seeking to spread an American gospel in ways not unlike the proselytizing missionaries of the nineteenth century.[55]

There was an irony in all of this. As the United States projected its power throughout the world, the dominant trend in its culture and public life was inward. The new Rome was obsessed with itself. Here was an underappreciated legacy of the inward turns of the interwar period. The immigration restrictions of the 1920s led to a diminishing percentage of the population that was foreign-born—the 14.7 percent of 1910 gradually fell to an all-time low of 4.7 percent in 1970. The trend extended beyond demography. The number of American high school students who studied foreign languages, for example, plummeted by more than half between 1915 and 1975. The national triumphalism of this period encouraged a self-referential and blinkered worldview that over time distorted how Americans perceived themselves as well as events beyond their nation's borders. While Europe struggled to get back on its feet, and as instability and conflict prevailed in the decolonizing world, Americans looked anew at their nation as a paragon of stability and prosperity. As the devastating Great Depression receded from memory, Cold War America proclaimed itself an "exceptional" nation, a country that had veered off the highway of history—avoiding extreme ideologies of fascism and communism—charting instead a backroad to an alternate universe of social liberalism, economic dynamism, and political stability.[56]

The great public monument of the Cold War, the arch in Saint Louis—a city that had been a crossroads from pre-Columbian times through the imperial successions of the eighteenth century and the great demographic and economic changes of the nineteenth and twentieth—embodied the new nationalist ethos. Designed by Finnish immigrant architect Eero Saarinen and completed in 1965, the arch was a monument to an imagined history of the interior of North America in which the United States was the only historical actor of significance. The Jefferson National Expansion Memorial, as it was officially named, downplayed the region's diverse history—its native peoples, its French and Spanish influences, its conflicts over slavery, its large population of German and Italian immigrants—replacing it instead with a celebration of entrepreneurial Americans who overcame all obstacles in their way, including the construction of the architectural marvel itself. It was a contrast from the great monument of the late nineteenth century, the outward-facing Statue of Liberty. The gift of America's first foreign ally, France, Lady Liberty celebrated America's republican origins and its welcoming spirit, not least toward the millions of immigrants who arrived upon its shores in the great wave at the turn of the century.[57]

This curious blend of nationalism and internationalism sustained the US effort through a half century of Cold War. It shaped some of the era's most transformative policies. One such example was the National Interstate and Defense Highways Act of 1956, which created the interstate system. This federal infrastructure enhanced the nation's security by connecting its internal military bases and industries while at the same time enabling the frenzied suburbanization that led Americans of the period to imagine themselves as the successors of the pioneers of days gone by. In other cases, nationalism and internationalism tugged policymakers in conflicting directions. This was evident in the case of immigration reform. The 1952 McCarran-Walter Act, the most significant immigration act since the restrictions of the 1920s, was an attempt to balance the contrary impulses of the era. The impact of the Cold War was impossible to miss: the act strengthened the federal government's ability to deny entry and deport those with Communist affiliations. The legislation also aimed at cultivating the strategic relations with Asian nations by removing—finally—the old prohibitions on Asian immigration and naturalization. But despite this liberalizing aspect, many internationalists opposed the bill because it perpetuated the old national quota system, which continued to advantage northern Europeans and others of "Anglo-Saxon stock." Truman vetoed the bill on the grounds that it "denies the humanitarian creed inscribed beneath the Statue of Liberty."[58]

The Senate overrode Truman's veto, but the days of the discriminatory national quota system were now numbered. The tide turned at the height of Cold War liberalism during Lyndon B. Johnson's era of the "great society." The 1965 Hart-Celler Act dismantled the discriminatory national quota system, replacing it with an overall limit on immigration that now also included the Western Hemisphere. The act also allowed for family reunifications above and beyond the overall cap on immigrant numbers. The results would not be apparent for some years but eventually were impossible to miss: the relatively closed borders of this global power were swung open to a more diverse group of immigrants, including those from Asia, Africa, and Latin America. The percentage of the population that was foreign-born climbed from 4.7 percent in 1970 to 11.1 percent thirty years later. This trend of increased incoming traffic found a parallel in commerce and finance. By the twilight of the Cold War, the United States became a net importer of capital, returning to the debtor status that it had held in the century before 1914.[59]

As the twentieth century entered its final decades, the United States once again became like a giant sponge, soaking in labor and capital—and foreign imports, not least oil. These changes eventually placed new strains on the nationalistic political establishment that had been created during the crises of the mid-twentieth century. Indeed, the half century roughly between 1920 and 1970 now looks to be an outlier in the grand sweep of American history in that it was characterized by low immigration, capital exportation, and (after 1945) geopolitical ascendance. This peculiar era was one in which the politics and culture of the United States was strikingly inward facing while simultaneously being the moment in which the nation projected its financial and military power around the globe as has no other empire in world history. The era of American history that most stands out from the rest is ironically the one that assumed normative status in the narratives of national exceptionalism that appeared in the second half of the twentieth century.[60]

COLD WAR AMERICA was not without its share of internal contradictions. The persistence of social and racial inequalities belied the promise of the American creed, both at home and abroad. Soviet propagandists lost no opportunity to highlight the gap between American practices and ideals, particularly when it came to civil rights, a matter closely followed by observers in the decolonizing world. As the dividends of the postwar economic boom diminished, social and political tensions heated up, reaching a boiling point in the 1960s and 1970s. The United States' fervent anticommunism was prone to self-destructive spasms of suppression and coercion, not least the McCarthyism of the 1950s. In addition to such illiberal tendencies, America's culture of anticommunism had the tragic result of narrowing the politically viable options on the table for diplomats. The roots of the greatest error of Cold War diplomacy—the war in Vietnam—lay not only in the decolonization of Indochina but also in a nationalistic domestic political environment that made escalation in a conflict in which US statesmen doubted their ability to win the path of least-perceived resistance. "What in the hell is Vietnam worth to me? What is it worth to this country?" President Lyndon Johnson asked in 1964. "It's damn easy to get into a war, but...it's going to be awful hard to ever extricate yourself if you get in."[61]

Even some of the greatest successes of the Cold War era yielded unanticipated effects. The US-led revitalization of the global capitalist system created new economic competitors. Indeed, the trend toward deindustrialization in the United States in the 1970s and 1980s was in part the product of the industrial development of allies like South Korea, whose industries boomed as a result of US procurements during the Vietnam War. The "American century" was unsustainable in other ways. The United States presided over an international economic order powered by fossil fuels. The eventual price was reliance upon foreign producers and the onset of climate change. Embodied by the massive, gas guzzling vehicles that plied the roads of the interstate highway system in the 1960s and 1970s, the Cold War effort of the United States devoured the world's carbon energy.[62]

That the post-1945 United States had its share of internal contractions is not surprising. It was no more exceptional in this regard than it was in being a nation that celebrated its distinctiveness. What is notable is how long the United States maintained its global preeminence despite its limitations and contradictions. The international crises of the mid-twentieth century had the fortuitous effect of preparing the nation for the looming struggle against the Soviet Union, both at home and abroad. The demise of the European order cleared the path for the ascendance of the United States, which was spared the massive internal reconstruction project that confronted the Soviet Union after 1945. As the most successful postcolonial nation, the United States held an intrinsic ideological advantage over the Soviets in this golden age of the nation-state.

The "highly unstable zigzag course" of the preceding era of global crisis became a lesson of what not to do for the Cold Warriors of the future. "Think of the difference between our course now and our course 30 years ago," Harry Truman declared in his farewell address of 1953. "After the First World War, we withdrew from world affairs—we failed to act in concert with other peoples against aggression—we helped to kill the League of Nations—and we built up tariff barriers that strangled world trade.... Think about those years of weakness and indecision, and the World War II which was their evil result. Then think about the speed and courage and decisiveness with which we have moved against the Communist threat since World War II." To be sure, there would be wobbles and tragic instances of overreach during the ensuing decades, but the wild zigs and zags that had characterized US statecraft were smoothed out into a more linear and coherent course after 1945—so much so that Americans came to imagine their history as one that had inexorably unfolded toward their global ascendance.[63]

CONCLUSION
From Triumph to Crisis

For all the vitriolic divisions in twenty-first-century American politics, there is at least agreement on one point: we are in the midst of a grave crisis. "Our Convention occurs at a moment of crisis for our nation," declared the Republican presidential nominee in his acceptance speech in July 2016. "We're gathering here," Democratic senator Elizabeth Warren informed an Atlanta audience in August 2017, "in a moment of crisis for our country." Politicians, of course, have incentive to proclaim crises when none exist; doing so is believed to increase participation, donations, and voter turnout. Yet one would need to be a particularly unflappable member of an optimist club to write off our current troubles as merely the invention of office seekers or journalists in search of website hits. It has been clear for some time that ours is an era of unusual volatility, at home as well as abroad. "That we are in the midst of crisis is now well understood," President Barack Obama stated in his 2009 inaugural address. "Our nation is at war. . . . Our economy is badly weakened.... Homes have been lost, jobs shed, businesses shuttered. Our healthcare is too costly, our schools fail too many, and each day brings further evidence that the ways we use energy strengthen our adversaries and threaten our planet."[1]

The crises of our age have come to many as shocking turns of events, unexpected and dislocating shifts in the very ground beneath our feet. The language used to describe the most unanticipated events of our era is revealing: 9/11 was "the day that changed everything"; the 2007–2008 financial panic was met with cries such as "the capitalist order is in freefall collapse!"; many observers labeled the outcome of the 2016 election a "political earthquake." "This is not normal!" blared another.[2]

This sense of crisis emerged not only from events themselves but also from their incongruity with popular understandings of the nation and its history that had taken root in the post-1945 era. In this inward-looking age of American global ascendance, the forward march of the United States had seemed inevitable, "seamless," in the words of one popular historian of this era of peak America. Just as Britain's Whig historians had crafted triumphalist narratives of progress in the glory days of the Victorian empire, Americans at the height of their nation's power constructed a linear history of their self-proclaimed exceptional nation. To be sure, as with so much else in our age of cultural and political polarization, there came to be competing versions: the left emphasized ongoing struggles waged over social and racial equality, while those on the right highlighted individual liberty, free markets, and national power. But for as much as they disagreed on the particulars, those from across the political spectrum were joined by the assumption that the historical development of the United States had a direction— as well as momentum.[3]

The jolts of our era have thrown such Whiggish narratives into disarray. Far from progressing in a straight, ascending line, the United States of the twenty-first century has swung back and forth like a pendulum. The nation that had been the world's foremost advocate of free markets and open trade is mired in debate concerning the extent to which it should revive its old traditions of economic nationalism and retrenchment from global politics. The first African American president was succeeded by a white president who exploited racial tensions for political gain as has no other mainstream national leader in living memory. The recently dubbed "hyperpower" now finds itself vulnerable to transnational terrorism and foreign meddling in its domestic institutions. These swings have not gone unnoticed. President-elect Obama declared on the night of his 2008 electoral victory that the American people possessed the power to bend "the arc of history...toward the hope of a better day"; eight years later talk of this nature was replaced by admissions like "the path this country has taken has never been a straight line. We zig and zag." It is a safe assumption that there will be similar disillusionment on the political right when its fortunes next fall.[4]

As WE TRY to maintain our balance amid this instability, we would do well to revisit America's previous moments of crisis. The temptation in unstable moments such as the present is the opposite—to look for comforting and redeeming national narratives, ones that underscore the enduring power of American ideals and the underlying continuities in the nation's historical development. It is perhaps not surprising that nostalgia permeates today's popular historical consciousness. The irony is that a moment of flux such as the present is precisely the time in which we should embrace the more complex historical record of volatility, unanticipated change, and moments of crisis. The interpretation of the nation's past presented in this book does not offer hard and fast rules of history, but it does bring a recurring and underappreciated theme into focus: the most transformative political crises of America's past have been entwined with sudden shifts in its position within the broader international system.

It is an irony of American history that its greatest periods of crisis were preceded by moments of international triumph. The only thing worse than a battle lost, the Duke of Wellington once said, is a battle won. The origins of the first civil war of the 1770s can be traced to the debts and strategic burdens accrued in the victory over France and her native allies in the Seven Years' War. The conquest of northern Mexico set the stage for the Civil War by thrusting to the fore of US politics the question of slavery in the western territories. The Great Depression and Second World War were preceded by the unprecedented expansion of US economic and cultural power in the first decades of the twentieth century, particularly after 1917. In all of these cases, the reigning political system was ill suited for the responsibilities and decisions that came with new strategic commitments.

The geopolitical shifts that followed 1763, 1848, and 1917, favorable to the United States though they were, unleashed bursts of economic and demographic change that further unsettled the political establishments of the day. Sudden changes in immigration patterns—the surges in the decades after 1763 and 1845 as well as the restrictions of the 1920s—disrupted politics in unanticipated ways. The rapid growth of new markets for trade and investment demanded political adaptations—imperial reform in the 1760s, territorial administration in the West in the 1850s, international engagement in the 1920s and 1930s—that proved beyond the capability of existing political regimes. Because the United States has been so entangled within the global system, its politics have been remarkably sensitive to international shifts, even those that were to its advantage.[5]

The early signs of the coming crises soon became visible as Americans struggled to adapt to new environments and to shoulder new burdens. Old allegiances and loyalties faded away; political parties began to realign, if not collapse altogether; social conflict intensified; international markets bounced around like pinballs; and great power rivalry intensified. Problems that had once been contained dangerously escalated. Observers took note, ringing the alarm bells. "The turning point in a disease is a crisis," a New York newspaper informed its readers as the nation rumbled toward civil war in the late 1850s. "At present the nation, considered politically, has reached this turning point, this critical moment.... Crisis is the proper and the best word to express the existing state of the country." Those committed to the status quo sought to restore order and confidence. "We are in an extraordinary degree self-sustaining, we will overcome world influences and will lead the march of prosperity as we have always done hitherto," Herbert Hoover declared after the Wall Street crash. But not all attempted to stabilize the existing order. Many instead advanced bold visions of change— evident in the mobilization of patriot resistance after 1763; Southern separatism in the 1850s; and the root-and-branch reform of the nation's politics, economics, and distribution of power after 1929. For some, crisis was opportunity.[6]

The early sparks of crisis eventually turned into flames that roared out of control. The post-1763 political divisions turned into full-on civil war in 1775; Lincoln's election triggered Southern secession, which in turn led to the deadliest war in American history; and the banking and unemployment crises of the winter of 1932– 1933 brought the American economy to its knees at the very moment members of the Roosevelt administration took their oaths of office. It was in such exigent times—in these rare moments which required the rapid mobilization and reorganization of national power—that new political forms swept away the old. "The dogmas of the quiet past are inadequate to the stormy present," Lincoln declared in the pivotal year of 1862. "As our case is new, so we must think anew and act anew. We must disenthrall ourselves, and then we shall save our country." New ideas, possibilities, and actors rushed onto the scene, not least the immigrants who arrived to America's shores. Transformative change followed: the 1776 break from Britain and the formation of the newly named United States, the transition from a war to save the Union to one that destroyed slavery, the reconfiguration of the nation's political economy during the New Deal, and the formulation of a new conception of national security during the dark days of totalitarian ascendance.

These bursts of creative destruction gave birth to political institutions that are still with us today, not least the Constitution itself, the oldest written national constitution in the world. The durability of these creations—the national currency established in the Civil War; the social welfare system of the New Deal; the international institutions built in the 1940s, such as the United Nations and NATO; even the very idea of the United States as a land of "one people," as the Declaration put it in 1776—has given them an aura of timelessness. But they were less the inevitable outcomes of an exceptional American political tradition than they were the contingent products of moments of acute crisis. Furthermore, these innovations were not simply the handiworks of the political elite. Crises have a way of empowering those who have hitherto been marginalized. The patriot cause unleashed social forces that ultimately gave birth to modern democracy; the African Americans and immigrants who served in the Union armies that reduced the Old South to rubble could not be treated after the war as they had been before it; and the white ethnics, working classes, and African Americans who swelled the ranks of organized labor formed the backbone of the New Deal coalition that would dominate American politics for a generation.[7]

Moments of crisis also brought to center stage foreign powers, the most overlooked actors in American history. Foreign powers were the fulcrum upon which the fate of the American nation has hinged in those rare moments in which its future—indeed, its very existence—hung in the balance. The United States owes its independence to the assistance of France, which not only provided desperately needed material support and military power but which also—in its potential to support the war effort—incentivized the establishment of the political union between the thirteen colonies. The conquest of northern Mexico in the 1840s was facilitated by the Comanche raids that cleared the way as well as the hospitable international order overseen by a British Empire that had a vested interest in the economic growth of the United States. During the Civil War, it was Britain's decision to remain neutral that allowed Yankee power to overwhelm the slaveholders' rebellion. That London financiers kept their hands in their pockets during the conflict had the unintended consequence of hastening the rise of Wall Street, the basis of so much of the nation's future global power. Had Britain and the Soviet Union failed to withstand the Nazi onslaughts of 1940–1942, there might not have been an "American century"—at least not the one that we got.

As the United States stabilized at the end of each of these periods of crisis, the nation bore the indelible imprint of the pressures that had reshaped it. America emerged from periods of crisis with new forms of politics and economics that positioned it for the international environments that lay ahead. The founding documents of 1787 endowed the vulnerable, slaveholding republic with the central powers it needed to survive in a hostile world while retaining enough elements of home rule so as to minimize the threat of internal rebellion from a populace conditioned to be suspicious of government authority. The post-1865 antislavery nation sucked in immigrants and capital, particularly to its industrializing North and developing West, while erecting protective tariffs and engaging in the formal colonial expansion that characterized this age of global empires. The United States of the decades after 1945, in contrast, restricted immigration, exported capital, dismantled tariffs, and helped create new international institutions that advanced its interests in a postcolonial age. For all of today's talk about the enduring hold of America's exceptional political traditions, what most stands out when one takes the global view of its history is just the opposite—the United States has reconfigured, even reinvented, itself during moments of crisis.

IF HISTORY DOESN'T impart predictive powers to its students, it does provide a baseline for assessing and measuring the present. In this age of screaming pundits, celebrity politicians, and the 24/7 news cycle, it is more important than ever to step back from all the noise to take stock of what is going on. How serious are our current predicaments when seen in historical terms? In comparing our current troubles to past crises, striking commonalities emerge—and one all-important difference.

First, the similarities. As in the past, politics at home have been destabilized by changes in the international system that followed an American triumph. The victory in the Cold War in 1991 might well be one of those poisoned chalices to which the Duke of Wellington once referred. One thing is certain: the sudden implosion of Soviet-led communism transformed the international landscape, eliminating America's ideological rival while freeing up resources and political energy previously devoted to the half-century-long struggle. The American victory did not end history, as was rather bombastically declared at the time, but it did accelerate the globalization of liberal capitalism, which had been gaining momentum since the 1970s. What unfolded after 1991 was a global version of the opening of the American West in the 1860s: the sudden end of a long-running political stalemate led to a frenetic rush for profit. European critics of the United States connected these historical dots, bemoaning the expansion of America's "cowboy capitalism" in this age of "neoliberal" globalization. The world's markets rapidly integrated, capital flowed across borders, and human migration increased. As in the nineteenth century, this occurred at a time of innovations in communications and transportation, with the internet playing the role of the telegraph and ever-expanding airports and massive container ships providing the infrastructure of globalization that the railroads and steamships of the Victorian days did.[8]

As in the aftermath of those victories of the past, America's Cold War victory brought with it new burdens that existing political institutions have struggled to shoulder. The political system that won the Cold War has been tested by the new, post-1991 environment. America's military, national finances, and public opinion have showed signs of strain under the weight of the vast strategic commitments that are the price of global ascendance, while at home its citizens have become accustomed to Cold War dividends in the form of tax cuts. The attacks of September 11, 2001, exposed new vulnerabilities in national security while entangling the United States in seemingly unending conflicts in the Middle East—"forever wars," as they came to be called. Meanwhile, the global capitalism of the post–Cold War period deepened socioeconomic divides in America (and elsewhere), skewing the distribution of wealth to its most unequal since 1929. America's consumer society and ballooning deficits came to be financed by foreign capital, particularly from East Asia—and particularly from China, which in 2015 was the largest holder of the 40 percent of the US national debt that was held abroad. The situation is reminiscent of the nineteenth-century days in which the United States was a debtor to its greatest rival, then Great Britain.

Another pillar of the globalization of our era—the increase in immigration—heightened political tensions, helping to fuel a surge of populist nationalism and nativism that harkened back to previous eras of anti-immigrant sentiment, such as the Know-Nothing days of the 1850s and the national quota restrictions of the 1920s. As the percentage of the US population that is foreign-born climbed to 13.4 percent in 2015 (not far behind its historic high of 14.8 percent in 1890), the Republican Party's views on border walls shifted from "Mr. Gorbachev: Tear down this wall" to the "build that wall" chants of the election of 2016.[9]

The United States has struggled to adapt to post–Cold War globalization despite its leading role in creating it. Just as the relative absence of foreign threats intensified preexisting divisions over slavery after the Mexican War in the nineteenth century, the end of the Cold War brought to a boil the culture wars and partisan divisions that had been simmering since the 1960s and 1970s. The moral certitude that underlay the battle against Soviet totalitarianism came to be redirected to domestic opponents—literally so in the case of the curiously persistent political languages of anti-communism and antifascism, which twenty-first-century Americans hurl more often at one another than they do at foreign adversaries. The nation's once-dynamic political system has ground to a halt amid this partisan stalemate. The federal government is now seemingly unable to fulfill basic functions such as passing budgets and filling vacancies in the judiciary, let alone of creatively adapting to the new global situation in which we find ourselves. The post-2001 war on terror at times revived the shared national purpose of the Cold War, but on balance, it might have done more to deepen internal divisions, not to mention fray international alliances, given the contentious issues it raised concerning surveillance, civil liberties, and foreign wars. At the very moment that the United States has needed to look forward and outward, we have turned inward, nostalgically pining for a return to an imagined past, which is itself fractured along partisan lines.[10]

Nations across the world are showing similar signs of strain and internal political conflict as they try to keep up with the pace of change in this volatile age of globalization. Britain's "brexit" from the European Union—similarly fueled by a nativism that was a reaction to the 13.5 percent of the United Kingdom's population that was foreign-born in 2015—was as unexpected as the outcome of the 2016 election. Populist nationalism is on the rise across much of the rest of Europe too. The recent Arab Spring brings to mind the wave of revolutions that swept across Europe in 1848, as illiberal regimes are losing their grip as their people demand more representative government and economic opportunities. The world has been further destabilized by transnational terrorism, rogue states, the onset of the extreme weather patterns of climate change, and the return to a multipolar order most vividly demonstrated by the rise of an economically powerful, but a potentially unstable, China.

Transformative moments of crisis in the past have been international in scope: 1776 was part of the broader age of revolutions; the Civil War was but one instance of violent nation making in the mid-nineteenth century; the New Deal was the American response to a set of circumstances that elsewhere gave birth to fascism and empowered communism. It is the international dimensions of our current troubles that most suggest we are on the brink of a transformative shift in the underlying tectonic plates of the geopolitical system. As the world hurtles from one crisis to another, the limits of its international political integration become ever more apparent. The United Nations is ineffective, lacking the power to stabilize a volatile world order in ways reminiscent of the political impotence of the British Empire in North America after 1763. Other post-1945 institutions, such as NATO, were designed for a Cold War world that no longer exists. Even the Anglo-American "special relationship," a foundation of the post-1945 world order, is showing signs of strain as the demography, economy, and historical consciousness of both countries shifts in relation to new circumstances. As the Cold War world recedes in memory, the prospect increases that the foreign policy of the United States will revert to the traits that characterized its pre-1941 past: skepticism of international institutions, prioritization of national economic objectives over international ones, and—particularly in its moments of crisis—unexpected swings in policy.[11]

WHEN ONE EXAMINES the present from a geopolitical perspective, in sum, there are echoes of past moments of crisis and reconfiguration. But there is something missing in the comparison. The difference, so far, between our era and earlier periods of crisis is that our crises have been contained. The tremors have not yet erupted into one of those major quakes that forever transforms the landscape— at least not in the United States. For all the shock of 9/11, the 2007–2008 financial collapse, and the election of 2016, none of these crises are yet to cascade into one of those rare moments of which Lincoln spoke, when old dogmas of the past collapse and new practices emerge in their place. Ours has remained an era of gridlock, not transformation; of pendulum swings, not definitive turns. It is a period marked by the politics of personal destruction, not the creative destruction of political institutions.

Cracks have emerged in the pillars of American capitalism and constitutional democracy, but so far, they have remained standing. Despite the handicap of operating in a hyperpartisan environment, the much-maligned political establishment of our age has proven effective at cushioning blows. The national security state has prevented another attack on the scale of 9/11, insulating the nation from the flames that the forever wars have fanned in the Middle East. Monetary policy, stimulus legislation, and international coordination softened the crash landing from the financial crisis of 2007–2008. The federal bureaucracy and free press have thus far held in check those who seek to depart from long-held constitutional norms. But for all the success of the nation's leadership classes and state institutions, they have not had to confront a crisis on the scale of those most transformative moments of the past.

The crises of our era have not yet demanded anything approaching a full-scale renovation of the nation's political or economic system. It has been possible merely to rearrange the deck chairs of the ship of state, rather than overhauling the aging engines that are sputtering in the boiler room below deck. For all the length and tragedy of the wars that followed 9/11, the United States has waged them with minimal disruption to the majority of its citizens—in stark contrast to the destruction that US interventions have unleashed in Iraq and Afghanistan. The majority of Americans have not been asked to sacrifice; instead, as the members of America's volunteer military force shoulder an immense burden, there have been further payouts of the Cold War dividend in the form of tax cuts, particularly for the top decile of the population. A similar point can be made of the slow recovery that followed the 2007–2008 financial crisis, which hit low-wage earners the hardest. The nation's political and economic establishment has proven adept at cloistering itself, and its middle- and upper-class patrons, from the volatility of a fast-changing world by outsourcing sacrifice to others. The poor have cushioned the blows for the rich; the people of the Middle East have borne the brunt of America's national security policy. Meanwhile, the nation's finances, public institutions of education, and infrastructure are crumbling before our very eyes, as are the international alliances that underlay America's power in the second half of the twentieth century. Stormier waters may well lie ahead.[12]

However events unfold in the short term, one thing is a near certainty: there will be a time when the American nation again encounters a crisis that unleashes transformative changes. All of its citizens will have to make sacrifices in order for the nation to mobilize its full power. Furthermore, if the past is any indication, the outcome of the next crisis will be determined not only by the willingness of Americans to face it but also by the actions of those beyond the nation's borders as well as the foreign-born within them. At some point in the future, the United States will confront another Saratoga moment in which its fate hangs in the balance and it is not fully in control of the outcome. As we navigate our way through that crisis, whenever it may be, we would be well served to remember something that American history teaches us: the more we look outward, the more prepared we'll be.

Acknowledgments

THIS BOOK IS based on how I taught US history to students at Corpus Christi College in Oxford, England, the last fifteen years. What those mostly British and European students wanted to learn about American history was not what made the United States different from other nations but rather how it was connected to the wider world. I am sure that I learned more from the many hours of tutorial conversation with these students than they learned from me. I owe them all warm thanks. This book also draws from the emerging global turn in US historiography. The years since the end of the Cold War, especially those of the twenty-first century, have witnessed something of a revolution in the study of US history. This research speaks to our present moment in ways similar to how the revival of "history from below" helped to make sense of the social movements of the second half of the twentieth century. Without this academic scholarship, this book could not have been written.

I would like to thank several people who made this book possible. First, editor Dan Gerstle is an indomitable force. I consider it a great privilege to have worked with him, despite his poor taste in sports teams. Thanks also to Stephanie Summerhays and Theresa Winchell, who helped tug the manuscript into its final port. My colleagues at the Kinder Institute and History Department in Missouri have been generous and patient, especially Christa Dierksheide, Justin Dyer, Catherine Rymph, Skye Montgomery, Billy Coleman, Victor McFarland, Allison Smythe, and Thomas Kane. A special shout-out to Jeff Pasley, who not only shared his unmatched knowledge of the late eighteenth century but also was a great buddy throughout. I am fortunate to have the opportunity to work with the Kinder Foundation on behalf of the noble goal of regenerating our public institutions of higher education. Very helpful feedback on ideas within these pages came from Brian Schoen and the Missouri Regional Seminar on Early American History, Michael Heale, Kristin Hoganson, Tony Hopkins, John Darwin, Brian DeLay, Alyssa Reichardt, Gareth Davies, Daniel Immerwahr, Marc Palen, Alice Baumgartner, and Brooke Blower. Also deserving of thanks are all the Harmsworth professors since 1998, whose influence on my take on US history will be evident. Last but not least, the "gold rush trio" of David Goodman, Ben Mountford, and Steve Tuffnell helped me refine the argument during an epic road trip along the world's greatest drive: the stretch of I-70 between Denver, Colorado, and Columbia, Missouri, with a pit stop at the Cozy Inn in Salina, Kansas. All errors and omissions are my own.

My partner, Julie Wood, made this project possible in ways direct and indirect. She is the best. Finally, much love to Georgia and Stella, who fill me with optimism when I look to the future.

Notes

Introduction

1. "Declaration of Independence," 4 July 1776; Richard Hofstadter, *The Age of Reform* (New York: Vintage, 1955), 35–36.

2. Pauline Maier, *American Scripture: Making the Declaration of Independence* (New York: Knopf, 1997), esp. pp. 44, 126, 167; Peter S. Onuf, "A Declaration of Independence for Diplomatic Historians," *Diplomatic History* 22, no. 1 (Winter 1998): 71–83; David Armitage, *The Declaration of Independence: A Global History* (Cambridge, MA: Harvard University Press, 2007), 63–69; Eliga H. Gould, *Among the Powers of the Earth: The American Revolution and the Making of a New World Empire* (Cambridge, MA: Harvard University Press, 2012), 113–117.

3. Armitage, *The Declaration of Independence*, 12–13; Maier, *American Scripture*, 131; Alyssa Zuercher Reichardt, "War for the Interior: Imperial Conflict and the Formation of North American and Transatlantic Communications Infrastructure, 1727–1774" (PhD diss., Yale University, 2017).

4. Lee quoted in Jack N. Rakove, *The Beginnings of National Politics: An Interpretive History of the Continental Congress* (Baltimore: Johns Hopkins

University Press, 1982), 98; Adams quoted in Larrie D. Ferreiro, *Brothers at Arms: American Independence and the Men of France and Spain Who Saved It* (New York: Vintage, 2016), xxii; Thomas Paine, *Common Sense* (Philadelphia: W. & T. Bradford, 1776).

5. Elizabeth Cady Stanton, "Declaration of Sentiments"; Martin Luther King, "The Negro and the American Dream," Savannah, Georgia, 2 January 1961.

6. Eric Foner, *The Story of American Freedom* (New York: Norton, 1999); Sean Wilentz, *The Rise of American Democracy: Jefferson to Lincoln* (New York: Norton, 2005); Arthur M. Schlesinger Jr., *The Cycles of American History* (New York: Houghton Mifflin, 1986); Fred Anderson and Andrew Cayton, *The Dominion of War: Empire and Liberty in North America, 1500–2000* (New York: Penguin Books, 2005).

7. This book would not be possible to write were it not for the recent scholarship that situates US history in international context. Among the works that have shaped my thinking include Ian Tyrrell, "American Exceptionalism in an Age of International History," *American Historical Review* 96 (October 1991): 1031–1055; Amy Kaplan and Donald E. Pease, eds., *Cultures of United States Imperialism* (Durham, NC: Duke University Press, 1993); Daniel T. Rodgers, "Exceptionalism," *Imagined Histories: American Historians Interpret the Past*, ed. Anthony Molho and Gordon S. Wood (Princeton, NJ: Princeton University Press, 1998) 21–40; David Thelen, "The Nation and Beyond: Transnational Perspectives on United States History," *Journal of American History* 86, no. 3 (1999): 965–975; Jeffrey G. Williamson and Kevin O'Rourke, *Globalization and History: The Evolution of a Nineteenth-Century Atlantic Economy* (Cambridge, MA: MIT Press, 1999); A. G. Hopkins, ed., *Globalization in World History* (London: Pimlico, 2002); Thomas Bender, ed., *Rethinking American History in a Global Age* (Berkeley: University of California Press, 2002); Ira Katznelson and Martin Shefter, eds., *Shaped by War and Trade: International Influences on American Political Developments* (Princeton, NJ: Princeton University Press, 2002); Bender, *A Nation among Nations: America's Place in World History* (New York: Hill and Wang, 2006); Ian Tyrrell, *Transnational Nation: United States History in Global Perspective* (London: Palgrave Macmillan, 2007); Eric Rauchway, *Blessed Among Nations: How the World Made America* (New

York: Farrar, Straus and Giroux, 2007); Kristin Hoganson, "Where the National and Global Converge," *Passport: The Newsletter of the Society for Historians of American Foreign Relations* (2009); Paul A. Kramer, "Power and Connection: Imperial Histories of the United States in the World," *American Historical Review* 116 (2011): 1348–1391; Hoganson, "Twenty Years since the Imperial Turn: Time for Trans-imperial Histories," *American Historian* (2015); Brooke L. Blower and Mark Philip Bradley, eds., *The Familiar Made Strange: American Icons and Artifacts after the Transnational Turn* (Ithaca, NY: Cornell University Press, 2015); Andrew Preston and Douglas Charles Rossinow, eds., *Outside In: The Transnational Circuitry of US History* (New York: Oxford University Press, 2016); James Belich, John Darwin, Margret Frenz, and Chris Wickham, eds., *The Prospect of Global History* (Oxford: Oxford University Press, 2016); A. G. Hopkins, *American Empire: A Global History* (Princeton, NJ: Princeton University Press, 2018).

8. Clay quoted in David Hendrickson, *Union, Nation, or Empire: The American Debate over International Relations, 1789–1941* (Lawrence: University Press of Kansas, 2003), 119.

9. Paine, *Common Sense*.

10. For foreign-born percentages over time, see www.migrationpolicy .org/programs/data-hub/charts/immigrant-population-over-time.

11. Bell quoted in Robert Fox, ed., *We Were There: An Eyewitness History of the Twentieth Century* (New York: Overlook Press, 2010). For medical and nautical uses of "crisis" in the nineteenth century, see Adam I. P. Smith, *The Stormy Present: Conservatism and the Problem of Slavery in Northern Politics, 1846–1865* (Chapel Hill: University of North Carolina Press, 2017), 14–15.

12. William H. Seward, "The Union," 12 January 1861.

13. Washington quoted in Alan Taylor, *American Revolutions: A Continental History, 1750–1804* (New York: Norton, 2016), 168; Jeremy Bentham, "Short Review of the Declaration" (1776).

14. Franklin D. Roosevelt, "The President's Christmas Greeting to the Nation," 24 December 1940.

15. "While freedom can be achieved, it may also be taken away." Foner, *The Story of American Freedom*, xiv.

16. Abraham Lincoln, "Second Annual Message," 1 December 1862.

Chapter 1: An Unexpected Result

1. Thomas Paine, *Common Sense* (Philadelphia: W. & T. Bradford, 1776); Franklin quoted in Walter Isaacson, *Benjamin Franklin: An American Life* (New York: Simon and Schuster, 2003), 284; Jefferson draft of the Declaration reprinted in David Armitage, *The Declaration of Independence: A Global History* (Cambridge, MA: Harvard University Press, 2007), 157–164.

2. Herbert S. Klein, *A Population History of the United States*, 2nd ed. (New York: Cambridge University Press, 2012), 34–60; Richard Hofstadter, *America at 1750: A Social Portrait* (New York: Vintage, 1973), 5; Johnson quoted in Linda Colley, *Captives: Britain, Empire, and the World, 1600–1850* (London: Random House, 2002), 201.

3. Bernard Bailyn, *Voyagers to the West: A Passage in the Peopling of America on the Eve of the Revolution* (New York: Knopf, 1986), esp. p. 26; James Horn, "British Diaspora: Emigration from Britain, 1680–1815," in P. J. Marshall, ed., *The Oxford History of the British Empire*, vol. 2, *The Eighteenth Century* (Oxford: Oxford University Press, 1998), 32.

4. T. H. Breen and Timothy Hall, *Colonial America in an Atlantic World* (New York: Pearson, 2004), 302; Alan Taylor, *American Revolutions: A Continental History, 1750–1804* (New York: Norton, 2016), 25.

5. "The road to Americanization ran through Anglicization," see T. H. Breen, "An Empire of Goods: The Anglicization of Colonial America, 1690–1776," *Journal of British Studies* 25 (October 1986): 467–499; "fashions" quoted in Alan Taylor, *American Colonies* (New York: Viking, 2001), 313–314; John Dickinson, *The Political Writings of John Dickinson* (Wilmington, DE: Bonsal and Niles, 1801), 119; see also the essays in honor of John Murrin in Ignacio Gallup-Diaz, Andrew Shankman, and David J. Silverman, eds., *Anglicizing America: Empire, Revolution, Republic* (Philadelphia: University of Pennsylvania Press, 2015).

6. London paper quoted in Bailyn, *Voyagers to the West*, 42; Young quoted in Hofstadter, *America at 1750*, 31; Benjamin Franklin, *Observations Concerning the Increase of Mankind, Peopling of Countries, etc.* (1751).

7. P. J. Marshall, *The Making and Unmaking of Empires: Britain, India, and America, c.1750–1783* (Oxford: Oxford University Press, 2005), 326–330.

8. Quote from Taylor, *American Colonies*, 424; Richard White, *The Middle Ground: Indians, Empires, and Republics in the Great Lakes Region, 1650–1815* (New York: Cambridge University Press, 1991).

9. John Darwin, *After Tamerlane: The Global History of Empire* (London: Allen Lane, 2007), 168–172. For Frederick the Great, see p. 169.

10. For the Seven Years' War, see Fred Anderson, *Crucible of War: The Seven Years' War and the Fate of Empire in British North America, 1754–1766* (New York: Knopf, 2007); Franklin quoted in Richard W. Van Alstyne, *The Rising American Empire* (New York: Norton, 1960), 26.

11. John H. Elliott, *Empires of the Atlantic World: Britain and Spain in America, 1492–1830* (New Haven, CT: Yale University Press, 2006), 301, 305; Taylor, *American Revolutions,* 51.

12. Justin Du Rivage, *Revolution against Empire: Taxes, Politics, and the Origins of American Independence* (New Haven, CT: Yale University Press, 2017); Pitt quoted in Elliot, *Empires of the Atlantic World,* 318.

13. Robert M. Calhoon, *The Loyalists in Revolutionary America, 1760–1781* (New York: Harcourt Brace, 1973); Marylander quoted in Taylor, *American Revolutions,* 216.

14. Andrew J. O'Shaughnessy, *An Empire Divided: The American Revolution and the British Caribbean* (Philadelphia: University of Pennsylvania Press, 2000); Taylor, *American Revolutions,* 144–146; A. G. Hopkins, *The American Empire: A Global History* (Princeton, NJ: Princeton University Press, 2018), 121.

15. Gordon Wood, *The Radicalism of the American Revolution* (New York: Vintage, 1993); Carleton quoted in D. W. Meinig, *The Shaping of America: A Geographical Perspective on 500 Years of History,* vol. 1, *Atlantic America, 1492–1800* (New Haven, CT: Yale University Press, 1986), 303.

16. Elliott, *Empires of the Atlantic World,* 319.

17. Bernard Bailyn, *The Ideological Origins of the American Revolution* (Cambridge, MA: Harvard University Press, 1967); "Moving forward while facing backward" is the phrase of William F. Buckley Jr., quoted in Adam I. P. Smith, *The Stormy Present: Conservatism and the Problem of Slavery in Northern Politics* (Chapel Hill: University of North Carolina Press, 2017), 227; "loyal subjects" from Brendan McConville, *The King's Three Faces: The Rise and Fall of Royal America, 1688–1776* (Chapel Hill: University of North Carolina Press, 2006), 255.

18. Jack P. Greene, *The Quest for Power: The Lower Houses of Assembly in the Southern Royal Colonies, 1689–1776* (New York: Norton, 1963); Alyssa Zuercher Reichardt, "War for the Interior: Imperial Conflict and the Formation of North American and Transatlantic Communications Infrastructure, 1727–1774" (PhD diss., Yale University, 2017).

19. T. H. Breen, *The Marketplace of Revolution: How Consumer Politics Shaped American Independence* (New York: Oxford University Press, 2005), xvi; Adams quoted in Taylor, *American Revolutions*, 105; Stockton quoted in Mary Beth Norton, *Liberty's Daughters: The Revolutionary Experience of American Women, 1750–1800* (Ithaca, NY: Cornell University Press, 1996), 171.

20. Michael A. McDonnell, *The Politics of War: Race, Class, and Conflict in Revolutionary Virginia* (Chapel Hill: University of North Carolina Press, 2012); Alan Taylor, *The Internal Enemy: Slavery and War in Virginia, 1772–1832* (New York: Norton, 2013); Paul Finkelman, *Slavery and the Founders: Race and Liberty in the Age of Jefferson* (New York: Sharpe, 2001). For political violence in this period, see Holger Hoock, *Scars of Independence: America's Violent Birth* (New York: Crown, 2017).

21. Paine, *Common Sense*; David M. Fitzsimons, "Tom Paine's New World Order: Idealistic Internationalism in the Ideology of Early American Foreign Relations," *Diplomatic History* 19, no. 4 (September 1995): 569–582; Eric Foner, *Tom Paine and Revolutionary America* (New York: Oxford University Press, 1977).

22. David Armitage, *Civil Wars: A History in Ideas* (New York: Knopf, 2017), 134–147.

23. Jonathan R. Dull, *The French Navy and American Independence: A Study of Arms and Diplomacy, 1774–1787* (Princeton, NJ: Princeton University Press, 1976); Sandwich quoted in John Brewer, *The Sinews of Power: War, Money, and the English State, 1688–1783* (Cambridge, MA: Harvard University Press, 1990), 177.

24. Franklin quoted in Larrie D. Ferreiro, *Brothers at Arms: American Independence and the Men of France and Spain Who Saved It* (New York: Vintage Books, 2016), xvi; Lee quoted in Jack N. Rakove, *The Beginnings of National Politics: An Interpretive History of the Continental Congress* (Baltimore: Johns Hopkins University Press, 1982), 98.

25. Peter S. Onuf, "A Declaration of Independence for Diplomatic Historians," *Diplomatic History* 22, no. 1 (1998): 71–83; David C. Hendrickson, *Union, Nation, or Empire: The American Debate over International Relations, 1789–1941* (Lawrence: University Press of Kansas, 2009).

26. Armitage, *The Declaration of Independence*, esp. pp. 64–66, which stresses the significance at the time of the first and final paragraphs of the

Declaration, and Howe quoted on p. 73; Eliga Gould, *Among the Powers of the Earth: The American Revolution and the Making of a New World Empire* (Cambridge, MA: Harvard University Press, 2012).

27. "Unprecedented" in Richard M. Ketchum, *Saratoga: Turning Point of America's Revolutionary War* (New York: Henry Holt, 1997), 437; Franklin quoted in Isaacson, *Benjamin Franklin*, 343; Vergennes quoted in C. H. Van Tyne, "Influences which Determined the French Government to Make the Treaty with America, 1778," *American Historical Review* 21, no. 3 (April 1916): 528–541.

28. For this interpretation of the Articles, see Du Rivage, *Revolution Against Empire*, 221–225 (Adams quoted on p. 222); "more than any other" quoted in Merrill Jensen, *The Articles of Confederation: An Interpretation of the Social-Constitutional History of the American Revolution, 1774–1781* (Madison: University of Wisconsin Press, 1940), 184.

29. Marshall, *The Making and Unmaking of Empires*.

30. George Washington, "Circular Letter of Farewell to the Army," 8 June 1783; Maya Jasanoff, *Liberty's Exiles: The Loss of America and the Remaking of the British Empire* (London: Harper Press, 2011); John Steele Gordon, *Hamilton's Blessing: The Extraordinary Life and Times of Our National Debt* (New York: Bloomsbury, 2010).

31. Knox quoted in Frederick W. Marks III, *Independence on Trial: Foreign Affairs and the Making of the Constitution* (Baton Rouge: Louisiana State University Press, 1973), 176.

32. Jay quoted in Peter Onuf, "The Expanding Union," in *Devising Liberty: Preserving and Creating Freedom in the New American Republic*, ed. David T. Konig (Stanford, CA: Stanford University Press, 1995), 50–80.

33. *Federalist 14*; David Hendrickson, *Peace Pact: The Lost World of the American Founding* (Lawrence: University Press of Kansas, 2003).

34. Madison quoted in Walter LaFeber, "The Constitution and Foreign Policy: An Interpretation," *Journal of American History* 74, no. 3 (December 1987): 697.

35. *Federalist 42*; Max Edling, *A Revolution in Favor of Government: Origins of the US Constitution and the Making of the American State* (New York: Oxford University Press, 2003).

36. *Federalist 11*; Jefferson quoted in Drew R. McCoy, *The Elusive Republic: Political Economy in Jeffersonian America* (Chapel Hill: University of

North Carolina Press, 1980), 132; Edling, *A Revolution in Favor of Government*, 209–210.

37. Max Edling, *A Hercules in the Cradle: War, Money, and the American State, 1783–1867* (Chicago: University of Chicago Press, 2014), esp. p. 83; Hamilton quoted on Mira Wilkins, *The History of Foreign Investment in the United States to 1914* (Cambridge, MA: Harvard University Press, 1989), 45.

38. Gaillard Hunt, ed., *The Writings of James Madison: 1787–1790* (New York: G. P. Putnam's Sons, 1904), 436–437.

39. Jeffrey L. Pasley, *The First Presidential Contest: 1796 and the Founding of American Democracy* (Lawrence: University Press of Kansas, 2013), 370; George Washington, "Farewell Address," 19 September 1796.

40. Hans-Jurgen Grabbe, "European Immigration to the United States in the Early National Period, 1783–1820," *Proceedings of the American Philosophical Society* 133, no. 2 (June, 1989): 194; Gordon S. Wood, *Empire of Liberty: A History of the Early Republic, 1789–1815* (New York: Oxford University Press, 2009), 247–250.

41. Thomas Jefferson to James Madison, 30 January 1787, *Papers of Thomas Jefferson*.

42. For Jefferson's thought, see Peter Onuf, *Jefferson's Empire: The Language of American Nationhood* (Charlottesville: University Press of Virginia, 2000).

43. Bethel Saler, *The Settlers' Empire: Colonialism and State Formation in America's Old Northwest* (Philadelphia: University of Pennsylvania Press, 2015), 28; Patrick Griffin, *American Leviathan: Empire, Nation, and Revolutionary Frontier* (New York: Hill and Wang, 2007).

44. Quoted in Marks, *Independence on Trial*, 207.

45. R. R. Palmer, *The Age of the Democratic Revolution* (Princeton, NJ: Princeton University Press, 1969); Lester Langley, *The Americas in the Age of Revolution, 1750-1850* (New Haven, CT: Yale University Press, 1996).

46. George Washington, "Farewell Address," 19 September 1796.

47. James Monroe, "Annual Message to Congress," 2 December 1823; Clay quoted in Jay Sexton, *The Monroe Doctrine: Empire and Nation in Nineteenth-Century America* (New York: Hill and Wang, 2011), 73.

48. Frank Thistlethwaite, *The Anglo-American Connection in the Early Nineteenth-Century* (Philadelphia, 1959); Ralph W. Hidy, The *House of*

Baring in American Trade and Finance: English Merchant Bankers at Work, 1763–1861 (Cambridge, MA: Harvard University Press, 1949); A. G. Hopkins, "The United States, 1783–1861: Britain's Honorary Dominion?" *Britain and the World* 4, no. 2 (2011): 232–246; Jay Sexton, "The United States in the British Empire," in *The Oxford History of the British Empire, Companion Series: British North American in the Seventeenth and Eighteenth Centuries,* ed. Stephen Foster (Oxford: Oxford University Press, 2013), 318–348.

49. Darwin, *After Tamerlane,* 172–173.

50. Pinckney quoted in Robert Bonner, *Mastering America: Southern Slaveholders and the Crisis of American Nationhood* (New York: Cambridge University Press, 2009), 6.

51. David Waldstreicher, *Slavery's Constitution: From Revolution to Ratification* (New York: Hill and Wang, 2010), 3; Don E. Fehrenbacher, *The Slaveholding Republic: An Account of the United States Government's Relations to Slavery* (New York: Oxford University Press, 2001), 15–48 (Wilson quoted on p. 38).

52. John Craig Hammond, "'Uncontrollable Necessity': The Local Politics, Geopolitics, and Sectional Politics of Slavery Expansion," in *Contesting Slavery: The Politics of Bondage and Freedom in the New American Nation,* ed. John Craig Hammond and Matthew Mason (Charlottesville: University of Virginia Press, 2011), 138–160.

Chapter 2: The Wrecking Ball

1. Abraham Lincoln, "Second Inaugural Address," 4 March 1865.

2. Lincoln, "House Divided," 16 June 1858; Brown quoted in Robert E. May, *The Southern Dream of a Caribbean Empire, 1854–1861* (Baton Rouge: Louisiana State University Press, 1973), 9.

3. Karl Marx and Friedrich Engels, *The Communist Manifesto* (1848).

4. For the traditional argument, see Eugene Genovese, *The Political Economy of Slavery: Studies in the Economy and Society of the Slave South* (New York: Pantheon Books, 1964). For the South and capitalism, see Sven Beckert, *Empire of Cotton: A Global History* (New York: Knopf, 2014); Edward Baptist, *The Half Has Never Been Told: Slavery and the Making of American Capitalism* (New York: Basic Books, 2014); Walter Johnson, *River of Dark Dreams: Slavery and Empire in the Cotton Kingdom* (Cambridge, MA: Belknap Press, 2013).

5. Population and cotton figures from Peter Kolchin, *American Slavery: 1619–1877*, rev. ed. (New York: Hill and Wang, 2003), 93–95; "forced removals" from Baptist, *The Half Has Never Been Told*, xxiii; James Henry Hammond, "Cotton is King," 4 March 1858.

6. Beckert, *Empire of Cotton*, figures on p. 243, "alarming" quote on p. 120; one-fifth from *Economist*, 21 May 1853.

7. Baptist, *The Half Has Never Been Told*, 248. William G. Thomas, *The Iron Way: Railroads, the Civil War, and the Making of Modern America* (New Haven, CT: Yale University Press, 2011), 36; Jay Sexton, *Debtor Diplomacy: Finance and American Foreign Relations in the Civil War Era, 1837–1873* (Oxford: Oxford University Press, 2005), 70.

8. Robert Bonner, *Mastering America: Southern Slaveholders and the Crisis of American Nationhood* (New York: Cambridge University Press, 2009); Paul Quigley, *Shifting Grounds: Nationalism and the American South, 1848–1865* (New York: Oxford University Press, 2012); Matthew Karp, *This Vast Southern Empire: Slaveholders at the Helm of American Foreign Policy* (Cambridge, MA: Harvard University Press, 2016).

9. Mexican abolition became effective in 1837, not 1829 as is often thought. See Andrew J. Torget, *Seeds of Empire: Cotton, Slavery, and the Transformation of the Texas Borderlands, 1800–1850* (Chapel Hill: University Press of North Carolina, 2015), 205n26; Alice Baumgartner, "The Mexican-American War," *Cambridge History of America and the World*, vol. 2 (New York: Cambridge University Press, forthcoming).

10. David Walker, *An Appeal to the Coloured Citizens of the World* (1829); Betty Fladeland, *Men and Brothers: Anglo-American Antislavery Cooperation* (Champaign: University of Illinois Press, 1972); Van Gosse, ' "As a Nation, the English Are Our Friends': The Emergence of African American Politics in the British Atlantic World, 1772–1861," *American Historical Review* 113, no. 4 (October 2008): 1003–1028; Edward B. Rugemer, *The Problem of Emancipation: The Caribbean Roots of the American Civil War* (Baton Rouge: Louisiana State University Press, 2008), "slave question" quote on p. vii.

11. Tyler quoted in Jay Sexton, *The Monroe Doctrine: Empire and Nation in Nineteenth-Century America* (New York: Hill and Wang, 2011), 89–90.

12. Joel Silbey, *Storm over Texas: The Annexation Controversy and the Road to Civil War* (New York: Oxford University Press, 2005); Calhoun's speech in *Papers of John C. Calhoun*, ed. Clyde N. Wilson and Shirley B. Cooke,

vol. 15, *1847–1848* (Columbia: University of South Carolina Press), 401–421.

13. For a comprehensive new history of abolition, see Manisha Sinha, *The Slave's Cause: A History of Abolition* (New Haven, CT: Yale University Press, 2016).

14. William W. Freehling, *The Road to Disunion*, vol. 1, *Secessionists at Bay, 1776–1854* (New York: Oxford University Press, 1991); David Brown, *Southern Outcast: Hinton Rowan Helper and the Impending Crisis of the South* (Baton Rouge: Louisiana State University Press, 2006); Karp, *This Vast Southern Empire*; May, *The Southern Dream of a Caribbean Empire.*

15. Clay quoted in Richard Carwardine, *Evangelicals and Politics in Antebellum America* (Knoxville: University of Tennessee Press, 1993), 323; reporter quoted in C. C. Goen, *Broken Churches, Broken Nation: Denominational Schisms and the Coming of the American Civil War* (Macon, GA: Mercer University Press, 1985). There were exceptions, of course, namely the Episcopalian and Catholic churches.

16. Illinois wheat in Don Fehrenbacher, *Prelude to Greatness: Lincoln in the 1850s* (Palo Alto, CA: Stanford University Press, 1962), 7–8; Thomas, *The Iron Way*, 52–53; Thomas P. Martin, "Cotton and Wheat in Anglo-American Trade and Politics, 1846–1852," *Journal of Southern History* 1 (August 1935): 293–319.

17. "Slap John Bull" quoted in Reginald C. McGrane, *Foreign Bondholders and American State Debts* (New York: Macmillan, 1935), 34; Sexton, *Debtor Diplomacy*, 69–78.

18. George Rogers Taylor, *The Transportation Revolution, 1815–1860* (New York: Holt, Rinehart and Winston, 1951); railroad mileage from Kevin Hillstrom and Laurie Collier Hillstrom, *Industrial Revolution in America: Iron and Steel* (Santa Barbara, CA: ABC-CLIO, 2005), 13; Mary D. McFeely and William S. McFeely, eds., *Personal Memoirs of U.S. Grant: Selected Letters, 1839–1865* (New York: Library of America, 1990), 774; Richard John, *Spreading the News: The American Postal System from Franklin to Morse* (Cambridge, MA: Harvard University Press, 1995).

19. Seward in *Congressional Globe*, 32nd Congress, 2nd Session, Appendix, 127; Philip S. Foner, *Business and Slavery: The New York Merchants and the Irrepressible Conflict* (Chapel Hill: University of North Carolina Press, 1941); Abraham Lincoln, "Inaugural Address," 4 March 1861.

20. For a dismantling of the tariff-caused-the-war myth with helpful references, see Marc-William Palen, "Debunking the Civil War Tariff Myth," *Imperial & Global Forum* (blog), 2 March 2015, https://imperialglobalexeter .com/2015/03/02/debunking-the-civil-war-tariff-myth/.

21. William Freehling, *Prelude to Civil War: The Nullification Controversy in South Carolina, 1816–1836* (New York: Harper and Row, 1966).

22. See the comments of Alfred Eckes in H-Diplo Roundtable XVII, 16, on *The "Conspiracy" of Free Trade: The Anglo-American Struggle over Empire and Economic Globalisation, 1846–1896* at https://networks.h-net.org/system /files/contributed-files/roundtable-xviii-16.pdf.

23. Marc-William Palen, "Global Ideologies: Economic Nationalism and Free-Trade Cosmopolitanism, c. 1846–1860," chap. 1 in *The "Conspiracy" of Free Trade: The Anglo-American Struggle over Empire and Economic Globalisation, 1846–1896* (Cambridge: Cambridge University Press, 2016); *The Economist*, 5 May 1849.

24. Michael F. Holt, *The Political Crisis of the 1850s* (New York: Norton, 1978), 111.

25. For the political economy of the Deep South, see Brian Schoen, *The Fragile Fabric of Union: Cotton, Federal Politics, and the Global Origins of the Civil War* (Baltimore: Johns Hopkins University Press, 2009). Engels quoted on p. 225.

26. Fitzhugh quoted in Nicholas Greenwood Onuf and Peter S. Onuf, *Nations, Markets, and War: Modern History and the American Civil War* (Charlottesville: University of Virginia Press, 2006), 328; John Majewski, *Modernizing a Slave Economy: The Economic Vision of the Confederate Nation* (Chapel Hill: University of North Carolina Press, 2009).

27. Greeley quoted in Eric Foner, *Free Soil, Free Labor, Free Men: The Ideology of the Republican Party before the Civil War* (New York: Oxford University Press, 1971), 27.

28. New Yorker quoted in Kenneth Stampp, *American in 1857: A Nation on the Brink* (New York: Oxford University Press, 1990), 233; Yankee editor quoted in James L. Huston, *The Panic of 1857 and the Coming of the Civil War* (Baton Rouge: Louisiana State University Press, 1987), 146.

29. Lincoln, "The Perpetuation of Our Political Institutions," address to the Young Men's Lyceum in Springfield, Illinois, 27 January 1838; A. E.

Campbell, "An Excess of Isolation: Isolation and the American Civil War," *Journal of Southern History* 29, no. 2 (May 1963): 161–174.

30. For nationalism in this period, see David Waldstreicher, *In the Midst of Perpetual Fetes: The Making of American Nationalism, 1776–1820* (Chapel Hill: University of North Carolina Press, 1997); Nicole Eustace, *1812: War and the Passions of Patriotism* (Philadelphia: University of Pennsylvania Press, 2012).

31. "War against Mexico," in Daniel Walker Howe, *What Hath God Wrought: The Transformation of America, 1815–1848* (New York: Oxford University Press, 2007), chap. 19 title; Pekka Hamalainen, *The Comanche Empire* (New Haven, CT: Yale University Press, 2008); Brian DeLay, *War of a Thousand Deserts: Indian Raids and the U.S.-Mexican War* (New Haven, CT: Yale University Press, 2008).

32. Aims McGuinness, *Path of Empire: Panama and the California Gold Rush* (Ithaca, NY: Cornell University Press, 2008); William Earl Weeks, *Dimensions of the Early American Empire, 1754–1865* (New York: Cambridge University Press, 2013); Peter A. Shulman, *Coal and Empire: The Birth of Energy Security in Industrial America* (Baltimore: Johns Hopkins University Press, 2015).

33. Polk as slaveholder in William Dusinberre, *Slavemaster President: The Double Career of James Polk* (New York: Oxford University Press, 2003), esp. p. 19; Comanche population in Hamalainen, *The Comanche Empire*; Southern conclusions from this period in Schoen, *The Fragile Fabric of Union*, esp. p. 9.

34. Quoted in William Gienapp, "The Republican Party and the Slave Power," in *New Perspectives on Race and Slavery in America: Essays in Honor of Kenneth M. Stampp*, ed. Robert H. Abzug and Stephen E. Maizlish (Lexington: University of Kentucky Press, 1986), 64.

35. Second Lincoln-Douglas debate, Freeport, Illinois, 27 August 1858; Robert E. May, *Slavery, Race, and Conquest in the Tropics: Lincoln, Douglas, and the Future of Latin America* (New York: Cambridge University Press, 2013).

36. Wilmot quoted in Baumgartner, "The Mexican-American War," *Cambridge History of America in the World*, vol 2 (forthcoming); Emerson quoted in James McPherson, *Battle Cry of Freedom: The Civil War Era* (New York: Oxford University Press, 1988), 47–77.

37. Webster quoted in Michael F. Holt, *The Rise and Fall of the American Whig Party: Jacksonian Politics and the Onset of the Civil War* (New York: Oxford University Press, 1999), 601; Timothy Mason Roberts, *Distant Revolutions: 1848 and the Challenge to American Exceptionalism* (Charlottesville: University of Virginia Press, 2009), 134–139; Andre Fleche, *Revolution of 1861: The American Civil War in the Age of Nationalist Conflict* (Chapel Hill: University of North Carolina Press, 2012). For the importance of political languages, see Elizabeth R. Varon, *Disunion! The Coming of the American Civil War, 1789–1859* (Chapel Hill: University of North Carolina Press, 2008).

38. William H. Seward, "Some Thoughts for the President's Consideration," 1 April 1861; Dean Mahin, *One War at a Time: The International Dimensions of the American Civil War* (Dulles, VA: Brassey's, 1999).

39. Carwardine, *Evangelicals and Politics*, 199. "It is seldom realized that, proportionately, this was the heaviest influx of immigrants in American history," David Potter, *The Impending Crisis, 1848–1861* (New York: Harper and Row, 1976), 241.

40. Hidetaka Hirota, *Expelling the Poor: Atlantic Seaboard States and the Nineteenth-Century Origins of American Immigration Policy* (New York: Oxford University Press, 2017).

41. Tyler Anbinder, *Nativism and Slavery: The Northern Know-Nothings and the Politics of the 1850s* (New York: Oxford University Press, 1992).

42. William Gienapp, *The Origins of the Republican Party, 1852–1856* (New York: Oxford University Press, 1988); Lincoln quoted in David Donald, *Lincoln* (New York: Simon and Schuster, 1995), 189; Gienapp, "Who Voted for Lincoln," in *Abraham Lincoln and the American Political Tradition*, ed. John L. Thomas (Amherst: University of Massachusetts Press, 1986).

43. Toombs to Yancey, Rost, and Mann, 16 March 1861, in James Richardson, ed., *Messages and Papers of the Confederacy*, vol. 2 (Nashville: United States Publishing Company, 1906), 3–8. For secession as statecraft, see Schoen, *The Fragile Fabric of Union*.

44. Carl Lawrence Paulus, *The Slaveholding Crisis: Fear of Insurrection and the Coming of the Civil War* (Baton Rouge: Louisiana State University Press, 2017).

45. David Brion Davis, *Inhuman Bondage: The Rise and Fall of Slavery in the New World* (New York: Oxford University Press, 2006), 205–230.

46. For runaways, the following draws from Eugene D. Genovese, *Roll, Jordan, Roll: The World the Slaves Made* (New York: Pantheon, 1972), 648–657, and John Hope Franklin and Loren Schweninger, *Runaway Slaves: Rebels on the Plantation* (New York: Oxford University Press, 1999).

47. Solomon Northup, *Twelve Years a Slave* (1855), 240.

48. Ex-slave quoted in Genovese, *Roll, Jordan, Roll,* 649.

49. Eric Foner, *Gateway to Freedom: The Hidden History of the Underground Railroad* (New York: W. W. Norton, 2015); R. J. M. Blackett, "Dispossessing Massa: Fugitive Slaves and the Politics of Slavery after 1850," *American Nineteenth Century History* 10 (June 2009): 119–136; Blackett, *The Captive's Quest for Freedom: Fugitive Slaves, the 1850 Fugitive Slave Law, and the Politics of Slavery* (New York: Cambridge University Press, 2018).

50. Michael E. Woods, "'Tell Us Something about State Rights': Northern Republicans, States' Rights, and the Coming of the Civil War," *Journal of the Civil War Era* 7, no. 2 (June 2017): 242–268; Frederick Douglass, "The Fugitive Slave Law," speech to the National Free Soil Convention at Pittsburgh, 11 August 1852.

51. Lincoln to Andrew Johnson, 26 March 1863, *Collected Works of Abraham Lincoln,* vol. 6, ed. Roy P. Basler (New Brunswick, NJ: Rutgers University Press, 1953), 149–150; William W. Freehling, *The South vs. The South: How Anti-Confederate Southerners Shaped the Course of the Civil War* (New York: Oxford University Press, 2002), chaps. 6–8.

Chapter 3: The Last Best Hope of Earth

1. Abraham Lincoln, "Special Session Message," 4 July 1861; "Second Annual Address," 1 December 1862; "Gettysburg Address," 19 November 1863; Gabor Boritt, *The Gettysburg Gospel: The Lincoln That Nobody Knows* (New York: Simon and Schuster, 2006), 256–286.

2. For the global politics of this period, see John Darwin, *After Tamerlane: The Global History of Empire* (London: Allen Lane, 2007), chap. 5; Michael Geyer and Charles Bright, "Global Violence and Nationalizing Wars in Eurasia and America: The Geopolitics of War in the Mid-Nineteenth Century," *Comparative Studies in Society and History* 38 (October 1996): 619–657; David T. Gleeson and Simon Lewis, *The Civil War as Global Conflict* (Columbia: University of South Carolina Press, 2014); Jörg Nagler, Don

Doyle, and Marcus Gräser, eds., *The Transnational Significance of the American Civil War* (London: Palgrave Macmillan, 2016); Don Doyle, ed., *American Civil Wars: The United States, Latin America, Europe, and the Crisis of the 1860s* (Chapel Hill: University of North Carolina Press, 2017).

3. Herbert S. Klein, *A Population History of the United States*, 2nd ed. (New York: Cambridge University Press, 2012), 96; Peabody quoted in Jay Sexton, *Debtor Diplomacy: Finance and American Foreign Relations in the Civil War, 1837–1873* (Oxford: Oxford University Press, 2005), 79.

4. Seward quoted in Andre Fleche, *Revolution of 1861: The American Civil War in the Age of Nationalist Conflict* (Chapel Hill: University of North Carolina Press, 2012), 70, 73. For the cultural connections between the South and Britain, see Alison Skye Montgomery, "Imagined Families: Anglo-American Kinship and the Formation of Southern Identity, 1830-1890" (PhD diss., University of Oxford, 2016).

5. *NYT* quoted in Don Doyle, *The Cause of All Nations: An International History of the American Civil War* (New York: Basic Books, 2014), 106.

6. Thomas Schoonover, *Dollars Over Dominion: The Triumph of Liberalism in Mexican-United States Relations, 1861–1867* (Baton Rouge: Louisiana State University Press, 1978); Doyle, ed., *American Civil Wars*; Patrick J. Kelly, "The North American Crisis of the 1860s," *The Journal of the Civil War Era* 2, no. 3 (September 2012): 337–368.

7. Sheridan quoted in D. P. Crook, *The North, the South and the Powers, 1861–1865* (London: John Wiley & Sons, 1974), 262; Romero quoted in Doyle, *The Cause of All Nations*, 127.

8. Cobden quoted in Marc-William Palen, *The "Conspiracy" of Free Trade: The Anglo-American Struggle over Empire and Economic Globalisation, 1846–1896* (Cambridge, Cambridge University Press, 2016), 40. For British public opinion, the starting point remains R. J. M. Blackett, *Divided Hearts: Britain and the American Civil War* (Baton Rouge: Louisiana State University Press, 2001).

9. Frank Owsley, *King Cotton Diplomacy: Foreign Relations of the Confederate States of America*, 3rd ed. (Tuscaloosa: University of Alabama Press, 2008); Rathbone quoted in Sven Beckert, *Empire of Cotton: A Global History* (New York: Knopf, 2014), 248.

10. James McPherson, *Crossroads of Freedom: Antietam, the Battle That Change the Course of the Civil War* (New York: Oxford University Press,

2002); Pam quoted in Howard Jones, *Blue and Gray Diplomacy: A History of Union and Confederate Foreign Relations* (Chapel Hill: University of North Carolina Press, 2010), 218.

11. Sir George Cornwall Lewis, "Recognition of the Independence of the Southern States of the North American Union," 7 November 1862, Gladstone Papers, Add. MSS 44,595, vol. 510, British Library; Howard Jones, *Union in Peril: The Crisis over British Intervention in the Civil War* (Chapel Hill: University of North Carolina Press, 1992), 181–230.

12. *Times* quoted in Joseph Fry, *Dixie Looks Abroad: The South and U.S. Foreign Relations, 1789–1973* (Baton Rouge: Louisiana State University Press, 2002), 82; Lyons quoted in Phillip E. Meyers, *Caution and Cooperation: The American Civil War in British-American Relations* (Kent, OH: Kent State University Press, 2008), 190.

13. "Every people" quoted in Fleche, *Revolution of 1861*, 89; Russell quoted in Meyers, *Caution and Cooperation*, 190; Richard Huzzey, *Freedom Burning: Anti-Slavery and Empire in Victorian Britain* (Ithaca, NY: Cornell University Press, 2012). For Gladstone's views, see Peter Parish, "Gladstone and America," in *Gladstone*, ed. Peter Jagger (London: Hambledon, 1998).

14. Phillip Buckner, "British North America and a Continent in Dissolution: The American Civil War in the Making of Canadian Confederation," *Journal of the Civil War Era* 7, no. 4 (December 2017): 512–540; Gary B. Magee and Andrew S. Thompson, *Empire and Globalisation: Networks of People, Goods and Capital in the British World, c. 1850–1914* (Cambridge: Cambridge University Press, 2010), 173.

15. Sven Beckert, "Emancipation and Empire: Reconstructing the Worldwide Web of Cotton Production," *American Historical Review* 109 (2004): 1405–1438.

16. The South's structural disadvantages are discussed in Douglas B. Ball, *Financial Failure and Confederate Defeat* (Urbana: University of Illinois Press, 1991), figures from p. 23.

17. Bird quoted in D. P. Crook, *The North, the South, and the Powers, 1861–1865* (London: John Wiley & Sons, 1974), 40.

18. Richard Franklin Bensel, *Yankee Leviathan: The Origins of Central State Authority in America, 1859–1877* (Cambridge: Cambridge University Press, 1990).

19. "Niagara" quote in Melinda Lawson, *Patriot Fires: Forging a New American Nationalism in the Civil War North* (Lawrence: University Press of Kansas, 2002), 21.

20. Max Edling, *A Hercules in the Cradle: War, Money, and the American State, 1783–1867* (Chicago: University of Chicago Press, 2014), 178.

21. Quotes from Sexton, *Debtor Diplomacy*, 79, 96; *The Economist*, 18 January 1862, 57.

22. Alfred E. Eckes Jr., *Opening America's Market: U.S. Foreign Trade Policy Since 1776* (Chapel Hill: University of North Carolina Press, 1990), 28; Henry C. Carey to Abraham Lincoln, 20 June 1861, http://civilwarcause.com /carey/Carey7.html; *Harpers* quoted in Heather Cox Richardson, *The Greatest Nation on Earth: Republican Economic Policies during the Civil War* (Cambridge, MA: Harvard University Press, 1997), 126.

23. Lunch counter in John Steele Gordon, *The Great Game: A History of Wall Street* (London: Orion, 1999), 97; David K. Thomson, "'Like a Cord through the Whole Country': Union Bonds and Financial Mobilization for Victory," *Journal of the Civil War Era* 6, no. 3 (September 2016): 347–375.

24. Walter LaFeber, *The New Empire: An Interpretation of American Expansion, 1860–1898* (Ithaca, NY: Cornell University Press, 1963); Sven Beckert, *The Monied Metropolis: New York City and the Consolidation of the American Bourgeoisie, 1850–1896* (New York: Cambridge University Press, 2001).

25. Figures from Allen C. Guelzo, *Fateful Lightning: A New History of the Civil War and Reconstruction* (New York: Oxford University Press, 2012), 238.

26. The literature on foreign-born soldiers is growing after a long hiatus. For a recent overview, see Doyle, *The Cause of All Nations*, 158–184, which also discusses sources; Tyler Anbinder, "Which Poor Man's Fight? Immigrants and the Federal Conscription of 1863," *Civil War History* 52, no. 4 (December 2006): 344–372; Bell Irvin Wiley, *The Life of Billy Yank: The Common Soldier of the Union* (Baton Rouge: Louisiana State University Press, 1952), 311.

27. Michael Burlingame, *Abraham Lincoln: A Life*, vol. 2 (Baltimore: Johns Hopkins University Press, 2013), 480.

28. George E. Baker, ed., *The Works of William H. Seward*, vol. 3 (Boston: Houghton, Mifflin and Co., 1884), 227; Union Party Platform of 1864;

Philip Shaw Paludan, *A People's Contest: The Union and Civil War, 1861–1865* (Lawrence: University Press of Kansas, 1996), 284; Richardson, *The Greatest Nation of the Earth*, 165–167.

29. Newspaper quoted in Paludan, *A People's Contest*, 282.

30. Meagher quoted in Doyle, *The Cause of All Nations*, 175; Pickett quoted in Paludan, *A People's Contest*, 283; Kirby Miller, *Emigrants and Exiles: Ireland and the Irish Exodus to North America* (New York: Oxford University Press, 1985); David Sim, *A Union Forever: The Irish Question and U.S. Foreign Relations in the Victorian Age* (Ithaca, NY: Cornell University Press, 2013).

31. Lincoln quoted in Richard Carwardine, "Lincoln's Horizons: The Nationalist as Universalist," in *The Global Lincoln*, ed. Carwardine and Jay Sexton (New York: Oxford University Press, 2011), 29.

32. Boutwell quoted in Christian G. Samito, *Becoming American Under Fire: Irish Americans, African Americans, and the Politics of Citizenship during the Civil War Era* (Ithaca, NY: Cornell University Press, 2009), 218–219.

33. Harmon quoted in Susan-Mary Grant, "African American Soldiers," in *Themes of the American Civil War*, ed. Grant and Brian Holden Reid (London: Routledge, 2010), 195; Bensel, *Yankee Leviathan*, 138; Lincoln quoted in Eric Foner, *The Fiery Trial: Abraham Lincoln and American Slavery* (New York: Norton, 2010), 331.

34. Lincoln to Shepley, 21 November 1862, *Collected Works of Abraham Lincoln*, vol. 5, ed. Roy P. Basler (New Brunswick, NJ: Rutgers University Press, 1953), 504.

35. Stevens quoted in Hans Trefousse, *Thaddeus Stevens: Nineteenth-Century Egalitarian* (Chapel Hill: University of North Carolina Press, 1997), 133; Julian quoted in Michael Les Benedict, *The Fruits of Victory: Alternatives in Restoring the Union, 1865-1877* (Lanham, MD: University Press of America, 1986), 116.

36. Eric Foner, *Reconstruction: America's Unfinished Revolution, 1863–1877* (New York: Harper and Row, 1988), 533; Morton Keller, *Affairs of State: Public Life in Late Nineteenth Century America* (Cambridge, MA: Belknap Press, 1977).

37. Schurz quoted in Michael Les Benedict, *Preserving the Constitution: Essays on Politics and the Constitution in the Reconstruction Era* (New York:

Fordham University Press, 2006), 13; Ian Tyrrell, *Transnational Nation: United States History in Global Perspective* (London: Palgrave Macmillan, 2007), 92; Matthew Karp, *This Vast Southern Empire: Slaveholders at the Helm of American Foreign Policy* (Cambridge, MA: Harvard University Press, 2016), 251–256.

38. Grant quoted in Foner, *Reconstruction*, 560.

39. Richardson, *The Greatest Nation on Earth*; Leonard P. Curry, *Blueprint for Modern America: Non-Military Legislation of the First Civil War Congress* (Nashville, TN: Vanderbilt University Press, 1968); Richard White, *Railroaded: The Transcontinental and the Making of Modern America* (New York: Norton, 2011), 22–23.

40. This view of the frenetic settlement of the West draws from Richard White, *The Republic for Which It Stands: The United States during Reconstruction and the Gilded Age, 1865–1896* (New York: Oxford University Press, 2017). See p. 142 for abandoned homesteads; and James Belich, *Replenishing the Earth: The Settler Revolution and the Rise of the Anglo-World* (New York: Oxford University Press, 2009).

41. Jules Verne, *Around the World in Eighty Days*, chap. 3; Jay Sexton, "Steam Transport, Sovereignty, and Empire in North America, circa 1850–1885," *Journal of the Civil War Era* 7, no. 4 (2017): 620–647, and "William H. Seward in the World," *Journal of the Civil War Era* 4, no. 3 (2014): 398–430.

42. For the importance of the flows of capital and labor in this period, see Eric Rauchway, *Blessed among Nations: How the World Made America* (New York: Hill and Wang, 2006).

43. British supporter quoted in Doyle, *The Cause of All Nations*, 299; Carwardine and Sexton, eds., *The Global*, 5–6, 11, 29.

44. Immigration figures and foreign-born percentages in Roger Daniels, *Guarding the Golden Door: American Immigration Policy and Immigrants Since 1882* (New York: Hill and Wang, 2004), 5; Craig Miner, *West of Wichita: Settling the High Plains of Kansas, 1865–1890* (Lawrence: University Press of Kansas); Richard White, *The Republic for Which It Stands: The United States during Reconstruction and the Gilded Age, 1865–1896* (New York: Oxford University Press, 2017), 405–439.

45. Net capital growth in Mira Wilkins, *The History of Foreign Investment in the United States to 1914* (Cambridge, MA: Harvard University Press, 1989), 153.

46. Jean Strouse, *Morgan: American Financier* (New York: Random House, 1999).

47. Erika Lee, "Defying Exclusion: Chinese Immigrants and Their Strategies during the Exclusion Era," in *Chinese American Transnationalism: The Flow of People, Resources, and Ideas between China and America during the Exclusion Era*, ed. Sucheng Chan (Philadelphia: Temple University Press, 2006), 1–21; Paul A. Kramer, "Empire against Exclusion in Early 20th Century Trans-Pacific History," *Nanzan Review of American Studies* 33, no. 1 (2011): 13–32.

48. Eckes, *Opening America's Market*, 28; Rauchway, *Blessed among Nations*; Marc-William Palen, "The Imperialism of Economic Nationalism, 1890–1913," *Diplomatic History* 39, no. 1 (January 2015): 157–185; A. G. Hopkins, *American Empire: A Global History* (Princeton, NJ: Princeton University Press, 2008), 239–440.

49. Chandler quoted in Crook, *The North, the South, and the Powers*, 379; Blaine quoted in LaFeber, *The New Empire*, 105; Yankee booster quoted in David Pletcher, *The Diplomacy of Trade and Investment: American Economic Expansion in the Hemisphere, 1865–1900* (Columbia: University of Missouri Press, 1998), 77.

50. John Haskell Kemble, "The Transpacific Railroads, 1869–1915," *Pacific Historical Review* 18, no. 3 (August 1949): 331–343; Timothy G. Lynch, "Crucible of California Capitalism," *Southern California Quarterly* 94, no. 4 (Winter 2012): 410–422; William Wray, *Mitsubishi and the N.Y.K., 1870–1914: Business Strategy in the Japanese Shipping Industry* (Cambridge, MA: Harvard University Press, 1984).

51. Lodge quoted in Anders Stephanson, *Manifest Destiny: American Expansion and the Empire of Right* (New York: Hill and Way, 1995), 104; Ian Tyrrell, *Reforming the World: The Creation of America's Moral Empire* (Princeton, NJ: Princeton University Press, 2010), 60.

52. Paul A. Kramer, "Empires, Exceptions, and Anglo-Saxons: Race and Rule between the British and United States Empires, 1880–1910," *Journal of American History* 88, no. 4 (March 2002): 1315–1353; Stephen Tuffnell, "Anglo-American Inter-Imperialism: US Expansion and the British World, c.1865–1914," *Britain and the World* 7, no. 2 (August 2014): 174–195; *Nation* quoted in Sexton, *Debtor Diplomacy*, 7; T. Roosevelt to Cecil

Spring-Rice, 18 January 1904, in *Letters of Theodore Roosevelt*, vol. 3, ed. Elting E. Morison (Cambridge, MA: Cambridge University Press, 1951), 699.

Chapter 4: Zigzagging through Global Crisis

1. Franklin D. Roosevelt, radio address to the Democratic National Convention, 19 July 1940; FDR, "The Seven Hundred and Twenty-Third Press Conference," 4 March 1941.

2. The "Age of Catastrophe" is the label used by Eric Hobsbawm, *The Age of Extremes: The Short Twentieth Century* (London: Michael Joseph, 1994).

3. "Zigzag" quoted in Joan Hoff Wilson, *American Business and Foreign Policy, 1920–1933* (Lexington: University of Kentucky Press, 1971), xvi.

4. Northcliffe quoted in Kathleen Burk, *New World, Old World: Great Britain and America from the Beginning* (London: Grove, 2007), 448.

5. Woodrow Wilson, "Peace without Victory," 22 January 1917; Rai quoted in Erez Manela, *The Wilsonian Moment: Self-Determination and the International Origins of Anticolonial Nationalism* (New York: Oxford University Press, 2007), 90.

6. Brooke L. Blower, *Becoming Americans in Paris: Transatlantic Politics and Culture between the World Wars* (New York: Oxford University Press, 2011); Jenifer Van Vleck, *Empire of the Air: Aviation and the American Ascendancy* (Cambridge, MA: Harvard University Press, 2013); exports in Alfred E. Eckes Jr. and Thomas W. Zeiler, *Globalization and the American Century* (New York: Cambridge University Press, 2003), 73; 42 percent in Hobsbawm, *Age of Extremes*, 97.

7. Keynes quoted in Burk, *New World, Old World*, 448.

8. "Impunity" quote from Emily S. Rosenberg, *Financial Missionaries to the World: The Politics and Culture of Dollar Diplomacy, 1900–1930* (Durham, NC: Duke University Press, 2003), 132; 6 percent in A. G. Hopkins, *American Empire: A Global History* (Princeton, NJ: Princeton University Press, 2018), 447.

9. David Greenberg, *Calvin Coolidge* (New York: Holt, 2006), 12; for the 1920s as "the high tide of the American Empire," see Hopkins, *The American Empire*, 536.

10. Roger Daniels, *Guarding the Golden Door: American Immigration Policy and Immigrants Since 1882* (New York: Hill and Wang, 2004), 45, 59; "Second

Declaration" in Donald Gabaccia, *Foreign Relations: American Immigration in Global Perspective* (Princeton, NJ: Princeton University Press, 2012), 142.

11. Daniels, *Guarding the Golden Door*, 59, 62.

12. Alfred E. Eckes Jr., *Opening America's Market: U.S. Trade Policy since 1776* (Chapel Hill: University of North Carolina Press, 1995), 88.

13. For comparison of US tariff rates across time see Eckes, *Opening America's Market*, 107; Hobsbawm, *Age of Extremes*, 88, 94; Patricia Clavin, *The Failure of Economic Diplomacy: Britain, Germany, France and the United States, 1931–36* (London: Macmillan, 1996).

14. Sir Isaiah Berlin, "President Franklin Delano Roosevelt," in *Personal Impressions* (New York: Random House, 2012).

15. Robert Dalleck, *Franklin D. Roosevelt and American Foreign Policy, 1932–1945* (New York: Oxford University Press, 1979), 45, 54.

16. Kiran Klaus Patel, *The New Deal: A Global History* (Princeton, NJ: Princeton University Press, 2016); Eric Rauchway, *The Money Makers: How Roosevelt and Keynes Ended the Depression, Defeated Fascism, and Secured a Prosperous Peace* (New York: Basic Books, 2015); Hopkins quoted in Arthur M. Schlesinger, *The Politics of Upheaval: 1935–1936, The Age of Roosevelt*, vol. 3 (New York: Houghton Mifflin, 1960), 191.

17. Ronald Edsforth, *The New Deal: America's Response to the Great Depression* (London: Wiley, 2000), 77, 115; Franklin D. Roosevelt, "Inaugural Address," 4 March 1933.

18. Alan Brinkley, *Voices of Protest: Huey Long, Father Coughlin, and the Great Depression* (New York: Knopf, 1982).

19. FDR, commencement address at Oglethorpe University in Atlanta, Georgia, 22 May 1932; "fish nor fowl" quoted in Michael Heale, *Franklin D. Roosevelt: The New Deal and War* (London: Routledge, 2002), 5.

20. The argument developed in David Kennedy, *Freedom from Fear: The American People in Depression and War, 1929–1945* (New York: Oxford University Press, 1999), esp. 363–380; socialists quoted in Schlesinger, *The Politics of Upheaval*, 192.

21. Jordan A. Schwarz, *The New Dealers: Power Politics in the Age of Roosevelt* (New York: Knopf, 1993); for racial issues, see especially Ira Katznelson, *Fear Itself: The New Deal and the Origins of Our Time* (New York: Norton, 2013).

22. Liz Cohen, *Making a New Deal: Industrial Workers in Chicago, 1919–1939* (New York: Cambridge University Press, 1990).

23. Jefferson Cowie, *The Great Exception: The New Deal and the Limits of American Politics* (Princeton, NJ: Princeton University Press, 2016), 108–114; Cohen, *Making a New Deal*, 251–289.

24. FDR, "Inaugural Address," 4 March 1933.

25. Berlin, "President Franklin Delano Roosevelt"; Patel, *The New Deal*, 261–300; Rauchway, *The Money Makers*; Elizabeth Borgwardt, *A New Deal for the World: America's Vision for Human Rights* (Cambridge, MA: Harvard University Press, 2005); David Ekbladh, "'Mr. TVA': Grass-Roots Development, David Lilienthal, and the Rise and Fall of the Tennessee Valley Authority as a Symbol for U.S. Overseas Development, 1933–1973," *Diplomatic History* 26, no. 3 (December 2002): 335–374.

26. A. J. P. Taylor, *The Origins of the Second World War* (London: Hamish Hamilton, 1961), 295.

27. Brooke L. Blower, "From Isolationism to Neutrality: A New Framework for Understanding American Political Culture, 1919–1941," *Diplomatic History* 38, no. 2 (April 2014): 345–376; John Moser, *Twisting the Lion's Tale: American Anglophobia between the World Wars* (New York: New York University Press, 1998); Smedley D. Butler, "War Is a Racket," 1935.

28. Paul A. Kramer, *The Blood of Government: Race, Empire, the United States, and the Philippines* (Chapel Hill: University of North Carolina Press, 2006), 397–402, 425–428; Hopkins, *The American Empire*, 590; Hull quoted in Lloyd C. Gardner, *Economic Aspects of New Deal Diplomacy* (Madison: University of Wisconsin Press, 1964), 52.

29. David Reynolds, *From Munich to Pearl Harbor: Roosevelt's America and the Origins of the Second World War* (Chicago: Ivan R. Dee, 2001); FDR, Fireside Chat, 29 December 1940.

30. Charles Lindbergh, address at America First Committee meeting, New York, 23 April 1941, www.charleslindbergh.com/americanfirst/speech2.asp.

31. Harold Lasswell, "The Garrison State," *American Journal of Sociology* 46, no. 4 (January 1941): 455–468.

32. John A. Thompson, "Conceptions of National Security and American Entry into World War II," *Diplomacy and Statecraft* 16 (2005): 671–697;

Dawn Berry, "The North Atlantic Triangle and the Genesis and Legacy of the American Occupation of Greenland during the Second World War," (PhD diss., Oxford University, 2013); Warren Kimball, *The Most Unsordid Act: Lend-Lease, 1931–1941* (Baltimore: Johns Hopkins Press, 1969), 151–152.

33. Andrew Preston, "Monsters Everywhere: A Genealogy of National Security," *Diplomatic History* 38, no. 3 (June 2014); FDR, Fireside Chat, 29 December 1940.

34. John Keegan, *The Second World War* (New York: Viking, 1989), 88–102, 127–141; Hobsbawm, *Age of Extremes*, 7–8. "It is one of the ironies of this strange century that the most lasting results of the October revolution, whose object was the global overthrow of capitalism, was to save its antagonist."

35. David Vine, *Base Nation: How U.S. Military Bases Abroad Harm America and the World* (New York: Metropolitan Books, 2015), 17–44. See 32–39 for very helpful maps.

36. Theodore A. Wilson, *The First Summit: Roosevelt and Churchill at Placentia Bay, 1941* (Boston: Houghton Mifflin, 1969); Churchill quoted in Kennedy, *Freedom from Fear*, 461.

37. Henry R. Luce, "The American Century," *Life*, 17 February 1941; Philip M. Seib, *Broadcasts from the Blitz: How Edward R. Murrow Helped Lead America into War* (Washington, DC: Potomac Books, 2006); Reynolds, *From Munich to Pearl Harbor*, 175, 181; Kimberly Hupp, " 'Uncle Joe': What Americans Thought of Joseph Stalin before and after World War II" (master's thesis, University of Toledo, 2009).

38. This conclusion draws from a lecture in Oxford's Examination Schools given by Melvyn P. Leffler in Hilary Term, 2003.

39. Statistics from Melvyn P. Leffler, *A Preponderance of Power: National Security, the Truman Administration, and the Cold War* (Stanford, CA: Stanford University Press, 1992), 5.

40. Figures from Kennedy, *Freedom from Fear*, 655; Churchill quoted in Paul Kennedy, *Engineers of Victory: The Problem Solvers Who Turned the Tide in the World War* (New York: Random House, 2013), 350.

41. Bruce Cummings, *Pacific Ascendancy and American Power* (New Haven, CT: Yale University Press, 2009), 299–334; Richard White, *"It's*

Your Misfortune and None of My Own": A New History of the American West (Norman: University of Oklahoma Press, 1991), 498–533.

42. John Morton Blum, *V Was for Victory: Politics and American Culture during World War II* (New York: Harcourt Brace, 1976), 122–123.

43. Gallup poll in William L. O'Neill, *A Democracy at War: America's Fight at Home and Abroad in World War II* (Cambridge, MA: Harvard University Press, 1993), 211; Gary Gerstle, "The Working Class Goes to War," in *The War in American Culture: Society and Consciousness during World War II*, ed. Lewis A. Erenberg and Susan E. Hirsch (Chicago: University of Chicago Press, 1996), 105–127.

44. Reed Ueda, "The Changing Path to Citizenship: Ethnicity and Naturalization during World War II," in *The War in American Culture*, ed. Erenberg and Hirsch, 202–216; United States, *Selective Service and Victory: The 4th Report of the Director of the Selective Service, 1944–1945, with a Supplement for 1946–1947* (Washington, DC: US Government Publishing Office, 1948).

45. South not joking quoted in Julian E. Zelizer, "Confronting the Roadblock: Congress, Civil Rights, and World War II," in *The Fog of War: The Second World War and the Civil Rights Movement*, ed. Kevin M. Kruse and Stephen Tuck (New York: Oxford University Press, 2012), 39; Crawford quoted in Elaine Tyler May, "Rosie the Riveter Gets Married," in *The War in American Culture*, ed. Erenberg and Hirsch, 140.

46. Gunnar Myrdal, *An American Dilemma: The Negro Problem and Modern Democracy* (New York: Harper & Bros., 1944), chap. 1; Kruse and Tuck, eds., *The Fog of War*; Bond quoted in Wendy L. Wall, *Inventing the "American Way": The Politics of Consensus from the New Deal to the Civil Rights Movement* (New York: Oxford University Press, 2008), 151.

47. Aldon D. Morris, *The Origins of the Civil Rights Movement: Black Communities Organizing for Change* (New York: Free Press, 1984); Jacquelyn Dowd Hall, "The Long Civil Rights Movement and the Political Uses of the Past," *Journal of American History* 91, no. 4 (March 2005): 1233–1263; Keona K. Ervin, *Gateway to Equality: Black Women and the Struggle for Economic Justice in St. Louis* (Lexington: University Press of Kentucky). For the broad economic context, see Robert J. Gordon, *The Rise and Fall of American Growth: The U.S. Standard of Living since the Civil War* (Princeton, NJ: Princeton University Press, 2016), 535–565.

48. Mary L. Dudziak, *Cold War Civil Rights: Race and the Image of American Democracy* (Princeton, NJ: Princeton University Press, 2000); Carol Anderson, *Eyes Off the Prize: The United Nations and the African American Struggle for Human Rights* (New York: Cambridge University Press, 2003); Acheson quoted in John David Skrentny, "The Effect of the Cold War on African-American Civil Rights: America and the World Audience, 1945–1968," *Theory and Society* 27, no. 2 (April 1998): 237–285.

49. John Darwin, *After Tamerlane: The Global History of Empire* (London: Allen Lane, 2007), 470. "This colossal imperium was on an unprecedented scale. No previous world power had entrenched itself at both ends of Eurasia, or had had the power to do so."

50. David Armitage, *The Declaration of Independence: A Global History* (Cambridge, MA: Harvard University Press, 2007), 152–153; Hopkins, *The American Empire*, 639–687.

51. This interpretation of the origins of the Cold War draws from Leffler, *A Preponderance of Power*, Acheson quoted on p. 6; Odd Arne Westad, *The Global Cold War: Third World Interventions and the Making of Our Time* (New York: Cambridge University Press, 2005).

52. FDR, "Fourth Inaugural Address," 20 January 1945; Harry S. Truman, "Special Message to the Congress on the Marshall Plan," 19 December 1947; Bevin quoted in Geir Lundestad, "Empire by Invitation? The United States and Western Europe, 1945–1952," *Journal of Peace Research* 23, no. 3 (September 1986): 263–277.

53. Quotes from Campbell Craig and Fredrik Logevall, *America's Cold War: The Politics of Insecurity* (Cambridge, MA: Harvard University Press, 2009), 79.

54. Wall, *Inventing the "American Way"*; Julian Zelizer, *Arsenal of Democracy: The Politics of National Security—From World War II to the War on Terrorism* (New York: Basic Books, 2009), esp. p. 5.

55. Laura Belmonte, *Selling the American Way: U.S. Propaganda and the Cold War* (Philadelphia: University of Pennsylvania Press, 2008).

56. Foreign-born figures from Daniels, *Guarding the Golden Door*, 5; Paul Simon, "The U.S. Crisis in Foreign Language," *Annals of the American Academy of Political and Social Science* 449 (May 1980): 31–44; Daniel T. Rodgers, "Exceptionalism," in *Imagined Histories: American Historians*

Interpret the Past, ed. Anthony Molho and Gordon S. Wood (Princeton, NJ: Princeton University Press, 1998).

57. The 1960s visitors video of the Jefferson National Expansion Memorial is worth watching, *Monument to the Dream* (1967).

58. Gary Gerstle, *American Crucible: Race and Nation in the Twentieth Century* (Princeton, NJ: Princeton University Press, 2001), 259.

59. For foreign-born percentages, see www.migrationpolicy.org /programs/data-hub/charts/immigrant-population-over-time; "U.S. Turns into Debtor Nation," *New York Times,* 17 September 1985.

60. For a variation of this argument that emphasizes domestic politics, see Cowie, *The Great Exception.*

61. Thomas Borstelmann, *The Cold War and the Color Line: American Race Relations in the Global Arena* (Cambridge, MA: Harvard University Press, 2001); Frederick Logevall, *Choosing War: The Lost Chance for Peace and the Escalation of War in Vietnam* (Berkeley: University of California Press, 1999); Johnson quoted in Craig and Logevall, *America's Cold War,* 230.

62. Jim Glassman and Young-Jin Choi, "The *Chaebŏl* and the US Military-Industrial Complex: Cold War Geopolitical Economy and South Korean Industrialization," *Environment and Planning* 46 (2014): 1160–1180. Thanks to Daniel Immerwahr for this reference.

63. Harry Truman, "Farewell Address," 15 January 1953.

Conclusion: From Triumph to Crisis

1. Donald J. Trump, address accepting the presidential nomination at the Republican National Convention in Cleveland, Ohio, 21 July 2016; Elizabeth Warren, address at Netroots Nation conference," 13 August 2017; Barack Obama, "Inaugural Address," 20 January 2009.

2. Matthew J. Morgan, ed., *The Day That Changed Everything? The Impact of 9/11* (New York: Palgrave Macmillan, 2009); capitalism quote at www.theguardian.com/business/2009/sep/04/lehman-brothers -aftershocks-28-days; political earthquake at www.nytimes.com/2016/11/08 /us/politics/obama-2008-election-comparison.html; not normal from John Oliver, *Last Week Tonight,* 13 November 2016.

3. This paragraph refers to popular understandings of US history. For American exceptionalism, see Ian Tyrrell, "American Exceptionalism in

an Age of International History," *American Historical Review*, 1991; and Daniel T. Rodgers, "Exceptionalism," in *Imagined Histories: American Historians Interpret the Past*, ed. Anthony Molho and Gordon S. Wood (Princeton, NJ: Princeton University Press, 1998), which quotes Daniel Boorstin on the "seamless" nature of US history. For the British Whig historians, see T. B. Macaulay, *History of England* (1848), chap. 10; and Herbert Butterfield, *The Whig Interpretation of History* (London: Well and Sons, 1931). For a popular leftist narrative of US history, see Howard Zinn, *A People's History of the United States* (New York: Harper, 1980). For the right's rejoinder, see Larry Schweikart and Michael Allen, *A Patriot's History of the United States* (New York: Sentinel, 2004).

4. Barack Obama, "Victory Speech," 5 November 2008; zig and zag quoted in www.slate.com/blogs/the_slatest/2016/11/09/obama_takes_long_view _of_history_offers_hope_that_trump_will_respect_democracy.html.

5. Wellington quoted in Rory Muir, *Tactics and the Experience of Battle in the Age of Napoleon* (New Haven, CT: Yale University Press, 2010), 7. "Winning big wars proved as fatal to empires as losing them: a lesson from the history of the British Empire which Washington might take heart." Eric Hobsbawm, *On Empire: America, War, and Global Supremacy* (New York: Pantheon Books, 2008), 69.

6. New York paper quoted in Adam I. P. Smith, *The Stormy Present: Conservatism and the Problem of Slavery in Northern Politics* (Chapel Hill: University of North Carolina Press, 2017), 14–15; Herbert Hoover, "Annual Message on the State of the Union," 2 December 1930.

7. For constitutional lifespans, see Zachary Elkins, Tom Ginsburg, and James Melton, "The Lifespan of Written Constitutions," http://jenni .uchicago.edu/WJP/Vienna_2008/Ginsburg-Lifespans-California.pdf.

8. Francis Fukuyama, *The End of History and the Last Man* (New York: Free Press, 1992); For a European rejoinder to widely held criticisms of US neoliberalism, see Olaf Gersemann, *Cowboy Capitalism: European Myths, American Reality* (Washington, DC: Cato Institute, 2004).

9. "America's Forever Wars," editorial, *New York Times*, 22 October 2017. For the revival of American anti-imperialism and isolationism, see Ian Tyrrell and Jay Sexton, "Whither American Anti-imperialism in a Postcolonial World?," in *Empire's Twin: U.S. Anti-imperialism from the Founding*

to the Age of Terror, ed. Tyrrell and Sexton (Ithaca, NY: Cornell University Press, 2015). For economic inequality, see Thomas Piketty, *Capital in the Twenty-First Century,* trans. Arthur Goldhammer (Cambridge, MA: Belknap Press, 2014). For US debt held overseas, see "Foreign Holdings of Federal Debt," Congressional Research Service, https://fas.org/sgp/crs /misc/RS22331.pdf. For foreign-born percentages, see www.migration policy.org/programs/data-hub/charts/immigrant-population-over-time.

10. For the language of the Cold War and its incongruity with the twenty-first century, see Daniel Rodgers, *Age of Fracture* (Cambridge, MA: Belknap Press, 2011), 15–40, 256–271.

11. John B. Judis, *The Populist Explosion: How the Great Recession Transformed American and European Politics* (New York: Columbia Global Reports, 2016). For Britain's foreign-born population, see www.migrationobservatory.ox.ac .uk/resources/briefings/migrants-in-the-uk-an-overview/.

12. All empires that have risen eventually have fallen. See Paul Kennedy, *The Rise and Fall of the Great Powers: Economic Change and Military Conflict from 1500 to 2000* (New York: Random House, 1987); John Darwin, *After Tamerlane: The Global History of Empire* (London: Allen Lane, 2007).

Index

Allison Smythe

Jay Sexton is the inaugural Kinder Institute Chair in Constitutional Democracy at the University of Missouri. Previously, he spent nearly two decades at the University of Oxford in the UK, where he remains an emeritus fellow of Corpus Christi College. Sexton lives in Columbia, Missouri.